The Great Karate Myth

Barefoot Zen: the Shaolin roots of Kung Fu and Karate

Zen Shaolin Karate

The Great Karate Myth

Unravelling the Mystery of Karate

by Nathan J. Johnson

The Wykeham Press
London & Winchester

In this book you will discover...

❖ Kicking, punching, blocking and striking, techniques, all commonly associated with Karate, are actually modern, of *limited* practical value, and do not reflect the true technical functions of the antique (ancient) kata (solo choreographed sequences of Karate techniques)

❖ The 'Sai' (an ancient Chinese 'pronged' weapon used in pairs) is quite literally the key to understanding most 'classical' so-called Karate kata and their applications. Many modern reformers' dissatisfaction with the *unarmed* interpretation of these kata (actually designed for use with weapons) can now be justified.

❖ In the old tradition of 'To-te' (Karate's forbear), only three kata were generally needed for mastery of the art. This remains true today, for both Karate and Kobudo (weapons), and challenges the modern inclusion of up to *fifty* kata in Karate alone.

❖ The reality behind Karate's World famous Sanchin (three battles or conflicts) kata, the mysterious legacy of Southern Chinese Quan-fa (Kung Fu) and one of the most important forms in both traditions.

❖ Seisan kata (Hangestsu in the Shotokan style), a cornerstone kata practiced in most Karate styles is (in its original Chinese form) *unquestionably* one of the main kata intended to train the practitioner in the use of 'Sai' weapons.

❖ How to practice, and correctly apply, Goju Ryu's top kata, 'Tensho' (Rokushu), essentially an arrangement of Southern Chinese Quan-fa (Kung Fu) techniques, simply detailing six methods of escaping from wrist grips.

❖ The original Chinese Naihanchin kata (Shotokan Tekki), the bedrock kata for the branch of Karate known as Shuri-te (Shorin Ryu) is a *two man grappling sequence from China!* – Not a 'block-strike' kata as is usually taught.

❖ How and why such huge mistakes were made. And their implications.

First published in the United Kingdom
in 2006 by The Wykeham Press

© 2006 The Wykeham Press of London & Winchester
P.O Box 437, Winchester SO22 5WN UK

Text copyright © N. J. Johnson 2006

Layout and design by Kenneth Lymer
Additional layout by Shanir Patel

Hardback ISBN Number 0-9549609-3-9
Paperback ISBN Number 0-9549609-2-0

Disclaimer

Please note that the author and publishers of this book
are NOT RESPONSIBLE in any manner whatsoever for
any injury, illness or accident that may result from following
the instructions within. Further, if you do intend to engage in
the activities described and illustrated in this book, you are
advised to consult a physician, prior to doing so.

If your free DVD does not accompany this book, simply send
proof of purchase (till receipt or purchase invoice) to the publishers:
The Wykeham Press P.O. Box 437, Winchester SO22 5WN (UK).
Please allow 28 days for delivery.

Contents

Notes on General Terms used in the Text

IT WOULD BE IMPOSSIBLE to write a book such as this without the inclusion of jargon and technical terms. I recognise this can represent a potential stumbling block, particularly for the beginner. Also, some of the names of Karate masters and pioneers can present problems in terms of pronunciation. However, I trust that this book is as user friendly as possible. The various sections have been kept fairly small and the text has been broken with descriptive sub-headings.

It would be pointless to try and simplify all the technical terms used throughout, but a selection of commonly used terms is explained in a 'glossary of terms' at the end of the book.

The terms Karate, To-te, Kung Fu and Quan-fa that figure prominently in the text are used interchangeably, so are the terms kata and quan. For example, sometimes I have found it is easier to use the Japanese term 'kata' (a choreographed sequence of Martial Arts moves), even though a Chinese 'quan' is being referred to. Broadly speaking they mean the same thing; however, mostly, one term will be used over another to stress a point. Moreover, the terms 'Karate' and 'kata' are perhaps easier for the general reader to relate to.

In this book, the term 'Kobudo' – 'Ko' (ancient), 'bu' (warrior), and 'do' (way) – has been used where the weapon-based techniques it describes could be (and were often formerly) rendered as 'Kobujutsu'; a term that delineates 'Ko' (ancient) 'bu' (warrior) 'Jutsu' (technique), pertaining to technique(s) actually used in feudal Japanese (and Chinese) societies. I have chosen to use the term 'Kobudo' simply because contemporary use of these ancient civil arrest techniques is now a modern 'study' – a 'do' or 'way' -- rather than a present-day means of maintaining civil order.

The terms 'Karate' and 'Martial Arts' are written with the first letter in capital throughout, unless the author is quoting another writer. Okinawan names are written using the (conventional) family name first, followed by the given name, thus, Miyagi Chojun is used rather than Chojun Miyagi, again, unless another author is being quoted. Use of terms man, he, his, etc. is not intended to privilege men over woman, it is merely used to facilitate the recording of material that is, by its very nature rather difficult to record. Man, etc. is therefore used in the best of Anglo Saxon traditions as a non gender-specific term.

All dates used in the book are current era unless specified by B.C.E (before current era)

The text is an historic expose. Pictures are only contextual and do not attempt to fully prove textual hypothesis.

Due to the nature of the subject, the DVD demonstrates aspects of this book where the pictures contained can only support textual hypothesis and catalogue the five kata that form the basis of Ko-do Ryu Karate and Kobudo.

It happens by a common vice of human nature,
that we trust most to, and are most seriously frightened at,
things which are strange and unknown
Caesar, *De Bello Civili, Bk. ii, sec. 4*

Faith, fanatic faith, once wedded fast
To some dear falsehood, hugs it to the last
Thomas Moore, *The Veiled Prophet*

Preface

THIS PREFACE IS GIVEN to enable the reader to grasp something of the 'gist' of this book's exposé – right away! Initially I did not think I could explain such a challenging and controversial discovery in a few words; however, just prior to publication, I was discussing 'The Great Karate Myth' with a friend who works in television when he explained something he called, the 'elevator sale' – the ability to explain or 'sell' an idea in the space or duration of a short elevator ride. I was horrified, thinking I would find that impossible. How could I explain the full extent of my discoveries in a 'sound bite'? He suggested that I 'cut to the chase' and got directly to the point. He got me to do it on film, so, I thought, long and hard about how to do the same for the preface of this book.

Eventually I decided on the story of 'The Emperor's New Clothes'; hoping and assuming that the reader would be familiar with the tale. Sufficient to say; a couple of 'salesmen' invite the emperor to view the rarest and finest fabric in the world, claiming it can only be seen by wise people and that it is invisible to the eyes of fools. The emperor (unable, of course, to actually see the non-existent fabric), immediately admires and praises it, and his courtiers swiftly follow suit, extolling the virtues of the 'miraculous' material. When the 'salesmen' offer to sew the fabric into a new suit of clothes for the emperor, he accepts, and a deal is struck.

The Emperor wears the 'invisible suit' in public, receiving adulation and flattery; with all 'admiring' the fabric and the 'cut' of the suit too. All, that is, but a small boy who has not been party to the general deceit and cries out: "The king isn't wearing any clothes!" Someone in the crowd tries to suppress the boy, but (as the song about it goes) he persists ... "The king is altogether as naked as the day that he was born!" he yells.

In tandem, *what if I were to suggest that the art of Karate never truly existed as an un-armed art of self defence, and that its original source material was never designed for plebeian fisticuffs, but for something infinitely more sophisticated yet practical?*

What if I could offer evidence ... proof?

For example, Karate, despite its mystique and reputation, has largely failed the litmus test of 'The Ultimate Fight Challenge' matches and other similar no-holds-barred tournaments, in which it has performed dismally. So called 'traditional Karate' has *not* held up to the scrutiny (read opposition) of those ignorant of, or uninterested in its 'protocols', its etiquette, grades and titles. Titles like Sensei (teacher) mean little inside a steel, 'combat cage' – just one of the harsh modern experimental laboratories that showcase a variety of 'full contact' combat methods today.

Returning to the parable of 'The Emperor's New Clothes'; once the little boy dared to shout that the Emperor was not wearing any clothes, the crowd was won-over. The Emperor was indeed discovered to be naked!

It is no wonder that Karate competitors were comprehensively defeated. They were trying to use the wrong tools for the job! (Or rather, they were *missing* the right tools). Karate historians have pointed out that Karate was never intended to be used in an arena, and that knowledge has been used to explain 'traditional'

Karate's poor performance in such scenarios. The 'calibre' of the competitors has been called into question too. But that is 'barking-up-the-wrong tree', so to speak. The problem is a technical but profound one.

Modern combat tournaments have nothing whatsoever to do with ancient Karate kata (upon which modern Karate is founded) and the original Karate techniques can not be employed under such circumstances. But not for the reasons usually given. Despite popular belief ... let me re-phrase that: despite *global* belief in Karate being an ancient *un-armed* art of self defence, it can now be demonstrated that 'empty hand Karate', as it is currently portrayed and recognized, is a much later 'fabrication' based on techniques intended for entirely different purposes; purposes outlined in this book!

The 'emperor' might not be wearing any clothes, but all is not lost ... read on.

Introduction

KARATE: A MYSTERIOUS deadly Martial Art whose 'master exponents' can easily kill with a single blow; defeat multiple opponents in style and with grace, or tackle dangerous wild animals unarmed. Karate: a fearsome art in which the split-second timing of a fist or foot-strike determines life or death. Karate: the study and application of multipurpose-Martial Arts-routines, comprising techniques, 'inscrutably' designed to be used equally well, with or without weapons. Karate: an art conceived for use by warriors who had lost their weapons on the bloody battlefields of ancient Japan. Karate: an art through which exponents may cultivate the abilities to easily smash through rock, brick, stone and bone, and (fatally) pierce human flesh, even delaying the time of an opponent's death ... These and other misinformed and inaccurate stereotypes figure amongst some of the most grotesque and misleading caricatures, distortions and hackneyed misrepresentations of Karate extant. Certainly very common, they are equally as false, attesting more to populist Oriental mythologizing than to the technical material contained in authentic kata – elegant, solo choreographed sequences of movements that record Karate's ancient techniques, the true source of Karate and the inspiration for this book.

Karate

Karate is a household word and a popular activity currently engaged in by several millions of people worldwide. 'Karate' (kah-ra-tay) is a modern Japanese term (dating from the early to mid 1900s) and is written using two 'Kanji' or Japanese characters (ideograms), 'Kara' and 'Te'. Kara means 'empty' and Te means 'hand' or hands. No weapons are implied, so (simplistically) Karate means 'empty hands'. Strictly speaking, the term Karate was intended to refer to un-armed techniques designed for civil rather than military use.

 Kara (empty) and 手 Te (hands) – empty hands

Today, there are many styles of Karate, but most can be traced back to two main prototypes created or rather *synthesised* in the (ancient) Okinawan cities of Shuri and Naha, and despite the intense eclecticism that underpins much modern Karate, Naha-te (Naha 'hand' – Karate) and Shuri-te (Shuri 'hand' – Karate) still represent the two fundamental categories into which Karate is traditionally divided.

Many methods that went to make up the core or basic early Karate techniques actually originated in China, where health and self defence methods (civil arrest techniques) were very popular, particularly during the Ming dynasty (1368–1644). Eventually, the techniques developed by the Chinese masters reached Okinawa, an Island in the Ryukyu chain, some 300 miles south of the tip of Japan, 300 nautical miles north of Taiwan and 400 nautical miles east of China.

By the late seventeenth to early eighteenth century, a small and somewhat elite group of Okinawan Karate-ka (Karate practitioners) secretly began to mould the Chinese techniques

Okinawa

into several versions of their own, which they referred to only as 'Te' (Tey) or 'hand'. There were in fact three leading schools of the day, each located in the three major Okinawan cities of Shuri, Naha, and Tomari. Each school had its own distinctive characteristics meticulously recorded in kata – solo choreographed sequences of techniques – although by the twentieth century, the Tomari kata were largely absorbed into the Shuri and Naha styles.

In 'The Great Karate Myth', you will discover (among other things) why traditional (kata based) Karate, latterly portrayed as a fearsome Japanese art of unarmed combat, appears to be relatively ineffective in violent modern 'real fighting' arenas, and why Karate (despite its true merits) is now being seriously questioned regarding its efficiency as a practical means of urban self defence – one of the many reasons for its study today.

The focus of attention in this book – and the necessary starting point for any serious investigation into the phenomenon of Karate – is the traditional kata.

Kata has long been the time-honoured vehicle for the preservation and transmission of Karate. Controversial re-interpretation of vital Karate kata form the backbone of this book, alongside startling new information regarding the original purposes of the techniques that comprise so-called 'traditional' Karate in general. In some respects 'The Great Karate Myth' de-constructs Karate as it is commonly perceived.

Here then is Karate 'laid bare', its roots, original purposes and fundamental methods critically analysed to reveal an art that has little in common with popular stereotypes regarding its objectives. Here – perhaps for the first time – is Karate, freed from commercial distortions and divorced from popular misconceptions and historical inaccuracy to reveal the *myth* !

Karate Today

Today, most Karate styles divide their practice into three types of training: kihon (basics), kata (forms) and kumite (sparring), respectively. However, kihon, the constant repetition of basics – isolating techniques and repeating them in drill fashion – is a relatively new invention, as is modern free-fighting or sparring. Indeed, modern basics often include the repetition of techniques not actually found in the traditional kata; high kicks for example. Of the three types of training mentioned, kata is the most traditional and is said, by the masters, to *be* Karate and Karate to be kata! Yet kata, sometimes described as the 'soul' of Karate, and revered by traditionalists, are also a source of great confusion and much disagreement between the various schools that practice them, particularly with regard to 'applications'. In reality many applications taught as 'traditional' are in fact very modern (dating from the 1950s) and could not be further from the original intentions for – and purposes of – the kata, as this book will show. Admittedly, as well as ancient kata, there exists a plethora of *modern* kata, but they are not dealt-with or discussed at any length here, being (typically) re-workings of already misrepresented classical kata.

It may be largely unknown to the general public that, within Karate, there is currently something of a crisis in confidence in the meaning and application of historically important kata, a situation that can only be denied by the most entrenched or blinkered of experienced practitioners. Many disconsolate Karate-ka have spent, and continue to spend, countless hours trying to fathom, unravel, and apply, misconceived, improperly passed-on or downright bogus kata, portrayed as 'traditional'. But true kata do exist, they have simply been jumbled-up (modified) and their functions confused, confounded and twisted into an ever tightening 'Gordian knot'. This book is intended to untangle that knot. It was not written to be deliberately controversial or to directly criticise established Karate, yet the explanations and applications for kata presented here and on DVD, unquestionably represent a major breakthrough in the field of Karate, its history, and philosophy; but more importantly in the *practical* applications of its *primary*, ancient (key) kata, including the fundamental kata of both major streams of Karate.

The most logical *proof* of what constitutes a genuine kata can only be found in the clear demonstration of its exact function – the reason for its existence, and the reason for its format. I hope to illustrate therefore, that for both Karate and Kobudo (weapons) kata, *it is function that ultimately dictates form!* This in turn will reveal the original uses for ancient techniques now known as Karate.

Much of this book is concerned with explaining and describing what constitutes 'key' Karate kata, alongside kata devised to be used with civil arrest 'tools' (Kobudo weapons) by tracing the lineages of genuine kata and establishing their correct versions. But, the strength of this book lies not in its revising or detailing of history, philosophy or theory, which are all arguable, but in its demonstration and *proof* of how to mechanically *apply* these kata – precisely. The kata speak for their-selves, and it is on that basis that this work will stand.

In Support of Tradition

Karate is an art steeped in traditional Oriental values. To entirely remove these traditions and values would constitute a grave error and reduce Karate to nothing more than a jumble of techniques for brutalizing our fellow human beings. Indeed, the human ego can do little more than *violate* if it is left unbridled, untutored, uncultured, and if, in its arrogant indifference to meaningful tradition, it becomes consumed by its own ambition whilst carelessly sweeping aside the past in favour of a 'brave new world' (starting, of course, at year zero). In such cases, harsh lessons always lay ahead and failure is almost inevitable (the actions of certain dictators spring to mind here). In the same vein, the abandonment of traditional Karate kata only leads to the need for a new set of paradigms, sequences, or training routines.

Generally, the reckless eradication of tradition, usually produces a moral, ethical and cultural vacuum of such destructive proportions, that new traditions must quickly be invented to plug the hole, and of course, they don't have 'old grandma's recipes', figuratively speaking. Is it not therefore wise to prudently consider the accumulative knowledge of those who came before us? And in the case of Karate, the antique kata; a language in movement left to us by the true masters.

Modern Karate, by looking only forward and rushing at a helter-skelter pace, incurs the risk of loosing its life-blood and abandoning that which created it – yet that which it struggles to understand – traditional kata. Indeed, it is only through the preservation of traditional kata that a truly worthwhile art of Karate will survive. The late Nagamine Shoshin (1907–1997), a celebrated Okinawan 'Shorin Ryu' (Shuri-te) Karate master, wrote in his book, *Tales of Okinawa's Great Masters*, (Boston, Tokyo, Vermont: Tuttle 2000) p.xvii:

> … karate has been popularised for its utilitarian and competitive elements and, for the most part, monopolized by young people … the classical values of the art have been ignored … kata is the central vehicle of this profound tradition … without restoration of these values, true classical Okinawan karate will become extinct.

Indeed, Karate has undergone several processes of modernization, but modernization does not automatically produce improvement. Often, quality is sacrificed in favour of quantity or appearance, and utility is compromised as a result. Modernism easily facilitates novelty, fads, the updating of fashions and built-in obsolescence (to generate more business). But *authentic Karate kata don't 'update'*, they are not like, for instance, electrical goods (the new ones are best ... the old ones ... outdated). I recently heard a Karate black belt refer to 'updated' kata as though he were indeed discussing such goods. He stated that he was glad to possess the 'latest'. With regard to authentic Karate kata, metaphorically speaking, fire and the wheel have already been discovered. *If human beings ever physically 'update', then classical kata will need to be 'updated' too!*

The point made above is of vital importance because there is currently a widespread (and seldom challenged) belief in (Western-style) 'progress' that *insists* things (constantly) change. This is in stark contrast to the extremely conservative ancestrally based *spirit* of Eastern traditionalism. The kata illustrated in this book are specific designs – templates – complete, in their purposes and aims. They are fully functional – once properly de-coded – and traditional in the most useful sense of the term; the ways of 'doing things' they record are tried, true and tested, and cannot easily be supplanted. That these kata have indeed been somewhat modified in the past must be admitted, but only in the context of the lack of knowledge of the functions, largely prevalent during their cultural migration during the nineteenth and twentieth centuries.

Whilst I understand the sentiments of Nagamine Shoshin, mentioned earlier, perhaps the overall picture for the survival of traditional Karate is not necessarily one of doom and gloom. The revered Lakota (Native American) elder, Wallace Black Elk (in speaking of his spiritual traditions) suggested that no tradition ever dies until the last person who honours it dies, to which I would add – in respect of the development of modern kata – if you practice classical kata then, metaphorically speaking, think carefully before you reach for your magic lamp should you hear the cry, "New lamps for old, new lamps for old."

Kata – General

Fighting can be learned without kata, animals do it just fine, but the (unarmed) art of Karate facilitates much more than just fighting, and humans can be more than just animals, a basic tenet that meaningful approaches to Karate seek to establish in encouraging practitioners along paths of ennoblement and self development. The kata provide the necessary 'reference points' for the classical art. They record and preserve immutable truths.

One advantage of kata is that it can be practiced alone. If performed correctly, kata (both Karate and Kobudo weapons) develop and maintain 'muscle memory' for the various techniques that they catalogue. Such 'muscle memory' when coupled in application with speedy (touch) reflexes, produce accurate and effective techniques. Kata practice also provides a first-rate holistic workout, a method of reflective introspection (meditation), and an enjoyable opportunity to refine and polish technique. Also the ancient kata have the 'pleasant flavour of antiquity'.

In respect of genuine Karate kata, a set number of limbs and the science of using them in a specific, eminently logical, systematic dignified and humane way forms the backbone of the art *as laid down in the 'Okinawan Ryu-ha Kihon Kata Tradition'* – the rule of thumb 'systems manuals' (see chapter two). In these important kata, the observation and categorisation of fundamental human physiological (and psychological) realities (posture, breathing, blood circulation, leverage, triangulation, the direction that joints bend or move in and when they are strong and when they are not, etc) are fully laid out.

Unfortunately, fundamental breakdowns in the transmission of the purpose for key (antique) kata have occurred with the passing of time. Since the seventeenth century, war, disease, cultural devastation and radical political reforms have befallen Southern China, the birthplace of To-te ('China Hand') and the cradle of quan (kata/forms) later to be utilised and 'adapted' to create Okinawan Karate. At that time, many traditions were lost or distorted. During the eighteenth and nineteenth centuries Okinawa suffered similarly too. With her population weakened by poverty and disease and decimated by the ravages of the pacific war, and with her cities and infrastructure bombed virtually flat during that period, Okinawan cultural confidence hit an all time low and the development of Karate suffered a significant setback. Consequently, much needed (specific) research into the interpretation of many of its *imported* and seemingly cryptic kata could not be properly undertaken, let alone concluded before the art was exported far beyond the borders of the former Japanese Empire.

The Great Karate Myth

Karate is a passion for me, and my choice of title for this book is not meant to be derogatory, it is merely intended to capture the attention of those who, instinctively, or otherwise, are, or will-be, drawn to a fascinating, enigmatic and intriguing art – Karate. As well as being a general exposé, this book is intended for the growing number of practising Karate-ka of all grades who are frustrated and disillusioned by the many inconsistencies they find in (modern) mainstream explanations of kata, yet instinctively feel, trust, or believe, that there may be something missing, unexplained, hidden, or of real significance within the antique kata. This book is also intended to explain the obvious difficulties in applying 'ritual' and formal traditional kata to freestyle fighting, rough and tumble fighting and real self defence situations, and to argue that the (antique) kata were never intended for such.

The material for 'The Great Karate Myth', and the discoveries presented herein were methodically and painstakingly researched on a non-commercial basis and represent a culmination of over thirty years of experience, fifteen of which were devoted solely to the kata presented within, and the applications meticulously outlined. Readers are invited to judge the results for themselves. Moreover, it is my fervent wish that 'The Great Karate Myth' becomes a 'seminal' or influential work.

It is also my wish to re-establish the kata detailed in this book, and their logical applications, under the banner of Ko-do Ryu Karate and Kobudo, and to promote them as a trans-cultural human resource. Collectively they represent a classical art of sufficient depth to constitute a 'Ryu' (school/style) in its own right.

Because the issues raised in this book have major implications for the art of Karate, and because its contents are challenging, the experienced reader is invited to set aside partisanship, and all readers are respectfully asked to 'suspend disbelief' until the various establishing points have been made in the text (and viewed on DVD).

In terms of technical content, this book supersedes my other published work on Karate.

Acknowledgements

I would like to take this opportunity to thank past and present staff members of the Students Union at Southampton and Portsmouth universities (and staff members at Oxford, Manchester, Bristol and West Sussex universities), and those patient university staff members who politely reminded me it was time to 'lock up', when I forgot the time, absorbed as I was with my practice, teaching and research.

Moreover, I have had the pleasure (and occasionally the pain) of being fortunate enough to work with certain individuals whose physical abilities in Karate, were only eclipsed by their intelligence. Those people include: Sensei(s) Martin Johnston, Dave Franks, David Blachford, Roy Smith, Steve Nowaki, Kevin Owen, Kevin Luce, Garry Mcglone, Professor Andy Cundy, Dr. Daniel Langton and Dr. Robert Wallis. Thanks to my long term friend, Sensei Simon Budden, for his insights into how a proper Karate club should be run, and for letting me weary his ears with my ideas.

My thanks go to, Dr. Elliot Cohen and Dr. Duncan Thomas, who as well as developing solid Karate skills, provided a great soundtrack for the DVD. Special thanks go the film-maker extraordinaire, James Watson, for making a 'silk purse out of a sow's ear'.

I would also like to thank, Tom Maxwell, Matthew Turner, James and David Faid, and Sensei Steve Rowe – of Shi Kon Budo – who has always acted as a sane, steady and reliable voice in the sometimes crazy world of Martial Arts. I also thank Shanir Patel for his organisational skills, Kenneth Lymer for the book design and layout, and The Wykeham Press for publishing this book.

Finally, I am deeply grateful to *all those*, far too numerous to name here, who helped with the arduous and often daunting task of 'restoration', mostly by being willing 'spare pairs' of arms that helped to test-out various hypotheses over some fifteen years of unremitting labour.

Nathan J. Johnson
Winchester, England 2006

Chapter One
The Great Karate Myth – A Synopsis

ALTHOUGH PERHAPS somewhat unconventional, this entire chapter is designed as a (thesis-sized) synopsis. Whilst not aiming at completeness, it is intended to give readers immediate access to the substance of the book. Thereafter, much of the material is repeated, developed, explained, and expanded-upon in the rest of the book.

'The Great Karate Myth' challenges many popular misconceptions about Karate by tackling the myths behind the purpose and functions of its traditional kata and replacing them with hard evidence and precise applications. The kata described herein, and demonstrated on the DVD, fall into two basic categories; those that I shall designate as *Karate Kata*, meaning empty hands/weapon-less kata, and those I shall designate as *Kobudo Kata* – ancient weapons kata. I do this because, in many cases, the two have unfortunately become confused.

In respect of Karate kata, as I have said, explanations of many kata are extremely problematic in terms of practical application and have, for many years, been a veritable 'battleground' of opinion, disagreement, doubt and uncertainty for many thousands of Karate teachers, tens of thousands of experienced practitioners, and many hundreds of thousands of inexperienced enthusiasts or observers worldwide. Many unworkable theories and much 'exoticism' present in the field of Karate stems from this collective confusion which is ably fuelled by film and computer-game inspired fantasy, naivety, and false expectation regarding the actual purpose and function of antique kata.

It is now almost universally the case that one can visit several different dojo (practice hall/s) all ostensibly teaching the same kata and find many different sets of applications for these same kata! Indeed, it has become the norm for 'multi layered' applications to be put forward (although admittedly, most applications don't progress beyond basic block/counterattack combinations). Seldom is an alternative considered – an alternative that insists that there were once quan (kata) with *specific applications*. Metaphorically speaking, a wrench can be used to hammer in screws, but …

The great Okinawan Karate pioneer, Miyagi Chojun (1888–1953) stated that (closed-fist) Sanchin, Tensho (Rokushu) and Naihanchin (Tekki) kata – detailed in this book – are the (three) *fundamental* kata, of *all* Okinawan Karate. He was right (in the context of weapon-less kata). But paradoxically, the actual *applications* of these important kata do not support Karate as it is currently portrayed or imagined. Even more striking is the fact that many Okinawan Karate kata (originally imported from China) practiced the world over and traditionally considered to be methods of weapon-less self defence, *were unquestionably designed as weapons kata*, employing tactics, strategies, and combat-engagement-distances suitable for use with and against weapons, but *unsuitable* for practical use in unarmed combat.

This book offers irrefutable evidence that key Karate kata, routinely practiced as unarmed self defence, are, in actuality, weapons kata simply practiced without the weapons! This accounts for the exotic appearance of many kata and is a major reason for the confusion regarding applications. This historic misunderstanding (or deliberate adaptation) has ultimately led to the current widespread dissatisfaction amongst many serious

Karate practitioners in their various attempts to apply supposed unarmed kata in *practical* and *spontaneous* ways. Consequently it is not Karate politics alone that has caused the formation of more modern Karate styles than can easily be counted.

Nagamine Shoshin wrote in his voluminous *The Essence of Okinawan Karate-Do* (Tokyo: Tuttle 1976) p.56:

> There are as many theories concerning the origins and executions of the kata as there are schools of karate. Some have theorized, for example, that the movements of the kata derived from mimicking the protective movements of animals. Others have speculated that the kata grew out of ancient dance forms ... Unfortunately, the lack of a comprehensive theory of the movements and how they are executed results in less interest in simple practice of the basic movements of the kata.

Of course, it is the case that some (modern) kata were not constructed for practical application at all, being constructed instead for martial display, exercise, the cultivation of general martial 'prowess' and to provide a culturally-based physical education curriculum for Okinawan schoolchildren, one that would, within twenty years of its inception, be adopted by mainland Japanese university students.

It is likely that kata created or modified during the last century were constructed or adapted on the *assumption* that the original source material found in the Chinese prototypes represented a weapon-less, unarmed art. But, at work here is one, or at the most, two possibilities: ignorance or concealment. Ignorance insomuch as the weapon-based function of many kata may have been unknown to the early (Okinawan) inheritors of Chinese quan, or, the total concealment of the fact that the antique quan – from which many Karate kata were created – were originally weapons kata.

During the last century, new kata were indeed created by re-ordering and re-assembling the component parts of existing kata. For example, the popular Pinan (Hein kata of Shotokan) – reportedly created to make Karate more accessible to Okinawan schoolchildren – were completed perhaps as late as 1908, and are quite clearly composed of elements taken from the much older Wanshu (Enpi), Passai (Bassai), Ouseishi (Gojushiho), Chinto (Gankaku) and Kusanku (Kanku dai) kata. If, indeed, as I suggest, these 'antique' kata were originally constructed to catalogue (conceal) techniques designed to be used with weapons, then component parts taken from them to form new kata become extremely problematic in terms of unarmed combat, no matter how clever contemporary explanations or applications may seem to be.

Selected Chinto solo techniques

Selected Chinto solo techniques with weapons

More Chinto solo techniques...

...with weapons...

...and applied

Opening Kusanku solo technique without sai

Applied Kusanku opening technique

Perhaps stemming from the Oriental habit of respecting the 'old masters' and their guidelines, whilst no one doubts the existence and practicality of, for example, a car, few have dared to suggest – metaphorically speaking – that, no matter how attractive the bodywork may be, a car will not run if the fuel tank is removed, and the radiator disconnected and 'mysteriously' but very neatly welded onto the tailgate. As ever with certain types of 'tradition', distortion appears at times of strife and under circumstances of great duress. Left un-repaired, and given enough time (and support), distorted elements of a tradition eventually become established, though in this case, in respect of kata applications, no one can – so to speak – seem to drive the 'traditional Karate' car at all, despite many attempts to do so. The fault here lies with the mechanic, not with the undoubted existence or possibility of a working car, and the functional engineering of the designers.

Pieced together on the small island of Okinawa, where its practice and development was shrouded in secrecy, Karate is now a globally practiced art, particularly popular with children. Clearly, the average ten year old taking Karate classes is not going to want to know where the kata came from, or be willingly lectured on the tiresome names, dates and details (errors too). No, the average junior Karate student just wants to get on and 'do it', enjoy it, and pass the grades, etc. The same can be said for many adult Karate students too. In fact, this has been how Karate has 'ticked along', for years.

Partisan loyalty develops fairly early in Karate students. Because modern humans are in many ways still 'tribal', it is easy to see why. As people learn to do things a certain way, that way becomes the norm for them. Within Karate, this situation has lead, in the past, to the collective entrenchment of ideas and practices that are often fiercely defended, no matter how peculiar they are or questionable they may be. Thus, ways of doing things are seen by those involved in them as, 'our way of doing things', 'our style', akin to an almost family-like state of affairs.

However, what I explain here is extremely important! I am not merely concerned with stylistic nuances or with obscure technical differences between styles that seemingly practice the same kata, but with the *radical* difference between the purposes those kata were originally designed for and those they are used for today. They are definitely not the same! If I am going to challenge the status quo of any 'collective', people will of course instinctively defend their 'way of doing things' and I am well aware of this. But I have chosen to be blunt in my exposé, to trust in the intelligence of my readers, and to tell the tale as directly as I can.

Market forces are a fact of life, and Karate too has its leading brands, and admittedly, it is easy to become comfortably cocooned in the 'safety in numbers' and alleged authenticity of 'corporate' Karate, the bastion of tradition, but actually the product of intense 'eclecticism'. It is the age-old story of that which was once new becoming traditional. So, once tradition is created, the whole 'shebang' gets passed down, 'warts and all', particularly because, excepting the professionals, Karate is, for most people, just a hobby – an amateur interest. The teachers have mainly taught in turn what they were taught, and things that don't add up or are not clearly understood have been passed on as 'tradition'. But the situation is changing.

Karate has now reached such large worldwide audiences that *several millions* of modern Karate practitioners are now asking the sorts of questions that, in the main, were largely *unasked* by *several hundred* Okinawan practitioners of *early* To-te. There are now increasing numbers of Western and other practitioners with many years of experience, who no longer want to have their basic techniques (honed through years of sweat and effort) 'corrected' by a new generation of visiting (corporate placed) younger, but unjustifiably higher-ranked, overseas Sensei, whilst the most important questions regarding kata still go unanswered.

Please do not mistake my motives here. This is not a matter of 'sour grapes'. Neither is grade an issue. And I am not against corporate Karate. Indeed I have learned – the hard way – about its benefits, and what it does well (as I will acknowledge later). I can readily see the need for people to consolidate, in the way major Karate styles have done. Groups and societies need to set norms and standards, whatever the subject, unless an 'avant-garde' non-leadership is professed, in which case someone will spring-up and become the leader anyway. It is clear that regulations for governance and conduct, etc. must be established and maintained within Karate groups, and standards set for grading.

Even though I can in no way be considered as a conventional Karate practitioner, I have spent a more than significant part of my life fervently engaged in Karate practice and research, so I am appalled by the number of 'self confessed – five years of training – instant experts', who turn themselves and their few friends into 'founders', 'masters', 'researchers' or what-have-you. These modern (often) internet-based 'experts' do not hesitate to analyse, categorise, theorise and 'cherry pick' the hard work and research of others, giving only fleeting and grudging acknowledgement to sources, whilst passing off (distortions of) other peoples work as their own 'research'. Feeding off the flesh of a fragmenting corporate Karate, the very Karate that gave them something to occupy themselves with in the first place, these 'experts' are swift to advertise their own 'superiority'. I am not one of these 'species' of 'expert' and I distance myself from them and their intrigues. Karate has been and is my life, and whilst my findings may indeed be challenging, they are expressed in earnest. Furthermore, I respect the major Karate founders and those honest individuals who have, by the sweat of their brows kept Karate alive, not with a bunch of eccentric flow charts, wacky theories and naive opinions, but through sweat and effort in the dojo.

Yet there remain many important and longstanding questions that need precise answers. 'Traditionally' those who questioned were reproached with admonitions such as, 'train harder/faster, trust tradition', or, 'one day you will understand'. But with regard to Karate kata application, such advice actually attests to a fluid and uncertain tradition, a tradition in the making rather than an established one, a tradition that has struggled to make sense of its own legacy and has therefore often resorted to ambiguity, vagueness and in extreme cases, face-saving tactics when challenged with the difficulties of fully explaining kata. Consequently, many, and often seriously conflicting explanations for the anomalies in Karate kata have begun to creep in. Add to this the new breed of 'instant Karate instructors' and it's no wonder that confusion has reached a critical point.

Modern Karate – Not One Practice but Three

Compounding the confusion mentioned above is the fact that (aside from Karate basics, kata and sparring) currently, much modern Karate consists of three largely separate and arguably conflicting approaches:

1. 'Traditional Karate' which includes kata and formal *choreographed* applications.

2. 'Freestyle Karate', which includes sport Karate and free-sparring that utilises natural/informal movements, high kicks and Westernized punching techniques.

3. 'Self Defence Karate' which does not rely upon (or in many cases even) practice kata, orienting itself instead to the rehearsal of perceived scenes of confrontation focusing on modern urban street conflict. Traditional dojo deportment and etiquette are of little interest to the devotees of urban combat.

It is important to note that free-sparring is relatively new to Karate. It only started out (in the main) in Japanese universities during the 1920s and 30s, when students and teachers alike were anxious to provide Karate with a competitive framework similar to Judo and Kendo. Prior to this period, Karate sparring was pre-arranged, and the performance of solo and group *kata* was the main focus of attention. Currently, many modern Karate styles claim to practice both traditional and competitive Karate.

The Difficulties of Applying Kata

It is quite astonishing how many Martial Artists tirelessly work their way through innumerable quan/kata trusting that they will

36

one-day arrive at the applications intuitively. Many, despite having a deep-seated desire to apply the techniques automatically, remain unable to apply the techniques *spontaneously*; that is, without pre-arranging the attacks and the defences, despite a remote feeling that somehow they do (or will be able to). A point I will revisit later.

One major difficulty experienced by Karate-ka trying to apply techniques from kata is that of knowing which technique to apply, when and how. By this I mean that real fights aren't choreographed and demand a degree of spontaneity that more closely resembles free-fighting than it does 'traditional' (rehearsed/formal) kata applications.

A swift scan of your own imagination can easily raise nominal solutions to various perceived self defence scenarios, and the modern (film-fed) psyche has been relentlessly bombarded by, and become so used to, choreographed fight scenes, as to almost believe they represent reality; the most typical example being that of a lone Martial Arts expert defeating several 'bad guys' by using techniques that work flawlessly. Many demonstrations of Karate kata applications reflect this choreography, their focus of attention being of course on the hero who lashes out continuously, connecting with winning shots, kicks, or strikes that 'take out' the bad guy(s). Seldom do we envisage the good guy's techniques failing, and him (and by proxy you) taking 'punishment'.

It is this process of imagination that validates much that passes for 'Traditional' Martial Arts. By this I mean that many things that are commonly imagined to work in a fight would not and do not, as so many modern combat specialists are now proving! It is fortunate that for most individuals, the whole subject of how one might respond in various fight situations has only ever to be dealt with in the imagination (or on screen). Happily, despite quite natural fears of violent confrontation, broadly speaking, most people, most days, do not have a (real) fight.

I suspect that 'To-te' (ancient Karate) was originally intended to be practiced only by professionals and generally used in policing and the keeping of civil order, rather than for demonstration, sport, recreation or consumption by the general public. In that sense, the art would have originally been less theoretical than it has become today because it was actually being employed, and, as I will point out shortly, not in the ways commonly imagined today, or even for the reasons commonly believed in today. Re-appraisal of the nature and intentions behind the creation of the antique kata sheds new light on the problems currently being experienced by those interested in how techniques from traditional kata are meant to be applied without pre-arranging. Moreover it will shortly become apparent why Karate-ka have been unable to achieve this.

Due to a change in the emphasis put on *modern* interpretations of ancient (Karate) kata as being unarmed block, strike and punch/kick techniques (which I will later illustrate they are not), incredibly, the assumed link between the constant rehearsal of fixed choreographed sequences (the so called 'bunkai' or 'traditional' unarmed kata applications) and practical combat efficiency in a vulgar fist fight, remains totally unproven; a puzzle I have long wanted to solve. I argue; *the techniques and the (working) distances recorded in the antique kata are not those of a stand up fist fight but of weapons or grappling!*

'Traditional' Karate techniques stemming from kata, if applied at all, and even if applied at speed, generally present in a 'stop start' fashion using time-consuming fixed blocking techniques and impractical positions that appear cumbersome and unwieldy and are unworkable against an unarmed compound attack (combination blows). In 'traditional' Karate, often, an attacker, whose attack has been 'blocked', is still capable of launching further attacks, yet he does not do so and remains (relatively) still while the defender counterattacks. A fast furious combination attack usually has to be dealt with in 'free-style' mode, meaning the elegant and (time consuming) classical kata techniques (often requiring full steps to execute) 'go out the window', so to speak. Just take a look at free-sparring!

Below, you can see a typical 'bunkai' in which the attacker is still capable of delivering another attack yet does not do so.

A typical modern example of 'Bunkai'

If you are an experienced Karate practitioner, ask yourself now, when was the last time you used an 'X' block, a 'sword-hand-block', a 'double block', an 'augmented forearm block', a 'double punch' (punching with both hands at the same time), etc. in free-sparring? A determined (not to mention skilled) opponent never stays still for long enough for many so-called 'classical' techniques to be used. Consequently, many established (but actually quite modern) Karate kata applications are now quite properly being rejected as naive and impractical by a growing army of dissatisfied practitioners worldwide.

The Myth of 'Blocking'

Traditional (actually read modern) Karate has 'blocking' techniques – established methods for warding off and deflecting blows and even kicks. Indeed, Karate has especially formal methods of blocking attacks. Unfortunately, the co-responding attacks are equally as formal. Further, they are generally commenced outside of contact, or even striking distance.

When such attacks and responses were first demonstrated to Westerners, they were perceived to be extraordinary and mysterious, and Karate was greeted with awe and admiration as it swiftly captured the popular imagination. Fascinated by the crispness of the techniques, always demonstrated in attractive symmetrical postures and executed with precision and dignity, the West eagerly embraced Karate. Soon however, Western Karate-ka would gain their-own experience – relative experience. Comparisons with boxing were quickly made, and forays into American style kickboxing and other 'full contact' arts began to generate many questions regarding the efficiency of the highly ritualised block and strike tactics of the revealed 'traditional Karate'. Numerous pioneering Karate-ka soon began to notice glaring discrepancies between traditional Karate (including pre-arranged sparring), free-sparring (not pre-arranged) and requirements for practical self defence. In free-sparring and self defence, obvious difficulties lay in determining which block was required and being able to apply it in time. Another general difficulty – one often painfully discovered – was that of applying a 'traditional' blocking technique against fast and unconventional (non Karate) punches.

'Traditional' blocking methods are applied only after first pre-arranging a target with the attacker *calling-out* the method of attack to be used. It is often assumed that through repeated practice of this, the defender will eventually be able to judge the target and direction of a randomly aimed attack and apply the correct traditional block. But, there is no evidence for this – quite the opposite in fact.

In modern Karate, a common and often used attack is the middle level straight punch, executed after taking a full step forward and finishing with the same hand and leg forward. In some respects this attack is rather similar in terms of commitment to thrusting with a pole/staff which I will discuss shortly. This same hand same leg forward, full step and punch, is often referred to as the 'lunge punch' or as 'oi-tsuki' – chasing punch. It is also known as 'jun-tsuki' – front punch. The 'lunge punch' is a (the) standard attack against which (modern) Karate defences are practiced. In this attack, the punching arm is thrust out and not withdrawn or retracted as it would be, in for example, a 'snap punch'; a type of punch in which the fist is speedily thrust out and withdrawn equally as quickly. Whilst the snap punch is commonly used in free-sparring, the lunge punch is not. The lunge punch is relatively easy to block using so-called traditional Karate blocks. This is because the punching arm remains extended long enough for the defender to apply a so-called traditional block, and, as I have said, the attack is pre-arranged. This is not the case for a snap punch which is pulled back and removed at such speed that all the defender can do is slap at it.

Traditional Karate blocking techniques are executed in two movements, a preparation stage (such as raising the hand prior to executing a downward block) and the actual block itself, although Funakoshi Gichin (1868–1957, the 'father' of modern Japanese Karate) stated that the two parts should become one. The attacker's traditional use of the formal stepping punch provides both the time and the (weapons style) distance for the defender to use these two-part blocking techniques. Oddly, the 'lunge punch' attack is commenced from a distance that is

41

actually out of range for weapon-less combat. In fact, the experienced eye will easily recognise the 'Maai' or distance used in modern Karate is very similar to that used in Kendo (a modern Japanese sport that uses 'Shinai', a split bamboo imitation sword).

Training against the 'lunge punch', whilst giving the time and opportunity for the defender to 'react' (actually choose a defence), relies on visual reflexes (looking, thinking, responding). Moreover, any skill acquired in this format does not necessarily translate usefully if the attacker is already in range. In other words, there is no time for such defences if the attacker does not need to step in to attack. Instead, makeshift, improvised, and more natural defences must be used, similar in nature to those

The 'Lunge Punch'

'Defence'

frequently seen in free-sparring or full contact Karate tournaments. This is what ultimately produces the 'kickboxing' type approach, where a fighter instinctively 'covers up' to prevent himself from being hit, and launches his counterattacks (or attacks) from behind his 'cover'.

It is fine for modern 'free-style' Karate-ka to use the double-cover, hunched shoulders, bobbing and weaving rhythms of modern boxing, but as effective as it is, it should be clearly understood that such movements, attitudes and postures are not implicit in Karate kata; they are modern, being largely influenced by Western sparring adapted from the functional no-nonsense craft of boxing. The combination punches of Western boxing, when used skilfully, are immensely practical, and the rhythm and cadence of such are impossible to deal with using a (static) Karate block/hit strategy.

Traditional Karate is a non-contact art. As soon as an element of contact is introduced, the blocking methods begin to fail. That is another reason why there are no formal blocking techniques in Western boxing, Thai boxing, modern kickboxing and full contact Karate. Such stylists do not carry their hands high whilst protecting their ribs with their elbows for stylistic reasons. They do so to avoid being hit! Those who have experience of trading actual blows from realistic distances seldom separate their arms very far from their bodies. By this I mean that they do not, for example, block downwards with a large sweeping block.

Such a technique will only expose the user to a follow-up aimed at the head. Similarly a large upwards block is not a practical (or sensible) option. It takes too long and leaves the user vulnerable. The practical solution adopted by 'contact' fighters is to 'crouch and cover-up' adjusting the arms minimally before 'exploding' with a counterattack,

Two variations of the 'downward sweeping block'

Reality check: Boxing 'bolo punch'

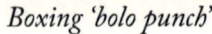
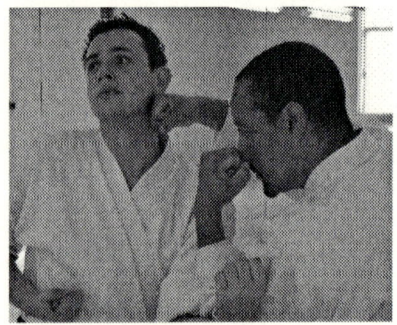

Boxing 'bolo punch'   *From another angle*

using, for example, devastating close-range power-packed hook punches. Inexperienced full contact fighters, in separating (extending) their arms away from their bodies in attempts to 'block', simply get hit as I have said, by a follow up, or react to what was only a feint and get hit anyway.

The overused 'stepping punch'

Another view

The reliance on the full step 'lunge punch' in traditional Karate is idiosyncratic. For example, in one International Goju Ryu organisation, out of some seventy-seven (demonstrated) kata-based applications (bunkai) purporting to reflect the scope and range of techniques in the kata, a staggering *fifty-five* (varying) defences are used against attacks always initiated with

THE GREAT KARATE MYTH

the same punch, the 'lunge punch', an attack initiated, as I have said, from outside the contact range. In short, there were fifty-five defences demonstrated against what was fundamentally the same (stepping) straight punch in each case. What's more, in most examples, an immediate counterattack was launched after the block, even though it was still possible (probable) that the attacker could or would launch another attack, particularly with his other (free) hand. This is certainly something seen in tournament fighting, where 'simultaneous exchange' (both people punching or kicking at the same time) is the bane of referees trying to decide who's scored.

In the 'bunkai' discussed above, there were eleven defences against a front kick demonstrated, ten defences against clothing grips, body grabs and rarely wrist grips, and there were two defences conducted against knife attacks. The knife attacks were delivered in the ritualised 'lunge punch' format, resulting in what amounts to a 'lunge punch' with a knife.

Similarly, in the official (former) Japan Karate Association (Shotokan) ballistic 'bunkai' to Naihanchin 1, 2 & 3 (Tekki) (see the companion DVD), the formal 'lunge punch' and weapons distances can clearly be seen. In this 'bunkai', multiple attackers assume remote (distant) positions relative to the defender whose 'application' of the techniques requires such a high level of choreography as to render it highly improbable, thus giving the defence a surreal and impractical look.

This is an extremely important point because it highlights exactly why modern Karate struggles to make sense of many so-called 'traditional' kata applications. Indeed, only Karate-ka would attack in the prescribed way and use the distance required to attack with a 'lunge punch'. Also, *such a format makes it appear that the attacks have been designed and orchestrated to fit (read justify) the defences!* It is precisely this 'putting the cart before the

Common 'Tekki' (Naihanchin) application

horse' approach that creates such improbable applications. I have decided (for the sake of brevity) that one filmed example (The Working Distance) of this common approach to Karate kata applications would suffice to make the following three important points (see DVD):

1. The distances being used in such applications are actually weapons distances.

2. The types of fixed attacks being used resemble the restriction imposed and the commitment needed in the use of a weapon; a pole or staff for example.

3. The common 'bunkai' for Tekki presents as a double whammy because a close quarters grappling kata is being used in the way perhaps a Kobudo (Sai) kata should be used, *yet no weapons are present!*

I will explain these important points in more detail in the following chapters.

The Pursuit of Correct Form

Essentially, 'ritual' attack and ritual defence – practiced according to proper or 'correct' form, executed with proper etiquette, deportment, attitude and spirit, is a very Japanese idea. But remember, the kata in question are Okinawan modifications of Chineses Quan-fa or Kung Fu forms. In the main, this (unarmed) ritual methodology is arguably totally inefficient and ineffective against a fluid, freestyle kickboxing-ground-grappling type of approach to combat. In reality, the 'attitudes' (postures) taken, combined with the types of techniques used in so-called 'traditional' Karate kata, plus the timing and the (weapons) distance used, all help to attest to the fact that much (modern)

Karate evolved out of techniques, attitudes, postures and distances originally designed for use with and against weapons.

In Japanese thought, sometimes correct form is more important than the result! Although this idea may have originated in Zen Buddhism, it has permeated out and become, in some respects, a cultural phenomenon. There is one famous story of a veteran American baseball player (who could hit a ball out of the stadium) hired by a Japanese team as a coach. He was soon dismissed and sent home; his 'form' was wrong! Many Japanese golfers actively pursue the ideal golf swing clearly defined by greats such as Arnold Palmer whose golf swing has become 'classical'. But, from a practical perspective, form is only an indication of function!

In summary, without wishing to be dismissive or seem flippant here, several methods of blocking the same – for argument's sake – straight punch is, from a *practical* perspective, unnecessary, when one or two will do. The usual reason given for practicing several middle-level blocks is that the block is selected according to the circumstances. Yet the standard Karate attack (punch) is invariable. I refer here to the stepping punch mentioned earlier. Defence against this attack is dependent upon the target being pre-selected. The whole process is operated by means of a *visual* reflex and is structurally slow, despite the relative speed of well-drilled exponents.

The only possible advantage that can be claimed to justify the choice of block is the potential positional advantage it may give.

Usually to be on the *outside* of the opponents attacking arm is best (the 'corner'); either that or the opponent's free hand must be 'checked', tied-up or trapped whilst you make your counterattack. These methods make it more difficult for the opponent to follow up. The Chinese (Quan-fa) habit of controlling the 'gates' (see

Finding the corner

chapter five) and using a simultaneous 'trap and counter', still remain superior in every way! These days, many Karate-ka will claim they do practice simultaneous block and strike combinations. Indeed, with greater exposure to Kung Fu, Karate kata 'bunkai' have become increasingly 'creative', making many of the so-called 'traditional' basic block and counter techniques logically redundant. Yet modern Karate-ka practice so many kata that each style has a vast collection of applications to justify! That is how the situation of fifty-five defences against a simple straight punch has come about. Clearly there must be some kind of attack to defend against in each instance, particularly if the techniques are always applied on a gap, that is, without contact.

However, using typical Chinese methodology, techniques will be utilised, for example, in Ko-do Ryu, under a variety of circumstances and applied with contact, from a pushing hands/ wrestling situation, hands-on and without pre-arrangement (see chapter five). Moreover, with contact, many techniques will be pro-active, rather than mere responses; combination wrist and arm locks, applied after contact, for example.

Even when the techniques from the kata are thoroughly learned in a prearranged way using visual reflexes, without the vital element of contact, no further progress is possible (see Contact Reflexes, chapter five). To work spontaneously, the application of techniques need to *be wired up*, so to speak; they require *contact*, and the ability to *feel* the direction and magnitude of a force in order to act instantly and appropriately (think wrestling rather than boxing). *A prearranged strategy based on knowledge of a sequence will never lead to spontaneity.* There is no magical trigger that will tell you what to do in time, only natural reflexes. Just consider again the difference between freestyle sparring – where one never sees a formal or properly executed block – and the formal application of kata techniques (bunkai).

Yet, even Karate free-sparring or free-fighting, with its eye-catching high kicks and 'kickboxing' format, although relatively effective and popular, is incapable of even partially reflecting the richness and variety of techniques found in traditional kata, whilst the methods advocated by modern self defence approaches do not, as I have said, reflect traditional kata either; far from it in fact – a point I will expand upon in chapter two.

Karate is often stereotyped as a violent art epitomised by flashy high kicks, but many kicking techniques are relatively modern. Even the 'traditional' kicking techniques represent less than ten percent of the technical material found in the antique kata where they are seldom directed at high targets (kicking techniques are briefly discussed later in this chapter and again in the appendix). The other ninety or so percent of Karate techniques are often viewed as a vast collection of somewhat exotic, but allegedly, 'lethal' 'blocking' and 'striking' techniques that are 'traditional', a little peculiar, and are somehow supposed to be more ruthlessly efficient than conventional methods of delivering impact force (Western boxing for example). The reality is quite different.

Karate Kata – Misunderstood Weapons Kata

In this book I describe at length how and why much so-called 'Traditional Karate', catalogued in solo choreographed sequences and presented as a weapon-less art, grew from (attempts to use) kata originally designed explicitly for use with a pair of Sai (a civil arrest tool used extensively in Southern China and dating from at least the Ming dynasty). I also explain that techniques intended to be used for *grappling*, were misconstrued as 'ballistic' block/punch/strike/techniques – thus creating the 'Great Karate Myth'.

The considerable frustration and criticism vocalised by many experienced modern Karate practitioners, unimpressed by, or unhappy with, modern, impractical and unconvincing *unarmed* interpretations of (many) traditional Karate kata, can now be justified, or at least understood. In fact, the misgivings expressed by these practitioners regarding the usefulness of traditional Karate kata, currently stretches to utter condemnation in some quarters. Sadly, this situation has already begun to affect the way traditional Karate is perceived, casting doubt on its value in the modern world.

One major source of the general confusion regarding kata hinges on *why* a given kata (intended, we are told, for unarmed self defence) is sequenced the way it is. If such was meant to illustrate possible ways of, for instance, fighting several enemies at once (now discredited), then what are the criteria for choosing one ordering of a kata over another? If it is random, why value a traditional kata over a kata of one's own devising? Clearly the kata were created by someone – by 'people'. But the eminent qualifications – if not the sheer genius – of those who created the kata presented in this book, can only become readily apparent if the precise *functions* are made absolutely clear. A true kata is properly sequenced or ordered for practical, logical and consistent reasons! Indeed, genuine kata have clear intentions behind their construction, and this must surely distinguish the 'real Karate' and Kobudo.

Grappling and Civil Arrest

So far, I have suggested much that constitutes supposed weapon-less kata-based Karate was predicated either unwittingly or wittingly upon techniques originally designed to be used with weapons. I will offer proof shortly. Meanwhile, it is also necessary to consider Naihanchin (Tekki 1, 2 & 3). My detailed research establishes that Naihanchin is a mainstream Shuri-te kata, comprised of techniques that in fact catalogue double armed grappling procedures designed to completely subdue and restrain an opponent via the twisting of wrist joints, and the 'locking' of elbow joints, to 'arrest' that opponent. Indeed I will describe Naihanchin later in this chapter under the heading, 'The Missing Grappling Techniques' and again, more fully in chapter eight, in which I will also fully explain the relationship between Naihanchin – actually a Chinese quan – and Chinese Ming dynasty civil arrest techniques. Grappling techniques were known as Chin-Na (to seize and grapple, pronounced 'chee – naa') in China where they were undoubtedly used to make unarmed arrests.

Note, the use of the term 'arrest' does not imply that the person being 'arrested' is necessarily a criminal as such, but just that their movement (and therefore their immediate liberty) is arrested, stopped, or jammed.

The Sai

The Sai, a pronged weapon, used in pairs, is quite literally the *key* to understanding many 'classical' so-called Karate kata and their applications, because these kata (open handed Sanchin, Seisan and Kusanku for examples) not only reflect the use of these classical 'tools' but are the exact physical records of how to wield them, how to orient them, and how to manipulate them.

The Sai – key to traditional Karate kata

Despite its (initial) appearance, *the Sai is not a stabbing weapon.* The pommel or 'knub' at the top of the handle is the main part of the Sai used in striking. The shaft is occasionally used to 'punish' (the hand that grips a weapon) but is mainly used to protect the user's forearms when the Sai is held (pointing backwards) with the pommel positioned thumb-side of the hand, and also in conjunction with the foil to catch and trap an incoming weapon when the Sai is used (pointing forward) with the pommel positioned little-finger-side of the hand.

Grappling and the Sai – The Connection

Chin-Na originally underpinned a 'civil arrest' tradition that utilised Sai to disarm and arrest an armed offender, and 'seizing and grappling' techniques to subdue and arrest an un-armed offender, without killing or maiming in either case. The object being to ensure an offender was given the opportunity – required by law – to be detained according to the due process of law and rendered up in fit condition to face trial. This was unquestionably a civil matter and not a military one, even though it must have involved or included members of the military too. The methods used and described above, were intended for use on behalf of the civil authorities and most likely pertained only to tackling and resolving incidences under civil jurisdiction.

About the Classification of Kata in this Book

Experienced Karate practitioners may find the following classification of certain kata, usually considered as unarmed kata and described in this book as Kobudo (weapons) kata to be unusual. This is understandable because, in the past, these kata have erroneously been designated as weapon-less kata – as unarmed self defence.

The Kihon or Fundamental/Basic (Weapon-less) Karate Kata
(Recorded by Miyagi Chojun as such)

The following three kata are fully explained and illustrated in chapters six, seven and eight.

'Closed-fist' Sanchin

Tensho (Rokushu)

Naihanchin (Tekki)

There are an uncountable number of – modern – Karate styles worldwide. However, the styles mentioned below can be considered as mainstream. The following list broadly establishes which of these styles practice which of the respective kata dealt with in this book. It is, however, beyond the scope of this book to give complete descriptions of these styles or of all the kata. Please note, as there are many varieties of Goju Ryu and Shorin Ryu Karate (formerly Naha-te and Shuri-te), I have decided to generalise them all under the simple terms Goju Ryu (hard, soft style) and Shorin Ryu (Shao-lin [Temple] style). Other listed styles are usually an amalgam of, or use kata selected from, either or both the Naha and Shuri strains.

Ryu can be considered as a generic Japanese term for a Martial Arts group or school. It can also be considered as a Martial Arts 'family' group (not necessarily with biological links) somewhat akin to a fraternity. 'Kan' means a (training) hall, Kai roughly means association, organisation/group, and 'Do' means (the) way, analogous to the Chinese 'Tao'.

Major Karate Styles that practice (Miyagi) Sanchin and Tensho:
   Goju Ryu (Okinawa and Japan: international)
   Goju Kai (Japan: international)
   Kyokushinkai (Japan: international)
   Shito Ryu (Okinawa: international)
   Karate Do Shotokai (UK)

Major Karate Styles that practice Naihanchi(n) (Tekki):
   Shorin Ryu (Okinawa: international)
   Shotokan (Japan: international)
   Shotokai (Japan: international)
   Wado Ryu and Wado Kai (Japan: international)
   Shito Ryu (Okinawa: international)

The following three kata can be found in *Uechi Ryu*, a major Okinawan Karate style in which they are considered to be 'empty hand' that is, weapon-less kata, a classification with which I respectfully disagree, as the evidence and proof of their actual functions is overwhelming (see below, and Sanchin/Sesian on film).

These three kata were later modified for inclusion in the Okinawan Goju Ryu Karate style, and subsequently their original functions have been obscured.

Uechi Ryu Kata
(Actually *Kobudo* Kata in their Original Chinese Forms)

Uechi (Kobudo) Sanchin and Sesian are illustrated in chapter nine:

1. Sanchin (the old open handed version)
2. Seisan
3. Sanseirui

Due to space limitations, the following Shuri-te kata are not dealt with at length in this book; the antique Wanshu (Enpi), Pasai (Bassai), Chinto (Gankaku), and Kusanku (Kwanku/Kanku-dai). However, my research confirms that, *in their original versions, these are weapons kata too*, although one must take into account 'modifications' made by the influential Okinawan Karate pioneer, 'Ankho' Yasatsune Itosu (1832–1915) who engaged in revising kata for popular modern consumption. The antique Rohai (Meikyo) and Ouseishi (Gojushiho) are most likely weapons-based kata too.

Some selected examples of the applications to these kata are given. Please bear in mind, there are several extant Okinawan and other 'versions' of most kata. For example, Passai (Bassai), can be found in at least the following *six* versions: 'Oyadomari-no Passai', 'Ishimine-no Passai', 'Tomari-no Passai', 'Matsumura-no Passai', 'Itosu-no Passai', and of course, the Shotokan 'Bassai'. Similarly, Kusanku can be found in the following versions: 'Shiho-Kusanku', 'Chibana-no Kusanku', 'Chatanyara-no Kusanku' and 'Kuniyoshi-no Kusanku'! One must also consider Matsubayashi Shorin Ryu's 'Kusanku' (arguably the 'Chatanyara' version), Funakoshi Gichin's 'Kwanku', and of course, modern Shotokan's 'Kanku dai' and Wado Ryu's 'Kanku'. The five Pinan (Heian) kata, being relatively recent inventions of Itosu's (circa 1905–1908) and designed to facilitate schoolboy Karate on Okinawa, were, as mentioned, constructed largely from existing antique kata, and are not treated here at all. The Goju Ryu kata Saifa, Seiyunchin, Shisochin, Sepai, Kururunfa, Suparinpei and Tensho kata are discussed in chapter three. Tensho (Rokushu) is fully discussed in chapter seven.

Sample Kusanku solo technique with and without sai

Application of Kusanku solo technique

The Proliferation of Kata

Modern Karate kata have proliferated to such an extent that it would be impossible to record them all, and kata are being invented even now to support 'home grown styles'. However, most modern kata are produced under the assumption that the prototypical antique kata (upon which they are often built) are unarmed self defence techniques of a ballistic (thrust, block, kick) nature, an assumption challenged in this book.

More does not necessarily mean better. More failure, for instance, is not 'better'. More kata does not necessarily mean better kata or better Karate. Proliferation of kata does not imply progress. In fact it has lead to much confusion!

One reason for the seeming proliferation of kata is the practice of 'adapting' or modifying an existing kata and giving it a new name, or adding an extra name to distinguish, for example, one 'Passai or Kusanku' from another. This practice has taken place for many years, and it seems that most people are content with this as long as the 'work' was, or is, done by an acknowledged (and famous) master. I would like to take a fresh look at this generally accepted practice by questioning whether the original modifiers were actually in receipt of the proper applications to the kata they modified in the first place.

Consider the ever-present Seisan kata, a kata that is absolutely central to much traditional Okinawan and Japanese Karate. Seisan is one of Okinawan Karate's oldest kata. Seisan means 'thirteen' and allegedly refers to the number of steps or techniques performed in the kata. In fact, chronologically, Seisan traditionally follows Sanchin and expands on the basic actions practiced in Sanchin kata.

Patrick McCarthy, the well respected Martial Arts expert, historian and author (holder of the prestigious grade of 'Kyoshi', 7th degree black belt, issued by the Dai Nipppon Butokukai, Japan), had this to say about Seisan kata in his *Classical Kata of Okinawan Karate* (Burbank, CA, 1987, Ohara), p.73:

> ... and in its many variations [Seisan] is the oldest kata still being practiced on Okinawa. (Parenthesis mine)

| *Uechi Seisan* | *Goju Seisan* | *Shotokan Hangetsu* |

Seisan is not only found – in modified form – in Goju Ryu Karate but also in extremely modified (and in places almost unrecognisable) versions in the popular Wado Ryu and Shotokan styles. In Shotokan Karate, Seisan is referred to as Hangetsu. Few people would suspect that the original version is still extant and can be found in the less popular (or well known) Uechi Ryu Karate style, one of the main so called Naha-te styles. It is quite easy to suspect that that the alterations made to Seisan kata were made without knowledge of the original function or application of the kata. Indeed, the Uechi Ryu Seisan certainly appears to be far more 'flowery' and 'Chinese' than the Goju Ryu Seisan or the (largely Japanese) Hangetsu. Further, I think Seisan (like other kata) was stripped of its suspected Chinese 'eccentricity' to be brought in line with the notions of a perceived (more) robust and practical emerging Okinawan art, an art openly declared to be an unarmed art – Karate!

Sesian without sai

Sesian with sai

A Sesian strike

In reality, the old version of Seisan is far, far more practical (than the modern versions) as long as the weapons it was supposed to utilise are included! Having been so radically altered, Hangetsu will not function as a weapons kata, and for me, its practicality as an unarmed/weapon-less kata lacks serious credibility. I will provide more (contextual) information on Seisan kata in chapter two, under the heading, 'What is the Okinawan Ryu-Ha Kihon Kata Tradition?' Further, in chapter three, I will demonstrate its pivotal role in the major Naha Karate traditions.

It is not particularly easy (for the untrained eye) to see how, or why, the old Sesisan (Uechi Ryu type) kata was transformed into the Shotokan Hangetsu kata. But we can begin by taking note that the (same) kata called Hangetsu in Shotokan is (still) called 'Sesan' in Wado Ryu, and that both versions can clearly be connected to Miyagi Chojun's (or Higaonna Kanyro's) version of Seisan, a point I will substantiate in chapter four. This situation probably occurred because Mabuni Kenwa (1889–1952) the influential founder of Shito Ryu Karate, and a friend/student of Miyagi Chojun, seems to have had some (indirect) influence on the kata eventually chosen to characterize the emerging Shotokan style of Karate. Also one must not rule out the considerable influence of Itosu Ankho who seems to have taught a modified version of Seisan.

A Goju Ryu practitioner who has learned Seisan kata will be able to recognise the Uechi Ryu Seisan and see elements of the original Chinese (Uechi) Seisan Kata in his kata, and a Shotokan practitioner will be able to see elements of Goju Ryu Sesan in his Hangetsu kata. But, neither the Uechi Ryu nor the Shotokan practitioner will be easily able to see the connection between their Seisan and Hangestsu kata respectively – the gulf is too great.

Practitioners of Japanese (Shuri-te based) Karate styles have inherited kata that have been considerably altered in format from their Okinawan originals. These changes have helped, in part, to obscure the actual functions. Fortunately, good examples of original Shuri-te kata were recorded by Nagamine Shoshin in his 'Okinawan Karate-do: The Preservation of a Legacy' Tokyo: (Shinjinbutsuorai-sha 1975). This seminal work was translated, re-titled and published by Charles E. Tuttle in 1976 as 'The Essence of Okinawan Karate-Do'.

In contrast to the 'shifting sands' of Shuri-te kata, which have changed considerably in the Shotokan and Wado Ryu formats, and unlike the kata of Goju Ryu, the Uechi kata remain virtually unchanged. George Mattson, a respected Uechi Ryu Karate Sensei of many years standing, recorded two of the three 'core' kata in 'The Way of Karate' (Rutland Vermont, Tokyo: Tuttle 1963). To come to the point, the ordering of these kata can be verified because they work! By work I mean they provide accurate mnemonics – prompts for when and how to manipulate a pair of Sai. Move by move, the purpose for each technique is clear and unambiguous once a pair of Sai is used. Moreover, the exact reason for the structure of each movement becomes readily apparent. The ordering of the kata sequences are justifiable and correct on that basis.

Many modern Karate-ka excel in solo kata performance, basics and sparring, and technical standards are extremely high in much

Karate. It's always the kata, or more specifically their applications that are problematic. After reaching the conclusions set out in this book, with respect, I can now suggest that one of the main reasons for the modern variations in kata hinges on the uncertainties regarding their applications.

One Technique, One Purpose

What defines the approach taken in this book towards the entire subject of Karate, and Kobudo, is the insistence that the 'kihon' (fundamental), empty hands kata (except Miyagi Sanchin – see chapter six), the formative Sanchin (the old open handed version), Seisan and Sanseriu, the key 'old style kata' presented here, have *exact* and *specific* applications! This goes against current thinking, which I suggest is somewhat misguided and reflects the fact that early Okinawan Quan-fa enthusiasts often found the Chinese quan (kata/solo forms) to be cryptic and somewhat impenetrable themselves.

Ambiguous applications for kata, devised much later than the actual kata themselves, and focussed incorrectly on weaponless combat to explain many techniques and kata designed, as I have said, to be used *with* weapons, have added hugely to the mystique of Karate, but has failed to deliver cohesion in Karate kata application/interpretation designated as being 'unarmed' combat. In short, this situation has created a climate of uncertainty, ultimately leading to the politically safe *'multiple application theory'* prevalent amongst modern traditionalists.

It is often claimed that, "Of course, kata techniques can be used with or without weapons … " And, "My hammer is also a screwdriver and a wood saw" – an approach that insists that a single technique in a given kata can do, A B C, or it can do, X Y Z, or it can do, 1 2 3, which means that, because the *specific* application of a given technique has been lost or is unclear, many 'applications' can, and are, attributed to it, and therefore unlimited possibilities can collectively be argued for a single ancient kata. Needless to say, generally speaking, I do not agree with this expedient but worn-out and utterly flawed theory. It is illogical, leads to abstraction or mystification and would not be tolerated in other fields (e.g. science, engineering, medicine, or general academia), although in the case of synthesised or radically altered or modified kata, modern interpreters are left little choice but to try and make sense of them however they can.

With the exception of Miyagi Sanchin, the kata in this book are *formula* rather than paradigms. Meaning, the applications to these kata are *specific* rather than conceptual. Nowadays it is usual for the kata to be perceived and considered in the way I will later consider Miyagi Sanchin (see chapter six). Miyagi Sanchin, like Itosu's five Pinan/Heian kata, is a synthetic kata. However, Sanchin in its various forms is central to Goju Ryu, Uechi Ryu and many other styles of Karate too.

Investigating the Sanchin Phenomenon

'Sanchin' (Sanchen, Fuzhou dialect – San Tzan, Mandarin dialect) translates from the Chinese, the Hogen (Okinawan dialect) and the Japanese as 'three' (san) and 'conflicts' or 'battles/struggles' (chin). Generally it consists of a simple and repetitive choreographed solo sequence of movements that commonly includes stepping (hoko), breathing synchronised with movement (kokyu), and technique (waza), presented in three distinct sections.

Within (Naha) Okinawan (and some Japanese) Karate styles, Sanchin kata is simultaneously considered to be the beginner's kata and paradoxically the most advanced or difficult kata to master. The same was reported – in respect of many Chinese Martial Arts – by Master Xia Bai Hua (long time Director of the Theoretical Wu Shu Research Institute, North of Beijing). He said (in an article published in *F.A.I.* vol 12, no 67):

> "In the Southern Shao-lin Temple Ancestors Boxing, 'San Chin' forms the basis for their breathing method, strength, stance and strategy, and consequently its study is both the preliminary and the advanced training." [Uechi Kanbun (1877–1948 – the founder of Uechi Ryu Karate) frequently claimed: "All is in Sanchin".] (Parenthesis mine)

It is rather difficult to talk in terms of the exact history of Sanchin kata because there are many versions extant (even in modern China), the origins of which lay shrouded in the mists of time. However, it is possible to unravel much of the mystery and iron-out some of the confusion regarding the open hand Sanchin taught in Qing dynasty China and taken to Okinawa during the nineteenth century, and the closed-fist Sanchin later developed by Miyagi Chojun.

The Sanchin kata of Miyagi Chojun

Sanchin, though often seemingly simple, provides a comprehensive framework for technique. Almost without doubt, the most popular version of Sanchin kata practiced at the time of writing is the Goju Ryu (Karate) version adapted by Miyagi Chojun. Miyagi was a student of the Okinawan Higaonna Kanryo (1853–1915). The common Goju version is somewhat shortened compared with older versions, and is more symmetrical. It eschews the (one directional) turns found in older Sanchin kata and takes only three steps forward and three steps back (actually one half step and two full steps forward and two full steps and one half step back). A longer version – including turns – is preserved in Goju Ryu Karate under the heading 'Higaonna Sanchin'. Both the Miyagi and 'Higaonna versions use clenched fists for the performance of section one, rather than the open hands of the Sanchin kata on which it was based.

In volume two of Higaonna Morio's (no relation to Kanryo) *Traditional Karatedo* (Performances of the kata – Minato Research and Publishing Company 1986) can be found, on page 29:

> Part 3 Sanchin Kata of Miyagi Chojun Sensei

Followed by a sub heading …

> 1. Why He Changed the *Kata*

Where it is stated that,

> Human beings naturally move forward, not backward … It was to develop this kind of backward movement that Miyagi Chojun Sensei revised Kanryo Higaonna Sensei's original Sanchin kata.

This statement implies that their source Sanchin kata had no backward steps. Indeed, as I will demonstrate later, it did not. However, I think that either Higaonna Kanryo or Miyagi Chojun added backward steps, as opposed to the three final sideways/backwards steps practiced in the original kata – as illustrated in this book, and as still practiced today, for instance in the Sanchin kata of the Uechi Ryu style of Karate. Moreover, on page thirty-seven of Higaonna Morio's controversial if somewhat skewed *History of Karate* (Okinawan Goju Ryu – no city given, Dragon Books 1996), he reports:

> In the early days Master Higaonna [Kanryo] taught Sanchin exactly as he had learned it from Ryu Ryu Ko Roshi [Roshi is a Buddhist term for teacher]. The breathing method was rapid

and the hand movements were performed with *nukite* (spear hand) rather than with the closed-fist ... It is not certain exactly when *nukite* in Sanchin changed to the closed-fist ... Kanryo Higaonna's adoption of the closed-fist was very likely related to his teaching at the Commercial High School [Okinawa circa 1905] ... (Parenthesis mine)

It can therefore (safely) be deduced from the above, that the Sanchin originally practiced by Higaonna Kanyro was performed with open hands and did not employ backward steps. This is significant, as I will explain later. Also, Miyagi Chojun changed the breathing pattern and added the now characteristic 'Goju' breathing method.

During 1989 I began to bring sixteen years of Kung Fu experience to bear on examining Sanchin kata from a 'Kung Fu' perspective rather than the usual 'Karate' punch, kick, block perspective. The results were exciting. At that time, due to partisan and other reasons, it was quite unusual for experienced Kung Fu practitioners to rigorously examine Karate kata! For (arrogant) Kung Fu Sifu of the day, involvement in Karate was considered to be 'slumming-it' (Sifu is a Cantonese Chinese term meaning 'father-teacher'). Most of the 'traffic' was in the other direction, and consisted of Karate-ka researching the 'parent' Kung Fu to study their 'roots' or discover that which they felt was missing from modern Karate. It should be borne in mind at this point that Sanchin is usually considered to be a major Chinese Quan-fa form in any case.

Because of the profound impact the proper application of *Naihanchin* kata (see chapter eight) had upon me, and because I was so surprised that there was such a thing as a kata with an *exact* application (one that did not deviate at all from the solo kata), I supported the traditional axiom that says (ancient) kata should as far as possible remain unchanged. I realised that if *major* structural changes had been made to the original kata, it would be impossible to discover the intended applications. Given that Naihanchin is systematic, 'non-flowery' and clearly formulaic, I reasoned that Sanchin was most likely formulaic too! What, indeed, I asked, were the underlying principles upon which this very famous and widely practised quan was founded? Subsequently however I recognised that the closed fist (Goju Ryu based) Sanchin kata I was investigating *had* been altered. Thus began my quest for an 'original' Sanchin. The open handed Sanchin kata, still practiced within the Uechi school of Karate proved to be the forerunner of the more common Goju Sanchin (see chapter three) Incredibly, this original Sanchin proved to be the (a) basic training kata for using a pair of Sai! (See illustrations on the opposite page and next after).

This was the last thing I had expected as Sanchin has always been promoted as the archetypal empty hands form. However, there are other (presumably unarmed) versions (see chapter six).

The Original (Open Handed) Naha-te Sanchin

'Uechi Ryu' Sanchin kata is an excellent example of an unaltered kata with a specific purpose. Sanchin figures prominently in all Naha-te Karate, and in its various versions is unquestionably one of Karate's most important Kata. A full analysis of Miyagi Sanchin can be found in chapter six. In the meantime, I will confirm that the oldest version known to Okinawan Naha-te Karate is the Chinese version, from which later versions were adapted. This version, actually the fundamental kata practiced in the Uechi Ryu Karate style (*not* Goju Ryu), can now be proven to be a primary training kata for a Sai weapons system! Its specific technical actions record and repeat (in drill fashion) how and when to 'flip' the Sai, where to strike, how to strike, and how to deflect and trap an incoming sword/pole/staff or other weapon attack! Incredibly, this information seems to be

70

Sanchin solo kata technique

Sanchin solo kata technique with Sai

unknown, and the kata has been taught and published (in the 1960s and subsequently) as a foundation *unarmed* kata, seemingly since at least the 1850s! I would go so far as to hypothesise that the (Uechi) Sanchin has not been altered since its creation – possibly in the late Ming/early Ching dynasty, during the seventeenth or eighteenth centuries.

I fully understand the gravity of what I say here. Many Karate practitioners will find this a little hard to swallow, let alone digest. Many will not want (their version of) Sanchin Kata, the basis of their unarmed Karate, turning out to be a weapons kata and will most likely never have considered it as such. I certainly did not want this kata to be a Sai kata. I virtually gave up Kung Fu to study Sanchin (the Uechi and Goju versions), and my colleagues and I diligently practiced the Uechi version with deep respect and attention to detail, only to discover eventually that it is a weapon kata, a fact that can no longer be seriously doubted. Furthermore, the kata makes far more sense as a Sai kata than it ever did as an empty hand kata.

I do not expect the general reader to be able to visualise much of what is being discussed here, or for experienced readers to readily accept the claims made, which is why this book has a companion film on DVD. This synoptic chapter and the descriptions given here are merely designed to draw the reader's attention to the *significance* of the book's contents and the discoveries outlined. The following chapters offer the detail. The film footage concludes the case. Seeing is, after all, believing.

Many people who practice the open handed Sanchin do not demand (or even expect) much in the way of *specific* applications and merely view the kata as a general training device. Benefits accrued from this type of Sanchin training are said to include, enhanced muscle tone, improved breathing and posture, the development of speed, power, strength, martial spirit and resilience, etc. Indeed, these are all fine qualities, but of themselves are insufficient to explain the structure of the kata. In short, these benefits, latterly pushed to the fore, are not, I repeat *not* the reason for the creation of, or the sequencing of this particular kata, which, as I point out, is a weapons kata. Even for those who esteem this Sanchin, in terms of laying the foundations for a system of unarmed combat, its presentation has often raised more questions than provided answers, and for many Karate-ka the practice of Sanchin is an article of faith, a source of great mystery, and the subject of much speculation, and has been for many years.

Attempts to explain the kata often take the kata at face value. For example, considering the stated applications of the first two sections of the kata – jabs with extended fingers – it is curious indeed to devote *two* of the three sections into which the kata is divided, to these repeated extended finger jabs (which, clearly are painful to execute against an opponent – ouch!) punctuated (in section one) by withdrawing the arm you are about to 'strike' with, in an arc. These 'strikes' are delivered at shoulder height and in line with the shoulder, they are not even centred! At the risk of incurring the wrath of practitioners of this kata, it does seem to be a very peculiar way of preparing for a no-holds barred unarmed confrontation, which is usually one of the stated aims of the kata.

Add the use of a pair of Sai, with the Sai-points forward and the pommels back – symbolised by the opened palms – and one can soon see that *the actions in section one actually record (empty handed) the path the Sai point takes as it is 'flipped' or rotated through 180° from being point forward to being pommel forward before the pommel is thrust forward towards the opponent's weapon-grasping hand, elbow or shoulder* (see the DVD).

The 45° slant of the open hands from the perpendicular in section one of the kata, illustrate the angle of grip used to hold the Sai. This grip and angle is similar to the grip and angle used with a tennis racket, or with a small wood-axe. It represents the strongest way for the gripping hand to withstand impact and thus avoid the Sai 'jumping' out of the hand on contact.

When I finally realised the purpose of (Uechi) Sanchin, I blanched. I did so for two reasons: one, because I realised the *function* of the (main) kata of a so-called 'traditional' Okinawan Karate style was to teach Sai (and that was difficult enough) and two, because I deeply suspected that the Uechi Sanchin was the same open handed version originally practiced by Higashionna Kanyro, the teacher of Miyagi Chojun, the founder of Goju Ryu Karate! I did not want to consider that Goju Ryu Karate was also founded on a kata intended to be used with a pair of Sai! In chapter three I will argue that the open hand (Uechi) version of Sanchin is indeed the version originally practiced by Higashionna Kanyro! No wonder Miyagi Chojun or rather Higaonna Kanyro, his teacher, before him (knowingly or otherwise), revised that Sanchin for empty hands compatibility, as I will also explain in chapter three. Higaonna may well have recognised several (for him) incongruous aspects of the (Chinese) kata construction (from a weapon-less perspective). Miyagi himself later made further revisions/modifications too. Clearly both were dissatisfied with the so-called 'spear hand strikes' that occur repeatedly in sections one and two of the kata. These were the first things to 'go', sometime before 1905, to be replaced by closed fists. A full study of these revisions is included in chapter six, under the heading 'Practical Sanchin'.

The reader may marvel at how a Sai kata could be confounded with un-armed combat and perpetuated as such for so long. But it was most likely a matter of the breakdown of tradition, the concealed nature of the techniques, and the instigation of a brand new belief system in a cultural milieu which was traditionally inflexible. Unfortunately, rather a lot of group and personal confusion seems to have followed. Deliberate deception by early teachers can not be ruled out! Even now it is rather difficult to (metaphorically speaking) stand up and shout, "The emperor isn't wearing any clothes!"

I am told that it takes two to three generations for something as culturally relative as Sanchin to become lost. I suspect the development and use of firearms in China was a significant and contributing factor in the decline in importance of certain weapons which clearly lost their significance and became obsolete technology. The purpose for the Sanchin (Sai) kata was probably lost as a result of the mass warfare, loss of life, plague and destruction that occurred during the Ming/Ching dynasty civil war and the weapons ban that followed it. I suspect that afterwards, the new tradition of viewing the techniques from the open handed Sanchin as being *unarmed* techniques became established.

Fortunately, the traditional worldview preserved Sanchin *kata*, and it became a Martial Arts enigma, yet, one still accorded great respect. Indeed, if one didn't know, one might never imagine what the kata was for, so cryptic does it (initially) seem, which makes me think, it could be the case that an empty hand, weapon-less version of a kata originally practiced with Sai, was simply invented to beat the weapons ban imposed by the victorious Manchu's, and thus preserve the skills of using Sai. This is an extremely important point, and I will return to it again.

Removing the kata from the 'Karate' context provided me with an opportunity to gain distance from its misinterpretation. Unless one is prepared to look objectively at the kata, and not from a partisan perspective, one is still likely to be affected by the party line, the half truths and the entrenched beliefs. Objectivity is an

Sanchin Solo technique without Sai

Sanchin Solo technique with Sai

act made difficult when one is enamoured of the kata, in awe of the (new) tradition, trusting in the teachers, uninterested in weapons, and sincerely seeking the so-called 'secrets' of unarmed combat said to be buried deeply within the kata. That was most certainly my experience, for many years.

One couldn't just pick up a pair of Sai and, for example, perform Uechi Sanchin with them. One has to be able to read the messages in movement built into the specific order and arrangement of the kata and perform accordingly. For example; the semi circle made by the withdrawing arm in section one of the kata (already discussed above), or the 'thrusting-out' of the open hands, palm down, the turning of them to be palm up, the circling of them into fists and the retraction of the closed-fists part way back to the sides of the body before they are opened to be palm up again, is a deliberate, exact and specific record of what to do when using Sai. It would be a somewhat tedious and long winded procedure if these movements merely represented three (unarmed) 'double spear hand strikes'. The movements in these two sections represent 'markers', records for posterity of how to intercept and trap an incoming weapon, when and how to flip the Sai, to change the grip and place the pommel forward before punishing the opponents weapon-holding hand/arm. And, in the case of section two, the action of flipping the Sai to strike with the 'knub' (pommel) is simply practiced simultaneously with both arms to create and maintain manual dexterity with the weapon.

The third and final section of the kata positions the user and the Sai in an extremely advantageous way. It illustrates a defensive manoeuvre in which the user places his forearms vertically aligned (one below the other) thus creating the maximum combined (perpendicular) protective surface by using them jointly to protect his body from, for example, a horizontal sword stroke or a 'swinging' pole/staff strike. The opponent's gripping hand (or weapon) is then struck (to break or bend it) and the weapon is trapped and 'driven' down to the floor with one Sai, and one of his holding hands is 'punished' with the 'knub' of the other Sai. A little exposure to the *correct* reading of the kata will satisfy even the most sceptical readers/viewers who will swiftly see the logical construction and true purpose of this much misunderstood kata, particularly when viewed on film.

Regarding the construction and application of original weapons kata; *no thought or intention was given to trying to apply the kata without the availability of the necessary weapons! Unless they are totally re-vamped, the weapons kata can not and do not double as unarmed kata.* In the next section I will explain why. I do so to avoid further confusion stemming from those who will wish it so, hope it is so, or even say it is so, that kata explicitly created for use with weapons can also sensibly be used barehanded. This, I suppose, is at the heart of the great Karate myth!

Although somewhat inadequate in terms of truly explaining the difference between armed and unarmed combat, the analogy given below is set out to distinguish *regulated* patterns in weapons play from the unregulated, chaotic *lack of pattern* in an unarmed violent assault. It has been suggested that acts of violence can be classified as habitual, and standard responses cultivated, but one serious problem for those who encounter them is they are often quite random in nature. Moreover they do in fact differ from person to person and are, when directly experienced, commonly ill defined; meaning they lack the structure and proper form of studied technique, the very type of technique Karate-ka are used to practicing against!

Empty Handed Combat and Armed Combat – The Difference

Empty hand (unarmed) combat and armed combat are not the same thing. They can not effectively use the same techniques and strategies, and the engagement distances (the working distance) differ, radically.

If, for instance, one considers using a pair of Sai to counter an opponent armed with a six foot pole/staff, it is easy to realize that despite the damage that can be inflicted by the pole, the operator's range and type of movement is restricted by the nature of the weapon. In plain language, the user of a pole – who will invariably grip the pole with both hands – places restrictions upon the use of his hands because they will be instrumental in manipulating the weapon which can only – roughly speaking – jab, hit up, hit down or swing using either end, etc. He will in fact be using a *system*. The same can be said for the use of a sword designed to be used with two hands. Similarly, a defender using Sai will be using a system too, and requisite responses are catalogued in kata – regulated systematic patterns of movement.

An experienced defender, skilled in the use of (a *pair* of) Sai, used them – sometimes together and sometimes singly – to block a thrust or a 'swing' before separating them, and employing them *independently* (separately but working together), one to detain/trap an offending weapon, and the other to 'punish' one of the attacker's arms, with the aim of so disturbing his grip and therefore control of the weapon as to disarm him and cause him to drop the weapon or become unable to continue using it. This is precisely the nature of the Sai when correctly used as a defensive (civil arrest) tool. These techniques would be rendered useless if the weapons – pole/sword *and Sai* – were removed from the equation, *largely because the opponent's tactics would no longer be limited or dictated by the use of a weapon.*

The attacker would, in effect, have four free and independent limbs for use in constructing (random) attacks, meaning his movements (intentions and actions) would be far more unpredictable. There might be method present, but no *system!* For example, he may charge and 'rugby-tackle', punch wildly, change tactics midstream, and utilise myriad feints or methods that were referred to by one prominent Quan-fa teacher as, 'killing the master with disorderly blows'. Contrary to some dismissive and overconfident Martial Arts views, brawlers have at their disposal an enormous range of 'changes' due largely to their capacity to 'half do' a technique, say a charge, then switch quickly to an entirely different *method*, like a fighter switching from boxing to wrestling and back again, but keeping to the rules of neither and adding distractions, like spitting, head-butting, or using the hands independently. It is therefore difficult for the defender to find a point of focus. There is not *one* weapon to engage with but *several* (fists and boots flying). The defender is invariably and somewhat instinctively drawn into the centre of a 'hub' of confusion, a maelstrom of random violence definitely without rhyme and often without reason. Inevitably he is drawn into launching a strike of his own, which ironically often leaves him exposed to a counter.

Tactics intended to be used with a pair of Sai do not (can not) be successfully utilised under such conditions, i.e. with no weapons involved. *Paradoxically, the use of weapons regulates the weapon–user and despite any creativity on an attacker's part, he will use regularly identifiable patterns of movement.* It is the sword that makes the swordsman dangerous, and it is to the neutralisation of the sword and its removal that the Sai operative would have applied himself. This is precisely what is reflected in (Kobudo) kata, which also represent regular patterns of movement.

One way to think about this is to imagine the eight directions (the compass points) around which the basic cuts of, for example,

Japanese swordsmanship are based, and to realise that the use of a sword requiring a two-handed grip (like a pole/staff), will limit or at least regulate the types and number of cuts or strikes possible.

For the purpose of this explanation, consider these basic well-known and well-defined cuts as numbering eight. In this respect I can liken them to a musical scale. Through the use of recognised scales, charted chord progressions, harmonies, refrains, and so forth, become possible, and two or more people can play together, each knowing when to change key, etc. – recognisable (Western) music that can be recorded, repeated and understood. However, if there were no such thing as musical notation or no one played scales, then the situation would be somewhat akin to different music groups who don't even agree where middle C is on a keyboard, or might ask innocently, "Middle C, what's that?" How would it be possible to change key, produce a harmony or a melody (kata) and prepare or practice? Like 'brawlers', 'musicians', not even bothering to tune the instruments they use, and untutored in music (employing no scales), and relying on mere impulse, could not make harmonious 'music', let alone write it down, and no one would be able to interpret their cacophony, predict their (non existent) chord changes, recognise harmonies, melodies, or verses and choruses, etc. In this sense, context is (almost) everything!

Obviously, fighting and music are not the same things. An 'art' reflects its purpose which in turn dictates the format, which in the case of using Sai would be Kobudo kata. The use of technologies will invariably produce strategies for application, for example, the invention of the rifle required the creation of rifle drills and target practice. 'Technologies of war' determine the protocols of war – the way it is conducted. This should not be carelessly confused with unscheduled barehanded fighting, one of the least desirable situations for most human beings to encounter (unless they want to).

Total solutions to unarmed self defence, commonly demanded from Karate, can not be viewed in the same way as disarming a swordsman or engaging in mass warfare. Unarmed tactics are 'low tech' and outcomes are actually far more unpredictable. Most such methods work best within their own format; Judo with Judo, Karate with Karate etc. That is, when a full display of the curriculum is required, or a system is to be taught or studied.

In matters of self defence, there may be no backup for a single unarmed defender and much of the 'repertoire' will be of little or no use. There will be no technologies (weapons), no army, and a big, strong and determined enemy (or several) represents a significant problem for those who are 'unequipped' and for whom there is no certainty. Many so-called bunkai (kata applications) would prove to be redundant at best and laughable or dangerous at worst.

Despite the romance of Karate and its image of mystique, and despite the awe in which the inexperienced often hold it, technology (in this case tools or weapons) is always more practical, being used by professionals or those determined to get results rather than fight with dignity, style or grace. Imagine, for example, a police officer attending a scene of serious violent behaviour without a night stick, baton, CS spray, handcuffs, backup, radio, etc. I raise this point because Karate is often viewed as a set of unarmed skills that can be used by the non-professional (ordinary members of the public) in serious situations of conflict. In respect of the intentions behind the creation of the antique kata, this is not strictly accurate if it is indeed accurate at all. Such is only believed because that is how Karate has been promoted, thus creating a mythical belief system that has endured and has gone largely unchallenged, except perhaps by those with (extensive) experience of real fighting, or perhaps by researchers.

Hands and Feet as Weapons

One of modern Karate's creeds is that hands and feet can become weapons. But the effectiveness of this notion remains largely relative. "Consider your hands and feet as swords," is an admonition promoted by Itosu Yasatsune in 1908. It has been perpetuated ever since. Even though Itosu was an Okinawan, his thinking comes from a peculiarly Japanese perspective, a perspective completely influenced by the virtual cult of the sword prevalent on the Japanese mainland during his lifetime. Indeed there are, within Karate, techniques described as 'shuto' – sword or knife hand blocks and strikes (in reality Sai techniques). However, the hands and feet are not swords. In fact, they are rather blunt comparatively, and need – if employed at all – to be used opportunely in powerful tactical (realistically pre-emptive) bludgeoning or punching movements, in order to be used to any great effect.

The idea of the hand being used as a sword has a certain emotional appeal, but on a practical basis there is one vital difference between arms and swords; swords are sharp! Arms can be (and are in real fights) grabbed, jammed-up and prevented from exercising free movement. Swords are not grabbed (at least by the blade) and distance must be taken from the cutting edge unless entry and closure are sought (closing with the enemy so that your swords are quite literally 'hilt to hilt'). As I understand it, one or two strong cuts with a keen-bladed Japanese sword are capable of amputating an arm! As usual, technology makes a difference. Of course, more subtle unarmed techniques can be employed, like finger pokes to vulnerable areas. Various 'clawing', hooking, and gouging techniques are commonly hailed as effective. But as ever, the problem is one of application, getting past the aggressor's in-built instincts for self preservation – particularly his body's reflexes. 'Flinch' reflexes, cover reflexes, crouching, bending, dodging, recoiling, and relentless aggression are all common features utilised by a powerful and determined aggressor. What's more, even though such an aggressor may be damaged by a well-placed strike (a difficult enough feat for the defender to accomplish given that the target will most likely be guarded and mobile) the attacker may take several moments to 'feel' the effects of said 'effective' strike, and in the meantime can make several 'effective' strikes of his own.

As clever as human beings are (learning methods, studying a subject, etc.), the brain can not get the physical body to do more than it is capable of doing. That is why, in all walks of life, we use technology – levers and pulleys to increase lifting power, for example; that is why we use weapons in war and conflict. Forearms and fists can be toughened for use as such, but they will (relatively speaking) represent a 'low tech' approach to combat, easily negated by the user of a weapon, or one superior in strength and (real) experience.

Another common misconception about Karate (mentioned in the introduction) is that, because an ancient warrior may either have lost his weapons (on a battlefield?) or he may be 'caught unawares', he studied Karate. But a proper study of Karate is very time consuming, requiring considerable practice, week in week out for ... what? – a 'just in case' situation?

My real issue is not with popular perceptions or misconceptions of Karate as a whole, but rather with the misconception of its antique kata, which in application should have seen the user sensibly armed with Sai, or preventing the *escalation* of violence (where appropriate or possible) with arresting techniques. That is my point!

To put unarmed self defence problems in context; being rushed, charged, bundled, rugby tackled and pummelled by a large and capable opponent represents a considerable challenge to a Karate-ka, but consider how cautious such an attacker becomes if he discovers that his intended victim is actually armed, say with a utility knife (box cutter) or some such. He knows that one little 'slash' might be all it takes. If he moves-in too fast or rushes the intended victim carelessly then … 'whoops' he might receive a very nasty cut, slash, or stab wound. Blood would gush out, *his* blood. Remove the (sharp) weapon from the scenario, and the aggressor can easily use superior height, bulk, greater aggression, etc. and, with far less caution. He can simply stalk his prey, closing it down, cornering and trapping it (you) in a dark alleyway (blocked at one end of course). Using superior strength, the 'bad guy' can wrestle his victim (you), kicking and screaming to the ground and …

Sound like a familiar nightmare? Indeed, I have employed this clichéd scenario to demonstrate that the myth of the power of Karate is so deeply embedded that many of us will still insist that a well placed front kick (choose your own target) and … the bad guy will fall. Actually he might, but then again …

I am not here advocating the carrying of knives, etc. to be used in self defence. Yet, civil arrest operatives employed coshes and batons/short sticks, staffs, rice flails (Nunchaku), etc. all of which were (are) undoubtedly effective in 'pacifying' miscreants without causing serious injury (provided only the limbs are struck). The Sai, of course, as I have said, was used to disarm an opponent prior to making an arrest.

There are other fundamental differences between the use of Sai and modern ballistic punch kick Karate (and unarmed self defence) too. Modern ballistic (punch/kick) Karate concentrates (mainly) on attacks to the body, head and occasionally the legs of an opponent. These attacks can be notoriously difficult to 'pull off' and many Karate-ka (fortunately) lack real experience in actually landing real blows on living flesh and blood. In contrast to the targets used by modern Karate-ka, the Sai user concentrates on delivering blows aimed mostly at the hands, forearms, elbows and shoulders of an armed opponent in order to make that opponent drop his weapon or be rendered unable to use it. In both instances, the distances are different and so are the tactics.

The extremely influential (late) Don F. Draeger, a former American marine, much admired and honoured by many leading Sensei in post world-war two Japan for his practical ability, his research skills and his knowledge of Japanese Budo (warrior way), said, when talking about Samurai warriors (I will give the whole quote in chapter two):

> Mere sparring tactics of a 'boxing' nature, which must rely for effect upon the natural parts of the body, hand, fist, foot, in delivering *atemi* (blows directed at anatomically weak points) by striking, punching, or kicking, were hopelessly ineffective and would be likely to result in more injury to the attacker than to the intended victim.

Draeger was stressing the importance of weapons for a (serious) warrior. To be unarmed in feudal times demonstrated low status, or meant that one lived under and was subjected to a regime that banned weapons. Many so-called 'empty-hand' quan/kata simply concealed techniques devised to be used with weapons, largely the Sai.

Sword hand block solo technique without Sai

Sword hand block solo techniques with Sai

Distance, a Crucial Factor

When a pole-user thrusts out a pole, he must quickly remove it to prevent the Sai user from trapping it, the very tactics the Sai user must apply to close down the long distance and make adequate contact with the pole, with, indeed, the aim of trapping it and disarming the user.

The time and distance taken for an attacker to effectively wield a pole/sword allows the defender using Sai to use, after initial contact, the sort of full steps often seen in Karate kata but absent from Western and other types of boxing techniques or violent confrontation where the opponent has both hands free.

Solo techniques without Sai (from the 'Chibana' Kusanku)

Applications with Sai

Once the missing weapons (Sai) are added to a kata like *the original* Seisan, it becomes easy to see that to remove those weapons from it would be like pulling the teeth from a guard-dog. I reiterate; countering the attack of the pole (originally synonymous with Chinese use of the spear), or the sword, was clearly one of the major uses of Sai techniques. The main task the user of a pole must undertake is to maintain the advantage of greater distance, and maximise the ability to inflict damage from that distance. In contrast, the Sai user must close this distance down, engaging the pole and sticking with it to neutralise its (distance) advantage, or in the case of the sword, trap it and limit or totally control its free movement. Anecdotes allege that good – not to mention expensive – sword blades were trapped and snapped with a sideways twist of a forged iron Sai.

To try to apply the principles of Sai defence whilst unarmed, against a similarly unarmed opponent, would be a mistake. The distances are totally different! And (I repeat), the defenders hands would not be limited by his holding, for example, a pole. The defender (not restricted by a weapon) would be capable of a huge range of variations employing either or both hands using, for example, violent hooligan-type kicks, headlocks, chokes, gouges, punches, slaps, hair-pulls, knee strikes, head-butts, charges, feints, distractions; he may spit, throw a projectile, push one person into another and hit the one who is unbalanced as a result ... The list is unfortunately endless. Sai *strategy* would not easily work under those conditions. Therefore the inevitable conclusion is that Sai – kata – techniques are redundant without the use of the very weapons they were intended to be used with. I'm not saying that defence against hooligans, violent criminals and the like is impossible; what I am saying is that one should not depend upon ancient Sai kata for source material.

Many kata employ frequent turns accompanied with, or by, apparent blocking actions, presumably designated to face a new opponent and block an attack. This is plausible if weapons are being used, but if not ... With the absence of weapons, attackers can be much bolder. This point has caused much vexation and frustration amongst modern practical-minded Karate-ka because the only way to apply the aforementioned turn and block (empty handed) is to choreograph it. In fact (unarmed), multiple opponents' kata 'bunkai' (applications) *have* to be choreographed; failure to do so produces a *user unfriendly* 'bundle' somewhat reminiscent of an outbreak of violence on a soccer terrace or at an ice hockey match. A good general example of this lays in the failure of the mistaken Naihanchin/Tekki applications demonstrated in the companion DVD. In the case of weapons kata, the employment of the actual weapons would provide the defender with the time and distance to respond, and the attackers would obviously be more cautious because of those weapons.

Kicking Away a Trapped Weapon

Within Karate, it is usually difficult for a teacher to explain the consecutive repetition of the same technique three times in many kata (a point picked up later), or the failure of the kata sequence to repeat a given technique on both sides of the body. The uneven numbers of kicks in most kata defy logic too, until one realises that the kicks and the ranges are most likely intended, if not to kick the opponent's trunk or limbs, then to kick away a weapon already trapped-down with the Sai, and that the techniques (like boxing or fencing) favour one side. A good example of a kick designed to kick away a trapped-down weapon is 'Mikazuki geri', or the crescent-moon kick, a singularly unpopular kick clearly not designed to kick the *body* of an opponent. The distance is awkward, and the kick would not 'impact' with any significant effect. This technique can be found in the 'Kusanku' and Pasai kata of Matsubayashi Shorin Ryu, in which it is classified as a foot block allegedly used to disengage from a hand hold. There are easier and more direct ways, however, of doing such. 'Mikazuki geri'also appears in the Heian godan, Hangetsu, and the Kanku-dai kata of Shotokan Karate. Funakoshi Gichin designates this kick as a kick to the chest, stomach, or private parts, in his *Karate – Do Kyohan*, (London and Tokyo, 1973, Ward Lock and Kodansha).

It is also rather difficult to explain why a technique on one angle is followed by a blocking technique and a kicking technique facing in a completely different direction, without of course recourse to the usual 'multiple opponent' explanation. However, if one considers trapping, hooking and twisting a weapon with a Sai and re-directing that weapon to the side, and then kicking that trapped weapon *from the side*, then the technique makes perfect sense. This example can be seen in, for instance, Kusanku kata.

The 'crescent-moon' kick

Application

'Tsumasaki-geri' ('toe tip kick')

Finally I wish to examine the famous 'tsumasaki-geri'or the 'toe tip kick', a peculiar kick executed (barefoot) somewhat like a conventional front kick except allegedly employing the tips of the toes rather than ball of the foot or the heel as the striking surface. A great deal of mythology and anecdote surrounds this kick, used for example in the Uechi Ryu Sesian and Sanseirui kata. Kicking with the tips of the toes is arguably a dangerous technique for the user, although of course it could also be argued that such a kick would penetrate deeply because of the relatively small impact area the toes provide. My personal view regarding the so-called 'toe tip kick' is that in its original use, whilst the toes were undoubtedly pointed, the intended impact point was the top of the foot, and the purpose of the kick was to kick a trapped weapon *from underneath*, with the intention of dispossessing the user.

Kata Were Not Explained to Early Karate-ka

It does seem that (clear) applications for kata were not provided in the early days of Karate. Indeed, Anthony Mirakian, an early American Karate pioneer and student of the late Yagi Meitoku (Goju Ryu), claimed that when he was studying on Okinawa as late as the 1950s, there was very little explanation of the meanings of the kata and that the applications were often left up to the student's own imagination and inquisitiveness. Such reports are common in Karate history.

Many early To-te and Karate teachers considered it to be extremely rude if students asked questions regarding the applications of kata, and consequently (generally speaking) students did not. Some, like Motobu Choki (who I will introduce in chapter two), did ask questions and were considered impolite, rude and coarse as a result. This cultural attitude illustrates the difference between Japanese deference to a hierarchical superior along with learning by rote mechanical means, and modern Western 'individuality'. These divergent attitudes, as they pertain to Karate, will be more fully discussed in chapter two.

It would be foolish to consider that only the Chinese, Okinawans and Japanese could create effective fighting methods. What they did seem to do was to catalogue weapons techniques in kata, or in the case of Naihanchin, for a specific type of grappling.

Ballistic techniques (punches, strikes and kicks) aimed at the head and body, although now universally accepted and generally believed to be authentic and viable constituent parts of Karate, can not be, and most likely *were* not originally the subject of or for organised kata, which seems to be a late invention, based, as I have suggested, on either a deliberate (or otherwise) attempt to apply weapons techniques barehanded, or (as in the case of Naihanchin) to treat grappling tactics as block, punch and strike techniques.

Bare-hand Ballistic Combat Doesn't Need Kata

This section is given to encourage caution in the expectations one may have regarding perceived self defence applications of (modern) Karate kata.

The Martial Artist and movie star Bruce Lee knew instinctively that there was something 'wrong' with forms (kata). He was dismissive of them, and famously discarded them. He wrote about the 'once fluid man cramped and distorted by the classical mess,' meaning that forms (kata) restrict the user and are unrealistic. Indeed, my sentiments are with him in this matter. It does seem to be a bit of a mess where inappropriate attempts are made to – metaphorically speaking – use the wrong key to try and unlock a door. Kata intended for Sai (remember, most traditional 'kata' were formerly Chinese Quan-fa forms) make poor tools for empty handed use (particularly in the arena). Please do not make the mistake – often made by the combat inexperienced – of failing to recognise the brutal efficiency of freestyle (non kata based) aggressive combination hand and foot techniques (proper hook punches – not Karate approximations, uppercut punches and blinding jab, uppercut, cross punch combinations, common to all effective full contact fighting). One must also consider the workmanlike (brutal) efficiency of Thai boxing, Greco-Roman wrestling and Ju-Jutsu, none of which can (sensibly) be recorded in fixed kata. These were the formats, along with Western boxing, that Bruce Lee quickly turned his attention to in the creation of his highly eclectic 'Jeet Kune Do' style – the way of the intercepting fist. It would be arrogant in the extreme to consider the originators of these methods to be primitive or to have failed to give 'form' to their techniques simply because they did not devise or utilise kata.

Street-fighters must be considered too, with their improvised tactics, distraction techniques, improvised or actual weapons, toe-punt kicks (for which they do not need to warm up), aimed aggressively at shins, knees and to the heads of fallen victims – an unpleasant thing to consider. Everyone is acquainted with pain; fear too. Both can drive humans to take desperate measures. It is a mistake to imagine that Karate kata were somehow conceived out of such desperation. Karate is not stylish street-fighting. Street-fighting is street-fighting!

Modern Karate-ka who practice kata but express an interest in getting 'real', frequently resort to the same few limited methods and targets, including head butting, knees to the groin and a rough, tough 'ragamuffin' collection of tactics that have little or nothing to do with traditional kata at all. In reality, ballistic unarmed combat is a gross and violent business, not an art. Any attempts to restrict freestyle unarmed ballistic combat and cramp and confine it into kata, would produce predictable and sterile patterns that would be of no use in application. Practical fist fighters (like Thai and Western boxers), hone their *skills* in application. Practical fist fighting is most effective if kept simple and direct. Much in the perceived Karate repertoire is far too sophisticated for use in a fist fight.

An untrained person can often be more than a handful, and many Karate instructors have experienced difficulties with beginners who 'just don't punch right!' There is often a (silent) groan from black-belts who have to deal with (instruct) the 'awkward' beginner. They must take him aside and teach him how to 'punch properly'. Once the student punches 'properly', that is, once his attack is given *form*, others can train with him. If a newcomer already has punching ability (say from boxing) it must be discarded for obvious stylistic reasons. A real opponent can be particularly tricky if he is violent and bellicose. His very disorder presents its own kind of problems in terms of the practical application of techniques from kata.

No-one should expect kata designed to be used with weapons to solve unarmed self defence situations, and Chin-Na (grappling) was not designed to be 'the answer to life, the universe and everything'. It was designed to be used under very specific circumstances (see chapter eight).

A scrappy Western style fist fight is just that. In Okinawan and Japanese though, it lacks form, it lacks dignity. Above all, in its unpredictability, it lacks structure! From a 'self defence' perspective, using stereotypes like, "most people are right handed, so an attacker will probably try to 'sucker punch' you with his right hand" – leaves the believer very vulnerable to, for example, a left footed shin kick, followed up by a 'bundle' (push/shove, grab/punch) and a headlock. Who is to know on the day? The chances are, the attacker won't know in his burst of violence. If the attacker does not even know, how are you supposed to? But surely, the Martial Artist *must* know what's going to happen, mustn't he? It is almost an article of faith that he does!

Let me 'wheel-out' the usual answers as to how the intrepid expert, well-versed in 'set pieces', is supposed to cope with the uncertainty outlined above … intuition, a hunch, experience? Lots of kata practise, mind training, telepathy, a fierce 'indomitable' spirit, or perhaps he can fall back on the knowledge that all attackers will most probably be mentally, if not physically, inferior morons who always telegraph their punches. I think not.

The police and other professionals use 'tools'; a baton, truncheon, night stick or similar, as I have said. A few blows with the Japanese iron 'Jutte' (similar to a Sai but with only one 'hook') will bring down the arms of even the most ferocious and belligerent of troublemakers. Chimpanzees will pick up a stick and thrash around with it during territorial disputes, yet it is the case that many still insist that Karate (kata) which were actually designed for weapons or pre-emptive arrest, solve all the problem of unarmed confrontation or a potential escalation of (gang) violence of the type that sometimes leaves its victims dead or seriously injured. Are we supposed to behave like the iconic film star Gary Cooper, the heroic sheriff, determined to confront a 'gunslinger' at high noon, in the dust and heat of the street, for a fair fight?

Ask yourself, when was the last time *you* attacked someone, for real? Many people reading this would most likely answer either never, or not since school days. Yet in the adult world there are those people, aggressive or disturbed enough to do violence to good people, *and they are often the ones with the real experience.*

In one's imagination (and certainly portrayed in films), a strongly focussed punch, kick or other fiendish strike, accompanied by a fierce ki-ai (spirit shout), will fell the bad guys, thank goodness! If only it were that simple.

Seizing and Grappling

One practical (but *strictly* relative) solution to the problem(s) of an unruly opponent is to grapple, seizing and controlling his arms to prevent them (him from) inflicting damage, *before he gets started!* Unfortunately the modern Western psyche is somewhat afflicted by the 'You can just hit him ... punch out his lights' syndrome, unhelpfully 'egged-on' by modern Karate's incompatible inclusion of the Japanese (Samurai) sword principle of 'ikken hisatsu' – one strike, one kill. It might be useful to consider that a crazed charging attacker, seemingly intent on tearing out his victims' hair and examining the roots, may have a similar objective in mind!

However, grappling in combat is an activity practiced the world over, and for a very good reason, namely; it is practical. For example, a tired boxer will cling to his opponent's arms, tying them up and restricting their movements (until the referee steps in and separates the boxers). Many real fights end up in grappling (wrestling) situations, a fact that can be supported by the total domination grapplers enjoy in modern 'no holds barred' 'Ultimate Fight Challenge' and other pioneering total combat scenarios; although, as I will illustrate later, Chin-Na grappling was not designed to be used in an arena, and Chin-Na is dissimilar to wrestling: Chin-Na is not 'body to body' but concentrates instead on the manipulation and control of an opponents wrist and elbow joints.

The views expressed above, plus my own personal experiences, and over thirty years of training, have convinced me that the originators of what would eventually become Karate kata recorded only weapon techniques and grappling/subjugation techniques in kata, because, only these two could be given proper *form and structure*, and moreover were legally, morally and socially acceptable methods with *a proven track record*. This idea may not seem to make much sense at first, because *ancient* Karate kata (look as if they) have 'punches' in them, and strange looking 'blocks' and 'strikes' too. However, in short (with the exceptions of Naihanchin and Miyagi Sanchin), where you see what looks like a punch in the performance of an *antique* kata, you can generally consider it to be a strike using the 'knub' (pommel) of a Sai, aimed at the weapon-holding hand/arm of an opponent. The two handed 'blocks' are generally weapon traps, and the 'strikes' are punishments inflicted on the fingers, hands and arms of an armed opponent.

Selected Kusanku 'blocks' and 'strikes'

Such methods – whilst having to take into account *engaging* an opponent – deal largely with what happens *after engagement or contact*. They are not about 'sparring', feinting, thrusting, jabbing, etc. thus leaving the combat engagement distance open or long. That is why they can not be effectively used in free-sparring. In both Sai and grappling kata applications, the attacker is quickly 'closed down' by having his weapons and/or arms 'jammed-up'/ kept restricted, either by the hook of the Sai, or in the case of grappling by swiftly seizing both limbs and locking one or both of the arms. Even if the initial mêlée is daunting, entry into the opponent's 'range' has (ideally) only to be effected once, and in respect of grappling was most likely done without attracting the target's attention. Unlike ballistic Karate, no 'hit gaps' were left, no space or distance permitted, nor a gap where an exchange of blows could occur. This was not a sport designed to score points, or part of a spectacle designed to please a crowd. Once the distance was closed, it was kept closed!

I think that Chin-Na grappling (not wrestling) techniques may well have originated as methods used to pacify an armed man who had not yet, unsheathed his sword(s), for example. These techniques were not intended for the battlefield but were most likely used in formal social settings/environments and in situations where, for example, one nobleman punching or slapping the face of another would constitute a grave insult, represent a 'loss of face', and most likely result in (undesirable) swordplay, thereby also risking death, family feuds and vendettas, with all the consequential waste of lives and resources. A dignified form of restraint would however better lend itself to 'negotiation'; communication, with little or no hurt being done to the offender's person or status. It may be the case that Naihanchin, for example, was designed to be used indoors and in situations where an arrest needed to be made yet weapons (including Sai) had been surrendered on entry to the building/room.

Sample Naihanchin solo techniques...

...Second angle...

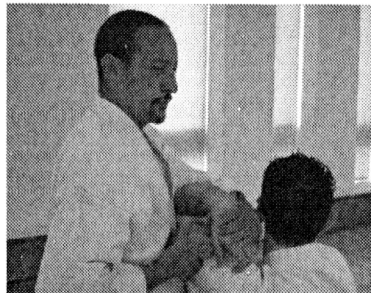

...Application

Although Naihanchin is (to the best of my knowledge) actually a Chinese form (see below and chapter eight), for the following explanation I will temporarily switch cultures from China to Japan. I do so because readers may more easily identify with a Japanese Samurai swordsman than with, for instance, a Chinese Ming dynasty cavalry officer. So, imagine that a young – and perhaps junior – Samurai warrior has had a few too many cups of sáké (rice wine) and has become unruly and quarrelsome. With his alcohol-fuelled bravado reaching a level of carelessness, and his behaviour becoming increasingly arrogant, erratic, and unreasonable, he becomes abusive or menacing and gives offence to a social equal or even a superior; an argument ensues. Enter the calm, trained, similarly ranked 'officer' who carefully intercedes in the argument, an argument he has noticed might become a swordfight at any moment, and presto! the offender is 'taken' almost unawares, firmly grappled, held, and 'talked to' – reminded of his social position and his 'Giri' (duty), reminded of the disturbance to the 'Wa' (harmony) of the immediate surroundings/observers, and offered the opportunity to 're-consider'.

Many societies all over the world, whilst officially frowning upon drunkenness, often excuse it if the offender causes little damage or injury, and if he apologises and does not become a repeat offender. In that sense, Chin-Na is virtually a pre-emptive art that paradoxically contradicts the famous 'Karate Ni Sente Nashi' (there is no first initiative in Karate). Please note that the example given above is merely that, an example. I am not here claiming that Chin-Na was devised especially to deal with drunkards. In chapter eight, I will repeat the important point of Chin-Na being an expedient but noble prevention of bloodshed, and stress more fully the context in which Chin-Na was most likely used in feudal societies, and how it should be viewed in its proper context today.

Regrettably, in modern times, many false expectations exist concerning the use of arm locks and such techniques, and many unreasonable demands are made on grappling the wrists to solve (modern) violent confrontation situations. It is very difficult to get a neat wristlock on someone who is viciously thrashing their arms around or brandishing weapons, and Martial Arts demonstrations of an unarmed person defending against a swordsman are seldom convincing to say the least. That is why I say that Chin-Na is just one of a series of measures that were employed in the past. It is pointless to consider the use of, for example, Naihanchin against a man already wielding a sharp sword! Naihanchin *could* be used, if the exponent was already in close proximity to the swordsman before that swordsman drew his sword – one would, for example, be positioned alongside him – and could thus physically prevent him from drawing and using the very tools or weapons that made him dangerous in the first place – his sword(s).

In respect of weapons kata, the move towards 'ballistic' (block, punch, kick) Okinawan empty hand Karate was most likely influenced by the ideas of Qing Chinese 'empty hand' pioneers who seem to have developed the idea that weapon (Sai) kata could be performed unarmed against similarly unarmed opponents.

It is of course entirely possible that former Han weapons teachers made redundant under the Manchu regime with its rigidly imposed weapons ban, could have re-invented themselves and perhaps even a new art by simply teaching weapons kata *without the weapons*, as I hinted at earlier. In the seventeenth century, the Manchu's were struggling to get the region of Fujian under control (remember, Fujian is where many 'Karate' kata originate) and even by today's standards, Chinese armies were huge. For example, Zheng Chenggong, a pirate general (whom I will discuss in chapter four), allied with a deposed Ming dynasty prince, allegedly had under his control a staggering 240,000 men at arms! All had to be equipped, armed, and trained. But what has this got to do with misunderstood quan? How could techniques designed to be used with weapons filter down to become barehanded 'fisticuffs' – 'Chinese boxing'?

Well, the much underestimated Chinese short single-bladed broadsword, used in pairs like the Sai, could have had something to do with it. The short broadswords, also known as the 'butterfly knives', were devastating weapons and the perfect counter to the entrenched Chinese military reliance on the spear, used by the massed ranks of the conscripted infantry. Indeed, this lethal art can be seen in the Wing Chun style of Kung Fu. Wing Chun preserves the use of these techniques by the inclusion of the 'Baat Cham Dao'or' (eight cutting broadswords) utilising a deadly pattern of eight cuts, and the 'Luk Dim Boon Kwan' or the six and a half point pole techniques which resemble the use of a spear rather than a conventional staff. The broadsword cuts, in fact, utilise the full range of basic anatomical possibilities in terms of human arm movement.

For what it's worth, I think the staff (a mere pole and not a spear) survived as a makeshift weapon because it could not easily be categorised as a weapon by the Manchu authorities. The pole had too many utility purposes for it to be banned, uses ranging from punting a barge or boat to an aid in walking, or dislodging or placing distant objects, such as lanterns or window shutters. It was also more notoriously used by brigands and 'ne'er do wells'.

It may be the case that the civil use of the Sai (a non edged weapon) against the pole (a spear without the point), was fashioned after the more deadly edged swords and the sharpened spear. It may not be well known that there was a clear distinction between the Sai, a police tool, and paired broadswords – military weapons.

Chinese broadsword sample solo techniques...

...Suggested application

Wing Chun broadsword technique (illustrated with sai)

Later proponents, perhaps raised on the idea of formalised unarmed Kung Fu, and lacking knowledge of Western boxing (and Western attitudes and tactics the Chinese would later consider 'barbarous'), created *a series of measured, structured unarmed attacks developed to fit the (former Sai) defences.* This of course is a total role reversal – attacks created to fit existing defences. Yet that is something we can still see in Karate today, with, for instance, the use of improbable double simultaneous punches being used to justify equally as improbable double simultaneous blocks.

Originally, as I have said, the Sai kata were developed to deal with the well-known routes, paths, angles, etc. of an attacker armed with a pole/staff or sword, whilst the grappling kata were designed to be used in contact and via contact reflex, once the targets arms were restricted, as I will illustrate in later chapters. I strongly suggest that the idea of using Sai kata without the Sai (very persuasive until one encounters Western-style violence) heralded the beginning of the notion of a ballistic-based art (non-weapon and non-Chin-Na based Quan-fa and later Karate) that could be laid down in kata format, first in China, then in Okinawa and Japan.

'Westernized' Karate reflects the Western experience and is why modern American full contact Karate, as pioneered by the great

Jo Lewis and the incredible Bill 'Super-foot' Wallace, reflects American culture. And, by the way, those two Americans could hit extremely hard (using essentially Western boxing punches rather than 'traditional Karate techniques). These formidable American fighters were master tacticians, who, using superb ring-craft, would 'close you down' (restrict your movements) and 'nail' you with punches that *felt* like a mule's kick because they were (actually) landed – hard! I once experienced a Bill Wallace 'hook punch' body-shot, when Mr. Wallace was in his prime – once again, ouch! – enough said.

The Kata as Defence against Multiple Opponents

The belief that Martial Arts can equip the practitioner to fight several (determined) opponents simultaneously (without weapons) is a myth that persists because it is so entrenched, yet it largely goes against common sense and experience. Just because something is ingrained or has become part of 'established thinking' does not necessarily mean that it is correct. One problem is that Karate teachers have often fostered the notion of 'multiple opponents' combat scenarios to explain kata.

Interestingly, the late great Wing Chun Kung Fu master, Wong Shun Leung, once told me, "I've only got one pair of hands, so I can only fight one person at a time." Conversely, a standard interpretation of the function of (allegedly unarmed) kata practice, within Karate, was given by Nakayama Masatoshi, the late Chief instructor to the Japan Karate Association:

> "Kata are the formal exercises of Karate. They have been passed on from the Chinese origins of karate centuries ago." And: "Imaginary [presumably unarmed] enemies surround the [unarmed] Karate-ka as he executes the four fundamental movements of the kata: uke (blocking) tsuki (punching) uchi (striking) and keri (kicking)" (Parenthesis mine).

This common and extensively accepted perception of Karate kata application owes more to the 'politeness' of the multiple attackers than it does to any practical reality (unless weapons are considered). It definitely has nothing to do with Naihanchin, despite the Japan Karate Association's official film depiction of Tekki (Naihanchin) as a defence against the attacks of multiple opponents. As mentioned, I have reconstructed that 'interpretation' on the companion DVD, for contrast with the proper application.

The Missing Grappling Techniques

The Chinese teachers, inventors of Naihanchin kata (*one kata in three parts*), one of Karate's most fundamental kata (with several million practitioners worldwide), do not seem to have passed on the *applications* to their Okinawan students! Naihanchin – kata application – is *a two man grappling sequence from China*, not a 'block-strike' kata as is usually taught. This in itself is astonishing.

Patrick McCarthy kindly had this to say about the Naihanchin discoveries (in N. J. Johnson, *Barefoot Zen*, York Beach Maine, 2000, p.177–178):

> I was fascinated to experience his (Johnson's) theory and application of Naifuanchin (Naihanchin) ... If one was to consider it for what it most likely is, a two man grappling-hands exercise without worrying about politics, uniform, name, etc. then I believe that Nathan's theory would be widely recognised. In fact I bet that if an Okinawan master had come forward and introduced that which Nathan has already done, he'd probably have been hailed from the highest sources.

Solo 'lock-up' position from Naihanchin and application

So, why didn't a Karate practitioner from Okinawa (the home of Karate) or Japan, recognize that Naihanchin is for grappling? There is no easy answer to that question. Maybe the Okinawans or the Japanese just simply did not come up with the understanding, or perhaps they did not challenge the (mistaken) block/punch application because it was developed on pre World War Two Okinawa (and in Japan) itself, where it has become a 'tradition' (worldwide too). The Japanese cultural habit of not wanting to be the 'nail that sticks up' (metaphorically speaking), could have prevented them from conducting critical research. Indeed there is a Japanese proverb that states, "A protruding nail eventually gets hammered down." Challenging the establishment (even when it is mistaken) is less acceptable in a conformist culture, with the result that the mistaken application to Naihanchin has been perpetuated. To suggest that such a mistake was made in the first place may seem arrogant, but then, not so long ago, merely to propose that the world was round, or that the earth spins and revolves around the sun, was considered to be heretical and carried a heavy custodial sentence, or worse!

Though the industrial age began in the West, no one would dispute Japan's industrial success, her manufacturing power and output, and the quality of her world-leading products and brands. Perhaps the same can now be said in respect of the global exposure to Karate and related arts, like Chinese Quan-fa (Kung Fu), and the commitment many thousands of practitioners make to these arts. Interest is intense these days, and there are professional instructors with a deep love of their subject. There has been much effort and research, and many innovative or restorative contributions made by the many Karate (and Quan-fa) teachers worldwide. After all there are now more Karate clubs *outside* of Okinawa/Japan than inside!

It would be foolish for the major discoveries detailed herein, with all their significant and far reaching consequences, to be rejected out of hand, or disregarded, just because the research was conducted in the West. But, unfortunately, sometimes old stereotypes prevail and are unwittingly (or otherwise) accepted by the poorly informed, or those who have become 'partisan'. What could a bunch of Westerners know about Karate that the Okinawans/Japanese do not? Well, it was most likely a firm grounding in Quan-fa, the grandparent of modern Karate that made the discoveries outlined in this book possible. Indeed, it was actually the ability to view the kata in a non-partisan way and look beyond the Japanese (cultural) veneer, added to what is fundamentally Chinese material, and analyse the kata logically and dispassionately – over many years – that led to such extraordinary results.

Substance – More Important Than Lineage or Rank

Reading partisan Martial Arts books or watching certain Martial Arts productions, I have noticed how the promoters of modern Karate, self defence methods or sport Karate, simply present 'themselves' and the training methods they advocate, but so-called 'traditionalists' stress the importance of history and lineage, and make long lists of who taught whom. I suppose (among other reasons) the purpose of this is to create a feeling of authenticity and tradition (somewhat like the phenomenon of 'royalty'). There is nothing inherently wrong with this, unless, in the case of Karate kata, the practices being proposed have become distorted, lost, corrupted or patently absurd. Under such circumstances it is naive in the extreme to do (follow) something simply because you have been told that is how master 'so and so' did it, long ago. Lineage (who taught whom), uniform, titles and rank, are of far less importance than substance, purpose, and the (correct) application of (the key) kata.

Currently we live in a world that is (for better or worse) global, and in many modern cities, multicultural. Clearly this has advantages and disadvantages. When an activity from another culture is learned, context can easily be lost. In respect of Quan-fa, To-te, and Karate, I think that has happened on – at least – the following three occasions:

1. When Chinese 'Quan-fa' was imported on to Okinawa to become 'To-te'.

2. When Okinawan 'To-te' was exported to Japan to become 'Karate'.

3. When Japanese Karate was absorbed into American and European mainstreams, Karate clubs, Martial Arts films, books, computer games, etc.

However, despite the radical revisions made to some kata, fortunately, other kata have been extremely well preserved. Karate is no longer a purely 'Oriental' or mysterious phenomenon. In its proper forms(s) it is – in fact – grounded in logic, with functions that can now be proven. The next chapter will explain (along with some relevant Karate history) how and why the differences in culture(s) have affected modern perceptions of Karate as an unarmed art, and how these 'misconceptions' have led to unrealistic and mistaken expectations regarding the use and purpose of the antique kata; leading ultimately to the 'myth' that is Karate today.

Detailed reconstruction of the famous Uechi Kanei
"Elbow Strike" pose using Sai.

Chapter Two
Karate – A Confusion of Purpose

Karate and Warfare

DESPITE KARATE NOT ORIGINALLY being intended for general military use, unfortunately, during the period from the 1920s through to the mid 1940s, Karate practice was explored as a possible adjunct to the military training of young men inculcated into Japans' increased militaristic and expansionist policies. This was not the first time that Karate had attracted the attention of the Japanese military. As early as the 1890s, the Japanese military authorities had shown an interest in the excellent physical development of certain Okinawan conscripts versed in To-te (as Karate was then called). But at that early stage in To-te's development, the Japanese military abandoned interest in it due to To-te's ancient Confucian-based ideology and lack of an accessible syllabus or curriculum soldiers could grasp during basic training that lasted for only six weeks or so. *Bayonet practice it definitely wasn't,* although by the second-world-war, some (patriotic) Karate-ka attempted to teach Japanese soldiers how to perform an upper block and kick to the opponent's groin, should hand to hand combat become the last means available to them.

In fact (aspects of), the history of Japanese Karate during that period has little to commend itself, particularly when it is alleged (according to the late English Karate teacher, Steve Cattle and the French Karate pioneer Henri Plée, who both published articles on the subject) that certain Japanese Karate-ka tested 'Karate' techniques on captive Chinese prisoners in the lead up to and during the second world war, inflicting trauma, and dealing out severe injuries and even death! This allegedly took place principally during Japanese incursions into Chinese territories between 1937 and 1945. To my knowledge, no senior Okinawan masters had any involvement in this, and figurehead masters such as Funakoshi Gichin (father of early Shotokan Karate), Miyagi Chojun (founder of Goju Ryu Karate), and Mabuni Kenwa (founder of Shito Ryu Karate), and many other venerable masters, would undoubtedly have considered such 'experiments' to be abhorrent, and I certainly do not intend to, nor do I, show any disrespect to their memory here.

If true, it is shameful but ironic that Karate, an art indebted to, and deeply grounded in, Chinese Quan-fa (Kung fu) and constructed by peace loving Okinawans, should have been so misused and besmirched. I raise this painful spectre not to denounce Japanese Karate, but to illustrate, albeit in an extreme way, what can happen when Karate 'aficionado's' become obsessed with the 'effects' of Karate strikes on living flesh and bone or its efficiency, in 'real life', for instance in a street-fight. Yet, I hear a small but persistent collective voice still asking, "But isn't that what Karate is ultimately for?" Karate commonly remains an art believed to be a method of 'self defence'. Indeed, as I have explained, 'modern' Karate advocates techniques for countering a variety of perceived assaults. It seemingly offers defensive and blocking manoeuvres, and a series of counter-attacking techniques mostly utilizing punching, striking and kicking techniques coveted for their aesthetic appeal, provisional defensive value, and their assumed destructive power. This is a myth!

In 1917 and again in 1922, prominent Okinawan [Kara] Te masters toured the Japanese mainland to promote [Kara] Te, and 'Karate' took off, eventually spreading to most parts of the world. Today, Karate is a household word. But to put the time-frame into perspective, Karate (formerly To-te Jutsu) only received its name in 1936 (the year my own mother was born), and had reached no further than Hawaii by that time (although an 'ex-patriot' Okinawan club may have existed in Los Angeles in 1927). In comparison, Ju Jutsu (the precursor of modern Judo) had already been established in London, England by 1898/99, at a club at Wardour St., by William Barton-Wright, a civil engineer of independent means. Even Prince Edward the (then) Prince of Wales went to investigate the club!

Karate and Culture

The misunderstanding surrounding the genesis and purposes of Karate kata and the moral and social principles that originally underpinned them, has led to much speculation regarding what 'works' and what doesn't work in a fist fight. For example, in respect of Karate, modern Western concerns often centre around what would 'work' in a bar or on the 'streets'. Because of the way Karate is commonly perceived, techniques originally cultivated in historically remote and geographically distant periods and regions (from a modern Western perspective), and from inward looking, traditional and *conformist* cultures, are often required to provide solutions to violence in a non-conformist modern Western society, a society that – it appears – has diminishing respect for authority and a growing penchant for extreme forms of violent behaviour.

In reality, a new and modern 'Westernised' Karate is beginning to appear, generated by disgruntled practitioners of 'traditional' Karate. Obviously dissatisfied with their results when trying to actually *apply* 'traditional' Karate, their search is to find what 'works' in a modern Western environment. The more successful of this new breed of combat-oriented instructors have developed practical methods that no longer even remotely resemble so-called 'traditional' Karate and have no use at all for kata. For these innovators, the 'mystique' of traditional Karate has vanished with their 'purging' of it. Quite frankly I'm not surprised. Just consider again the bizarre so-called 'double simultaneous blocks', applied against equally unlikely double simultaneous punches, or the time consuming full steps, or stop start staccato type movements that assume an attacker will remain still for long enough for one to apply them – these are enough to put doubts into even the most trusting of minds.

Take a look for example at this 'feet together – double block' from the kata Pinan Sandan (Hein Sandan in Shotokan) created circa 1905 by Itosu Ankho.

Solo techniques

Alleged-application

The most obvious question generated by the above photographs (why are the feet together when blocking – surely an unstable position?) only sets into action a chain of related questions such as, 'How can the defender be sure which hand to block high with, and which to block low with ... or, what if it isn't a block at all? Some Karate teachers claim that the kata were cunningly designed precisely to make us think in such a way. Needless to say I disagree.

There also exists a 'fraternity' of traditionalists bent on applying the techniques of ancient kata in modern urban environs, insisting that Karate can address all permutations of violence, regardless of cultural context, historical period or more critically, an aggressor's *motive*, method, and innate ability. Regrettably for them (as I have said), some of the techniques they are trying to interpret for use on modern city streets were designed to be used by an armed operative to counter (oriental) weapons like a sword or a six foot pole/staff, hundreds of years ago! And the techniques were not exclusively designed for urban use. Similarly, southern China's policing problems were not confined to metropolitan or urban areas. Many problems were associated with rural banditry, organised gangs of vagabonds, rogues and criminals who terrorised villages in armed raids. Terrorism, murder, burglary, robbery, theft, and so on, are not only urban phenomenon, and of course, as the gangs knew well, remote villages, although far less wealthy than the cities, could be raided for basic amenities like food and drinking water.

As I explained in chapter one, many major Karate kata perceived as unarmed self defence sequences, were originally developed as practical methods designed in application for use with weapons (or perhaps more properly 'tools') intended to facilitate civil defence or civil arrest in a particular cultural milieu, that of Southern China during the Ming and Qing dynasties to be more precise. I can not stress enough that these techniques make little sense with the absence of the weapons – or for the purposes of this discussion – in an inappropriate cultural environment.

Returning to the issue of the differences between (ancient) Eastern and modern Western culture; contemporary drug culture, the use of (modern) weapons, modern Western individualism, materialism and hedonism, a growing absence of social responsibility amongst some members of society, a certain 'streetwise-ness', constantly changing social values that can easily be bypassed (as opposed to a greater inflexibility in, for example, Japan or Okinawa), and a greater degree of disregard for authority amongst the young, all act to separate the cultures of the (ancient) East from the modern West.

Taking a simple look at the rigid formality and etiquette observed in traditional Karate and comparing it with the informality and lack of ritual, in say Western boxing (real), wrestling (and aggressive or loutish behaviour), one can get the feel of the effect culture has on the construction, purpose, attitudes and approaches to Martial Arts and (physical) confrontation. For example, generally speaking, the Okinawans, like the Japanese, place great emphasis on *form*, aesthetics, and the inclusion of religious and spiritual values and philosophical content, whilst Europeans and others (coming from different cultural bases) appear to be more 'results hungry'.

The Japanese Tea Ceremony

The aforementioned (Japanese) 'culturally embedded' attitudes, stretch right down to something as potentially simple as making a cup of tea. Tea is valued, and drunk, with differing degrees (or lack) of ritual, and under differing social circumstances, the world over. Yet in Japan, one can still find the highly ritualised 'tea ceremony', a ceremony so steeped in archaic etiquette and ritual behaviour as to (from a Western perspective) all but lose sight of it's utilitarian purpose – the delivery of a cup of tea! Most English tea drinkers (unaware of the Japanese tea ceremony) would find the Japanese tea ceremony baffling, time consuming (to say the very least) and as far removed from 'making' an 'English cuppa' as possible.

For me, the above observation succinctly parallels the differences between the (modern) Western requirements for, and attitudes towards, 'street fighting' (and self defence), and the modern *art* of Karate. People in the West regularly make a 'quick cuppa', during their tea breaks. In contrast, the elaborate and time-consuming Japanese 'tea ceremony' (modern Karate, in the parallel), is a highly ritualised and cultural set of *symbolic* behaviour(s) and actions, with profound social, cultural and spiritual significance(s) as well as a means of delivering a cup of tea.

Moreover, there is nothing inherent in the more elaborate ritual of the tea ceremony to suggest that the tea tastes any better (particularly to a Westerner) than Western tea, or that tea brewed during the Japanese tea ceremony is, in effect, nutritionally superior; however, the tea ceremony can be used as a vehicle to express nobility and 'high culture' as well as making a cup of tea. Similarly, the Sai and grappling techniques, found for instance in Seisan and Naihanchin kata respectively, represent a 'high culture' approach. These kata are clearly utilitarian in construction and practical in application, but at no point do they advocate brutality or employ ignoble tactics. Thus there is no ear biting, head butting, spitting, etc. involved in their practice. The Sai user merely seeks to disarm his opponent, whilst the grappler merely seeks to subdue, arrest, and remove his quarry.

Bu(do) Keeps Control among the Civil Population

In further support of the above line of thinking, I cite one of Okinawa's celebrated Bushi (warriors). The quote is from the 'Budo Makimono' (Warrior-way scroll) of the great Okinawan 'To-te' expert, 'Bushi' (Warrior) Matsumura Sokon, dated c. 1882, in which he classifies Martial Arts:

> *Meimoku-no-Bugei*, [purely technical 'fighting', without the true Budo spirit and purpose] signifies a person who has a physical understanding of Bugei. He may be a powerful and violent person who can easily defeat other men. He will have no self control, is dangerous, and can even harm his own family. Budo-no-Bugei [the true warrior way] is what I esteem. With this, you can let the enemy destroy himself – simply wait with a calm heart and the enemy will defeat himself.
>
> People who practice Budo-no-Bugei are faithful to their friends, their parents and their country. They will not do anything unnatural.

Matsumura then goes on to outline the seven virtues [of Bu]:

> 'Bu' prohibits violence, maintains discipline amongst soldiers, *keeps control among the civil population*, spreads virtue, creates a peaceful heart, helps keep the peace between people and makes folk or a nation prosperous ... (Italics mine)

The mere sight of an experienced, well known and well equipped Sai operative would have been enough to produce immediate conformity amongst most people during the period(s) under question, and like any tough veteran, his reputation would have been his greatest asset, providing he was tough, probably uncompromising, but above all, a skilled and dignified authoritative figure.

The above illustrates the gulf between the personal cultivation/ennoblement and collective social control described, and the requirements and attitudes for and of modern (Western) personal 'street defence'. Yet Karate is commonly viewed as a fiendish Oriental cure-all for such. No racial or cultural group has a monopoly on how to deliver sound and destructive blows, or how to be effective in real fighting. Karate is well-known, but kickboxing, shoot-fighting, cage fighting and 'ultimate challenge' style fighting (aggressive 'Westernized' forms of violent combat, motivated by winning), are all catching up and are currently regarded as 'real fighting'; what is more, their practitioners seem to win in 'real fighting' matches. Yet their methods incorporate no spirituality, use minimum etiquette, employ no philosophy, are not rooted in morality and of course do not practice kata.

I am fully aware of the old argument that true or real Karate is too dangerous to be practiced with full contact. Poking the eye, kicking the groin, strangulation techniques, breaking joints, delivering knockout techniques, are all far too dangerous to actually apply, so it is claimed. Well I am afraid that most of the above list (perhaps excluding eye poking or groin kicking) is used in the 'ultimate challenge-style- fighting', etc. for real. To date, no devoted advocates, practitioners of traditional Karate kata, have distinguished themselves (publicly) in such matches. Also, please bear in mind, there are no rules or etiquette required and equally none is used in street-fights! Yet many individuals still insist that is just what Karate's predecessor To-te Jutsu (or at least Karate) was essentially designed to deal with – raw violence. I think that is a mistaken assumption based on an incomplete understanding of the cultural, historical and spiritual milieu in which Quan-fa – Karate's grandparent – was originally generated, and the circumstances that led to its adoption on Okinawa. It is useful to understand how and why Quan-fa was transformed by secretive groups there who nurtured it, referred to it simply as 'To-te Jutsu', and eventually promoted it vigorously as (modern) Karate.

It is mistaken to confuse the current levels and climate of violence amongst certain groups in large modern Western cities (and elsewhere) with that of Okinawan village life in the nineteenth century, the setting for the codification of To-te Jutsu and its transformation into Karate. It should be understood *why* To-te Jutsu was pursued by the peaceful Okinawans in the first place.

Relevant History

In 1609, the Satsuma clan of 'Kagoshima' (formerly Satsuma on mainland Japan), sent some three thousand Samurai to Okinawa to annexe it. The inevitable subjugation of the already (largely) unarmed Okinawans led (indirectly) to the clandestine spread of To-te Jutsu – but not as erroneously believed – so that individuals could fight with or even defend against well-armed, well-trained and ruthless Samurai, but so that given the weapons ban in place, national pride and cultural independence could be maintained, and those with martial inclinations could at least pursue some kind of physical – albeit (supposedly) unarmed – Martial Arts training, unknown by, and unknown to, their oppressors; although this did not really begin to happen until the late eighteenth to early nineteenth century (c. 1800).

The Ryukyu island chain is fragmented, and Okinawa is small, relatively speaking. It only covers a total area of about 460 square miles. Okinawan lifestyle, cultural traditions and values were certainly not like those of the Bronx in New York, or Liverpool in England, then; nor are they now.

A couple of comparisons will help to make this point.

One of the old 'tough guys' of Karate, hailed for his 'practical Karate' was the unconventional and nonconformist Motobu Choki (1871–1944), one of the few serious Okinawan Karate practitioners with a reputation for 'street-fighting'. Standing 5ft 5in tall and weighing 190 lbs, the thick-set and extremely robust Motobu was a big man in comparison with other Okinawan or Japanese people of that time. Motobu used to get into frequent fights in the 'Tsuji' red light district, and claimed to have had over one hundred fights, *without ever being hit in the face !*

Although Western Boxing lacks the mystique and romance of Karate, the experienced Karate-ka is forced to respect it (however grudgingly). Yet even the likes of Jack Dempsey, Rocky Marciano and Cassius Clay (Muhammad Ali) got hit. I think that a record of over one hundred fights without even being hit in the face, does not necessarily attest to the combat efficiency of Karate, or the competence of the Karate-ka in question. One must consider the calibre of the opposition and the circumstances. For example, the late Gary Spiers, a ferocious 6ft, 280 lbs New Zealand former slaughter-man and ex Goju Ryu Karate-ka, settled in Liverpool (England) and formulated something called 'Applied Karate' which he promulgated during the mid to late 1980s. Spiers recounted several (terrible) fights that he had, and his 'credentials' were verified by the editor of Fighting Arts magazine, no stranger to 'security work' himself. The following quotes from *Fighting Arts International* (hereafter *F.A.I.*) No. 39 (Vol. 7 N 3), are graphic and rather unpleasant, but I use them to best illustrate my point:

> Spiers, "My face was literally cut in half, there was so much blood spraying out … through the hole in my nose that I couldn't see anything in front of me."
>
> O'Neill, "Did you go down?"
>
> Spiers, "No, I didn't …"

In the same article – one of several – Spiers recounts some pretty gruesome tales, including being stabbed, struck in the groin with a broken bottle, punched, hit and kicked in the face, and in turn inflicting severe trauma on opponents, such as biting off someone's ear, and apparently breaking someone's back. Here is a supporting quote from my book *Barefoot Zen*,

> In urban violence, imposing physique, intimidation tactics, vicious aggression and speed are mandatory, along with downright cunning, brutality and the cultivation of natural instincts for survival. These characteristics have always been present in the profile of the 'hard man', regardless of culture! These attitudes are learned *in situ* – that is, by observation, emulation and actual participation, and not by practicing forms in a sports hall. Such tactics and methods are free from etiquette and moral, social, or philosophical restrictions. That is partly why they work and precisely why there is nothing noble or culturally satisfying about them ... such tactics can not be recorded in a form.

I am not suggesting that Okinawa was (is) a utopian society. It undoubtedly had and still has its fair share of hoodlums, violence and crime, but the conformist Confucian-based traditional *culture* of Okinawa was (is) very different from the ever-developing, ever-shifting Western culture, and in many respects still is. Comparison of, for example, current crime statistics would tell its own tale.

A little information on the nature of Confucianism might help to explain the cultural thinking that led to the creation of Quan-fa, To-te and Karate, as opposed to mere 'street-fighting' (a common occurrence in any city). Confucius was born in China around 551 BCE and died around 479 BCE. After his death, his ideas permeated every level of Chinese society and 'Confucianism' became the virtual state religion from the Han dynasty (206 BCE) right up to the end of the Qing in 1911! Confucianism stressed the application of conservative 'tradition' that maintained peace and social order through good conduct and clearly defined patterns of obedience and filial piety. Old age was venerated and white hair too (the Ming/Qing dynasty's produced the Pak Mei or 'White Eyebrows' school of Quan-fa, named after its venerated founder, Pak Mei Too Jung). Advanced age was seen as something that symbolised the 'epitome' of knowledge and wisdom. Physically, the elderly may have been at their weakest, but it was considered that all good things flowed from their wisdom and knowledge. Dead ancestors were honoured and their spirits propitiated. The reverence and respect they were accorded allows us to understand the respect later given to the 'old Karate masters'. This is quite different from contemporary Western attitudes towards, and trends regarding, age.

One of the most influential Confucian concepts that affected the day to day life of the Chinese people was the concept called *li*. Li has two basic meanings:

1. Li as a sense of 'propriety' – how to behave correctly in a given situation.

2. Li as 'ordered ritual'.

This thinking, coupled with concepts derived from, or influenced by, Taoism (indigenous Chinese spirituality) and Buddhism (imported from India), ultimately led to the genesis of 'dignified' 'ordered' Martial Arts *rituals* – quan/kata – solo, choreographed sequences of techniques – and is why the arts unfolded the way they did in China and not elsewhere. In some respects, China was, to the Orient, what Rome was to Europe. And to some extent, the differences between Oriental and European thought and culture are reflected in the attitudes taken towards so-called 'un-armed combat'. Given that (from at least the Ming dynasty) China was the biggest exporter of culture in South East Asia and the Far East, it is easy to see why the Okinawans acquired a very thick 'veneer' of Chinese culture. But that is hardly surprising when one considers that before the Satsuma subjugation, Okinawa was essentially a Chinese 'vassal state'.

Early 'To-te' masters, whatever their understanding of the technical material they'd adopted, counselled strongly against fighting and violence. Actual fighting was frowned upon and considered shameful. The (social) disgrace of engaging in fighting was only mitigated if one had justice on one's side, and espoused and adhered to aphorisms like, 'Seigi Jindo' – peace and humanity, or maxims such as, 'Karate Ni Sente Nashi' – there is no first (hand/initiative) attack in Karate. Even then, fighting was still regarded as an unwelcome breakdown of 'Wa' – (personal) harmony, impinging upon social order. Actual fighting (rather than hard training) was considered to be no more than the (regrettable but urgent) treatment of a 'symptom'. Metaphorically, it was merely the repair of an object that should not have been broken in the first place. True To-te practice, however, was deemed to be a (general) long-term *preventative* or 'cure' for social disease, violence or disreputable behaviour, through physical *training* designed to occupy leisure time, focus attention, strengthen bodies, purify hearts and minds, and encourage nobility and virtue. Add to that, the well-known Okinawan penchant for peace and it becomes possible to get more of a cultural feel for the Okinawans – the perpetuators of old style Quan-fa, To-te, and the architects of modern Karate.

What follows is a paraphrased and partial quote taken from Itosu Ankho's ten precepts of To-te; (c. 1908) where in precept one he says, in part,

> ... To-te is not meant to be employed against an opponent (adversary) but rather as a means to avoid the use of ones hands and feet in a potentially dangerous encounter ...

Funakoshi Gichin

Possibly Itosu's most famous student Funakoshi Gichin, wrote in the 1956 re-print of his 1936, *Karate – Do Kyohan.* p.6:

> ... in the moment that one misuses the [Karate] techniques, for example in fighting in such a way that he injures another or himself, or brings dishonour upon himself, he nullifies any of these benefits [strength, poise, spiritual fortitude, humility, mentioned earlier in that text] and merits of Karate-do. Such misuse, arising from superficial understanding, is in fact self-defeating ... (Parenthesis mine)

A direct quote by Nagamine Shoshin, from *The Essence of Okinawan Karate-Do* p.14, will also help here:

> ... The *peaceful* and weaponless Okinawans are living proof of the possibility of a world without war. All people could live in peace if they followed the example of the Okinawans. (Italics mine)

Although Nagamine is speaking about the weapon-less nature of Okinawan society, their peacefulness (conformism) comes across quite strongly.

Metaphorically speaking, Ming dynasty Quan-fa, To-te Jutsu's ancestor, was designed to cure the 'illness' too, and not merely to treat the 'symptom'. Despite its obvious utility function, it was designed to underpin social cohesion, to be the visible presence of social (moral) authority, and to act as a deterrent to lawlessness and civil unrest. Its ideal was to create morally upright, dignified members of society (good police officers for example) by the collective disciplining of youth through a rigorous and noble 'way of life-style' replete with hierarchies that conferred status and undoubtedly created acknowledged masters who exerted genuine social influence. The various schools also employed technical methodologies that could be practiced, taught and demonstrated well into old age. They were not intended to be a means to merely solve immediate personal self defence problems. The idea of collective training for health and *social good* still underpins the practice of Martial Arts in China to this day. This is rather alien to the Western requirement of *self* empowerment (self defence).

The Chinese Art Goes off Course

Unfortunately, during the late Chinese Imperial, early Republican period (c. 1644–1911), the emphasis in Quan-fa shifted, and practice began to centre on nationalism, rebellion, and the training of 'angry young men' to repel foreigners, particularly after 1864 when the ranks of anti-foreign secret societies began to swell, culminating in the bloody 'Boxer' rebellion of 1900. The repressive Manchu regime imposed total control over the Han Chinese fondness for, and habit of, practicing Martial Arts. A Qing dynasty edict from 1727 (re-produced by Professor Douglas Wile in, *Tai Chi Ancestors*, Sweet Chi Press, New York 1999) p.5–6 proclaims:

> There are individuals who practice the martial arts, and calling themselves masters, seduce the masses and stir up ignorant people ... Belligerent young men flock to them, abandoning productive occupations and spending all day building themselves up and sparring with each other ... Sometimes they assume the name of religion to assemble thieves and bandits ...

During that period, secret societies and politically subversive groups began to arise. By modern standards, some had bizarre names like: 'The White Lotus Society', and 'The Fists of Harmonious Righteousness'. Styles began to mushroom and new weapon quan were constructed/invented and old ones 'revised'. These forms were practiced without the weapons being present, thus concealing the true intention of the quan from the Manchu authorities and possibly giving rise to a new perceived unarmed art. Fortunately, genuine old empty hand quan (like Naihanchin as opposed to weapon-based quan) continued to be practiced, but for new and different reasons.

Karate – Combat and Film – Some Misconceptions Examined

Regarding the influence of films on the Martial Arts, contemporary screen images of the Karate 'technician' as cold, clinical and ruthlessly efficient persist as part of the Karate warrior myth. Also, traditionally, the 'bad guys' in films seldom seem to be able to shoot straight or fight effectively. But the hero gets unlimited shots out of his six shooter, without the bother of having to reload, or if s/he is unarmed, no problem! Using Karate techniques, s/he can dispatch several opponents with relative ease. I guess the hapless 'bad guys' have the same weapons instructors teaching them unarmed combat.

I remember how, after the release of the influential and trend-setting Bruce Lee movie 'Enter the Dragon' in 1972/3, high kicks became extremely popular in many Karate schools. At that time, requests were sometimes made for instructors to teach techniques depicted in the film, and I recall the jumping side kick and spinning back-turning kicks (showcased in the film) becoming widespread, regardless of style. Even traditional Kung Fu styles with no precedents for such kicks, began to use them. I also remember a man who dyed his Gi (uniform) yellow to look like the tournament competitors in the same film, and turned up for our usual (packed) Karate class, only to be sent out of the Dojo, in disgrace (Gus, where are you?). I also remember two Caucasian Kung Fu students who dyed their hair black to try and look more Chinese. These points serve to illustrate *life* imitating *art*, and are given to show the influence of films, and to suggest that they (plus a little over-imagination) contribute to the many misconceptions regarding Martial Arts in general and Karate in particular.

Much that passes for Karate is demonstrative. This is by no means a recent phenomenon. Impressionable people (in the Orient too) have been fooled by unscrupulous self-promoters and 'masters' of tricks, for centuries. Outward shows of physique, strength and showmanship have always dogged the efforts of teachers with a less superficial understanding. But let's face it, people love a good show. Current poor public perceptions of 'traditional' Martial Arts can therefore be seen as the result of repeated exposure to misleading and showy displays. But exhibition forms are just that, they have always been a part of Chinese circus, fairs, banquets and market places, where they were originally used to draw crowds. Once assembled, these crowds could, for instance, be sold 'medicines'. Thus was the origin of popular acrobatic 'medicine seller', or 'street peddler Kung Fu', and its legacy can still be seen in modern Chinese Wu Shu (lit. to quell a spear).

In respect of showy or flowery forms, Douglas Wile (*Tai Chi's Ancestors: The making of an Internal Martial Art*, NY, Sweet Ch'i Press 1999 p.12) quoting Ch'i-chi kuang, has this to say:

> In chapter 4 of the [Ming dynasty Martial Arts treatise] 'Lien-ping shi-chi', Chi' expresses his opposition to flowery forms. [Showy, flashy, 'embroidered' forms]

Without obvious postures or techniques, you will be effective with [in] one move; if you *do* make the mistake of posturing and posing, you will be *ineffective* with [in] ten moves.

This theme is later taken up in Tang Shun-chi's 'Wu pien' which later repeats and develops Chi's work:

... The reason for postures in the martial arts is to facilitate transformations ... forms contain fixed postures, but in actual practice there are no fixed postures. When applied, they become fluid, but still maintain their structural characteristics. (Parenthesis mine).

This comment is certainly true in respect of the kata illustrated in this book, and is particularly relevant to weapons forms.

There are countless modern-day practitioners of scores of 'Martial Arts'. Many practitioners are content to follow instruction without question. Many simply practice what they like, and some merely practice what they think looks good. Modern styles and many 'home grown' styles have been influenced by Asian Kung Fu films, based as they are on maximising visual or dramatic impact. In contrast, the genuine kata were not devised for demonstration or to look grand, or to impress. True Karate is about training, not about 'showing'! Further, an ancient motif suggests that from a spiritual perspective, the real 'opponent' is oneself. Indeed, euphemisms like 'forging the body in the fire of the will', whilst a little clichéd, remain useful.

Karate Used Against a Swordsman?

Speaking of forging, I recently saw a poster in a University dojo advertising Karate as an art 'forged' out of the necessity of subject Okinawans to defend themselves (barehanded) from the

injustices of the Samurai.' This common misconception –
touched on earlier – about Karate being used by unarmed
peasants to bravely defend themselves against 'maniacal' sword
wielding Samurai, goes against common sense and history,
although this myth does actually rest on one recorded case – an
'exception' that proves the rule.

At the age of about twenty, or so, Matsumora Kosaku, an
Okinawan To-te Jutsu student/teacher (1829–1898) from
Tomari, allegedly got into a skirmish with a Samurai, whom – it
is claimed – he disarmed using a wet tea towel! For several days,
Matsumora had practiced the trick against his own (To-te)
students, with great success, although they were only armed with
wooden swords. When Matsumora confronted the (un-named)
Samurai (who was armed with a real blade), he apparently
succeeded. The Samurai was (temporarily) embarrassed, but,
unfortunately, in the engagement, Matsumora lost his little
finger – a vital component in the grip used with a sword and in
the Naihanchin grip (see Naihanchin kata). After the incident,
Matsumora – a marked man – had to go into hiding, and
remained exiled from his village for about ten years.

I'm not disputing the bravery and valour of the deed described,
I'm simply pointing to the outcome. Realistically I think
Matsumora was brave (or foolish) but lucky. He went on to
become a local political figure, and an Okinawan legend. One
must bear in mind that Okinawa's main *cultural* export is Karate,
and given that Okinawa has no military history as such, its Karate
masters became its heroic national figures – figures such as
Miyagi Chojun.

Miyagi Chojun

What is the Okinawan Ryu-Ha Kihon Kata Tradition?

The Okinawan Ryu-ha 'Kihon' Kata tradition was defined by the Karate 'great' Miyagi Chojun (Miyagusuku Chojun, 1888–1953), founder of the popular and now international Goju Ryu Karate style. In his important 1934 Essay, 'Karate Do Gaisetsu', responsible in part for legitimising Karate with the Japanese authorities, Miyagi states very clearly that the Sanchin, Tensho (Rokushu) and Naihanchi (Naihanchin) kata are the 'kihon' or fundamental kata of the entire Okinawan Karate Ryu-Ha, or (official) Karate 'Martial Tradition'. As previously noted, these kata represent the *two* Ryu (Families/schools) into which Karate is basically divided – Naha-te and Shuri-te. According to the late Yagi Metitoku (Goju Ryu), Naihanchin is Shorin Ryu's equivalent to Sanchin. Perhaps 'martial' is a misnomer when applied directly to these kata as envisaged in this book, but notwithstanding this, it is clear that Miyagi held these three kata in very high regard. It is my contention that he was right to do so, and his 'insight' paved the way for a renaissance of these three often misunderstood kata and their applications. What is not commonly known is that although Miyagi Chojun did not include Naihanchin kata in his evolving Goju Ryu style, he had studied and practiced the kata, as did his student Yagi Meitoku, and Yagi's student, Anthony Mirakian.

Naha-te Kata

(Closed-fist) Sanchin kata 'Three Conflicts' modified by Miyagi, who was most likely influenced by methods of 'triangulation' and breathing used in 'Preying Mantis' and 'Five ancestors Kung Fu'. It is best viewed as a system of basic holistic strength and posture building, and in application, basic Chin-Na and boxing/push hands techniques.

Tensho 'Change of Grips', originally known as Rokushu 'Six Hands' is a straight-forward catalogue of grip escapes systematically recording the methods of escaping from the fundamental configurations of grips an attacker can use.

Shuri-te Kata

Naihanchin kata is the solo representation of a pro-active collective of crossed arm grappling and restraining techniques, meticulously designed and engineered to arrest and subdue a single opponent with whom contact is never lost.

Three Original Naha-te Kata – Sanchin, Seisan, and Sanseriu

Sanchin, Seisan and Sanseriu, the open-handed kata, originally learned by Miyagi Chojun's teacher, Higaonna Kanyro, and also by Uechi Kanbun, the founder of Uechi Ryu, formed the basis for Goju Ryu (Miyagi's style), To'on Ryu (discussed in chapter three) and Uechi Ryu Karate, a style originally based solely on these three kata, which are, of course, kata intended for use with a pair of Sai.

Kobudo Sai

The Seisan kata is a very popular kata that hails from Fujian in Fuzhou, Southern China, and dates from a period during which the non native Manchu dynasty (1644–1911) imposed a ban on Martial Arts activity for the native Han people. Seisan Kata (like many others) is simply the practice of the techniques of the Sai without the actual presence of the weapons. As I have suggested, by this means, 'Martial Arts' (actually civil weapons training) was most likely preserved and disseminated under various guises, such as 'chi gung' health exercises, or as keep fit, callisthenics, gymnastics, or peasant fisticuffs (almost), under the eyes of the despised Manchu authorities (more on this later). The astute reader will realise that the implications of what I have said here, are huge for the art of Karate.

As will also be seen later, Seisan was allegedly the favourite kata of the founder of Uechi Ryu Karate, Master Uechi Kanbun. A (modified) Goju Ryu version of Seisan was also the favourite kata of Shinzato Jinnan (1901–1945), an early and senior practitioner of Goju Ryu, under Miyagi Chojun.

Returning to the kihon kata Sanchin and Naihanchin, these kata were championed and taught, respectively by Kanryo Higaonna (1853–1915) and Itosu Ankho (1832–1915). Higaonna taught Sanchin, Sanchin and more Sanchin (Miyagi Chojun, his most

Higaonna Kanryo

famous student only knew *one* other kata – Seisan – besides Sanchin, for the first seven or eight years of his training!).

Itosu Ankho enthusiastically taught Naihanchin, Naihanchin, and more Naihanchin. His student, Funakoshi Gichin, reports in his book *Karate – Do Kyohan* and in his memoirs, that he spent ten years learning solely these (three) kata (*one* kata broken into three parts).

Function Dictates Form

'*Function dictates form*', remains the phrase that best defines authentic kata. Unfortunately, as I made plain in chapter one, *modern* Karate kata applications have become so ambiguous and ill-defined, that many different teachers have produced as many different ideas/explanations/applications for antique kata. This situation has resulted in many 'stylistic' nuances appearing in the original solo kata, which has, in turn, ultimately led to the creation of many *different* 'Ryu'.

I would now like to consider this point more carefully. For example, a look at the way Funakoshi Gichin performed the 'back (leg bent) stance' in early photographs of Shuri-te kata, compared with the way he performed it in later ones, demonstrates the gradual evolution of the style later to be known as Shotokan (Shoto's Hall – Shoto was Funakoshi's pen name). Shotokan Karate subsequently became the market-leading flagship of (mainland) Japanese rather than Okinawan Karate.

Nagamine Shoshin, whilst maintaining a deep respect for Funakoshi and his achievements, complained about Funakoshi's deepening of the 'neko ashi dachi' (cat stance) and his transforming it into the Shotokan 'kokutsu dachi' (back leg bent stance). Nagamine bemoaned the creation of a new tradition where he felt none was required. The stance in the early photograph of Funakoshi is markedly higher and more closely resembles the original early Shuri-te 'neko ashi dachi' (cat stance), whereas the later photographs show a lengthening and deepening of the stance, more characteristic of the modern Shotokan 'kokutsu dachi' (back leg bent) stance. Such a modification represents a typical case of *kata* evolving to fit *desired* applications.

Perhaps Funakoshi's 'kokutsu dachi' was influenced by his association with Nakayama Hakudo. Nakayama was an extremely prominent Japanese swordsman and teacher of Kendo who offered Funakoshi the use of his own dojo (located at

Funakoshi's high and low backstances

Hongo-Yumi-cho, Tokyo) when it was not in use. 'Kokutsu dachi' does indeed resemble a sword-fighting posture. Later, in Japan, the length and width of the Sanchin and Naihanchin stances were similarly altered when certain kata were introduced, no doubt to conform to Japanese aesthetic and cultural values, particularly those based on Budo – the Japanese 'way of the warrior'.

In Shotokan Karate, the Sanchin stance is lengthened and turned into something called 'Hangetsu dachi' (half moon stance) practiced in a kata bearing the same name, whilst the Naihanchin stance is lowered and widened to become 'Kibba dachi', the 'horse riding' stance of the (Naihanchin) kata, re-named Tekki.

As noted earlier, Hangetsu is an adaptation of an already adapted Okinawan version of an original Chinese form (Seisan), a kata that, as I have repeatedly said, was designed expressly to be used with a pair of Sai. Whilst both Tekki (stance and kata, with its 'block strike' applications) is far removed from its original purpose, that of grappling a single opponent!

My point here is not to criticize established Karate *styles* per-se, but to illustrate that uncertainty, regarding the *exact* functions or applications of kata, is not a new phenomenon. Indeed, it's rather an old one. The Ming dynasty Chinese General, Ch'i Chi-kuang (1528–1587), a man who under his own initiative decided to teach Quan-fa to his troops, complained (in his manual on practical troop training), that one of the characteristics of (flowery) forms was a misunderstanding of the function of posture(s). In effect he was denouncing posturing and positioning without the practical knowledge of *application*.

A more recent example relates to the Shotokan style again and contrasts it with the apparently different (but very popular) Japanese Karate style of Wado Ryu (Harmony Way). Both

Otsuka Hironori

originated with Funakoshi's early Shuri-te or Shorin Ryu Karate. Otsuka Hironori, the founder of Wado Ryu, was an early student of Funakoshi and quickly became one of his top assistants.

Otsuka's Karate was largely built around the Karate first taught to him by Funakoshi in the 1920s (although there was input from other experts such as Motobu Choki). Otsuka retained the light, quick movements and the relatively high stances of the Karate from that period, whereas Shotokan became progressively more power-oriented and 'deeper rooted' in stances. Otsuka developed a series of 'kihon' or basic two-person drills, arguably unrelated to the kata, and quite different from the developing (essentially long range) Shotokan 'kumite' or sparring. The Wado Ryu Kihon drills bear the hallmark of Motobu Choki's ideas – higher hand positions (to protect the head), close distance, and the simultaneous use of both hands. Despite a common origin (originally the same kata), Shotokan and Wado Ryu have become markedly divergent, yet both are promoted as 'traditional'. Wado Ryu still retains the old names of the kata (Pinan, Sesian, Naihanchi(n), etc.) – names that were later changed by Funakoshi Gichin.

The reader may be happy to merely attribute the above situation to the exercise of freedom of choice, or technical developments made to 'improve a style' or create a new or different style. But both the styles mentioned above originated with the Shuri-te tradition, a tradition founded on the Naihanchin (Tekki) kata. Naihanchin used to be the main kata of study for Shuri-te, and in its proper form should still serve as the correct model or 'benchmark' – meaning; the maintenance of the original stance and the original height of the hand positions remain paramount.

Nagamine Shoshin, in his 'Essence of Okinawan Karate-Do', states (p.148),

> As for the kata of Naihanchi [n] [a.k.a. Tekki] (Shodan to Sandan) the composer is still unknown, yet these kata were known to the Shuri and Tomari schools even before the kata of Pinan [Heian] was invented [1905/1908]. This is proved by the fact that beginners used to learn Naihanchi [n] instead of Pinan. (Parenthesis mine)

Neither Shotokan nor Wado Ryu make (proper) use of Naihanchin, or have at their disposal the grappling application of which the solo kata is the record! (See chapter eight). Further, both Shotokan and Wado Ryu have made stylistic alterations to the original Naihanchin *kata*, based on misinterpreting Naihanchin – a grappling sequence – and representing it as a 'block strike sequence! Shotokan has deepened the *stance* thus restricting the quick sideways movement required to tumble and follow a tumbling opponent, and Wado Ryu has raised the *hand positions* – considering head-height positions to be a superior form of defence – thus surrendering the necessary, and all important *leverage* required to keep the opponent properly *locked* and *subdued*.

In a similar way, when (Higaonna Kanyro's) early Naha-te evolved into (Miyagi Chojun's) Goju Ryu, changes were made, particularly to kata. Currently, there is a school of thought that insists that (a given brand of) Goju Ryu Karate has been passed down from Higaonna Kanyro through Miyagi Chojun *unchanged*, but this is inaccurate and unrealistic, and merely represents partisan propaganda, as I will argue.

The upholding of tradition is a fine thing, so long as the reason for, and the understanding of, *why* something should be done one way as opposed to another, exists. With regard to kata, one needs certainty regarding the function!

Asymmetry in Kata

Many quan/kata practice or repeat particular techniques on only one side of the body and as I mentioned earlier, Seisan kata 'thirteen hands/steps' displays such a 'one-sided' approach indicative of a preferred (right handed) combat 'attitude', like a favoured side forward in, for example, Western fencing. The original Seisan kata clearly shows this characteristic, a hallmark of weapons usage. On the other hand, the correct Naihanchin kata – a non weapons kata – is symmetrical.

Naihanchin originated in China, making it in effect a Quan-fa form. In respect of the genesis of Quan-fa, one must take into consideration existing civil 'combat' methods, particularly civil arrest techniques generated in China during or before the Ming dynasty. There is sufficient evidence to suggest that such methods existed as early as the Chou period, 1122–221 BCE

Selected Sesian Sai techniques illustrate the asymmetry of many kata

This bronze statue of Chinese wrestlers (from the Chou Dynasty, 1122–221 BCE) bears uncanny resemblance to Naihanchin

Naihanchin is a symmetrical kata when properly structured and once the errors that crept in after the kata was broken into three parts are understood. The division of the kata necessitated the creation of two re-constructed openings (Naihanchin 2 & 3) and two artificial endings (Naihanchin 1 & 2. See chapter eight for a full discussion of this). The approach to unarmed conflict exemplified by Naihanchin – which I remind the reader, is one of the most traditional and revered of kata – illustrates that because the human anatomy is (largely) invariable, a fairly exact science can be constructed in terms of the application of leverage, based on skeletal articulation, adduction, abduction, the twisting of, limbs, and the locking of joints, etc. practiced on both sides of the body for obvious reasons, and giving rise to a symmetrical kata.

I think it fair to say that the civil defence techniques of Ming dynasty China set the precedent for the effective but non-brutal restraining techniques of a number of later traditions in China, Okinawa and Japan, including Ju-Jutsu (soft/pliant technique[s]), Judo (soft or pliant way) and Aikido (Harmony way). These modern Japanese arts are indeed based on joint locks, restraints and throwing techniques. However, the Naihanchin kata pre-dates the creation of these methods by at least three hundred years, and cannot therefore be seen as a derivative of them.

Although then still a work in progress, so to speak, I published the initial Naihanchin discovery in 1994, and released selected amounts of material in *Barefoot Zen* in 2000, although I did not *fully* identify and integrate other important source materials, notably the civil arrest techniques using Sai, and the civil arrest tradition of Ming and Qing dynasty China – major components of what would later become Karate. At that time (1995–1999), whilst I had privately aired my suspicions regarding weapons and kata, I had insufficient concrete proof before the publication of Barefoot Zen in December 2000, and I still could not fully explain the asymmetry of many kata (except to suggest that they be practiced on both sides). However, I now feel my research is complete, hence the present volume.

Some Karate-ka believe *all* kata can usefully be performed with or without weapons. But as I have already made clear, I disagree. The kata are the templates recording *how to* use, for instance, the Sai. Besides, Rokushu (Tensho) kata can not be practiced using weapons, and Naihanchin makes absolutely no sense as a weapons kata. Indeed I would go so far as to suggest that Higaonna Kanyro and Miyagi Chojun's modified versions of Sanchin, Miyagi's Rokushu, and the Naihanchin kata may well be the *only* Karate kata that are not mixed up with or derived from weapon-play. However, Goju Ryu Kata do seem to have been developed with the idea of 'Karate' (empty hands) in mind. Moreover, Miyagi Chojun's Sanchin kata and to a lesser extent Higaonna Kanyro's Sanchin kata are excellent revisions, well-tailored to suit ancient concepts of the 'empty hand' art – symmetrical close quarters weapon-less combat, based *on the control of an opponent's posture and balance.*

Leaving aside the Kobudo (Uechi) Sanchin for a moment, today the potential 'riches' inherent *in the many Southern Chinese empty hand (Sanchin?) quan* are routinely bypassed due to a lack of understanding (within the modern Karate world) of original

Chinese concepts and methods that underscore these kata. Even though (the) Sanchin (tradition) is the basis upon which many other quan rest, it is commonly misunderstood, and often favoured less than more demonstrative quan. Of central importance to *any* Sanchin is the fact that it should outline the rules of the game, so to speak. So, in theory, understand Sanchin and you can understand how the whole 'game' works, and how a given *system* unfolds. One should eventually be able to understand the similarities in related systems and styles too, vis-à-vis the fixed nature of the gate system, zoning, ranging, distancing and the fixed number of limbs employed regardless of 'style'. All will be involved in controlling an opponent's limbs through monitoring movements via pushing hands skills, whether they be referred to as 'tempting hands', or sticking hands, etc. Also, within a system, the kata will be progressive; for example, the Goju Ryu Sanchin is expanded (complimented) by Rokushu (Tensho) kata and both are weapon-less kata, whilst the Uechi Ryu Sanchin is expanded on in Sesian kata, its lineal development and originally the second kata studied in learning to use the Sai in that particular tradition.

Metaphorically speaking, in contemporary Karate (Goju/Uechi), Sanchin kata can be considered to be 'The Rosetta Stone' of Karate. The Rosetta Stone, although dating from a very late period in dynastic Egyptian history, was used to decipher the previously incomprehensible classical Egyptian hieroglyphs, including the earliest of dynastic inscriptions.

So, to summarize, Sanchin can be said to be a set of principles or a quan/kata (like other types of Quan-fa or Kung Fu/Gongfu forms) that can yield-up typical characteristics of Chinese Martial Arts: it can define a centreline and gate system (see chapter five); zoning at the wrists, elbows and shoulders; mastering the opponent's elbow position; controlling the corners (outside gate); occupying the inside gate and controlling the centreline; and in unarmed practice, 'floating', 'sinking', soaking-up (neutralising force) and 'spitting-out' (expelling force) to name just some of the characteristics suggested by these pre-eminent quan/kata. The purpose of (each) Sanchin depends of course upon its structuring.

A Possible Shao-lin Temple Connection

For centuries there has been a spiritual connection, association or dimension, claimed for various Chinese, Okinawan, and Japanese Martial Arts. Rightly or wrongly, the Shao-lin Temple tradition (Shorin-ji in Japanese) is usually considered to be the source of this. The Shao-lin Temple stood in a misty mountainous region in China's Henen (Ho-Nan) province. The name translates as 'Young Trees Temple' meaning that the temple was surrounded by young trees. It is said to be the home of Chan (Zen) Buddhism. Bodhidharma is traditionally hailed as the founder of Chan Buddhism. Under his direction, monks and nuns at the temple supposedly developed exercises in 'kinetic meditation' between pairs, Chi Kung (health exercises), and standing and seated 'Zen' (meditation). Combining these elements and supporting them with a profound understanding of human anatomy, physiology, and an insightful perception of the human 'condition' based on Chan Buddhism, the monks and nuns allegedly created 'Eighteen Monk Boxing'.

George Mattson, informs readers in *The Way of Karate* p.23, that:

> ... Bodhidharma devised a series of movements [Sanchin] that when done near perfectly, would give the performer the experience of enlightenment [the Buddhist aim of illumination and a state of 'grace']. Once he [the practitioner] accomplished this and knew within himself what enlightenment was, he could apply or practice this feeling in his everyday life. Even though this exercise was designed mainly to give the experience of

enlightenment to the Zen [Chan] practitioner, it came to be the foundation of the Chinese *ch'uan-fa* (literally 'fist way'), [Quan-fa] which the Japanese call *kempo* ... The exercise came to be called by different names, *and because of its seemingly simple and meaningless movements, it eventually came to be disregarded by the majority of later karate proponents.* Fortunately, a few of the Chinese masters recognized and understood the importance of this exercise. As time passed however, Zen and Karate became less and less associated. These few masters passed the exercise on to their students, telling them that it should never be altered or left out of a training session. They told their students that this exercise [Sanchin] was the foundation of karate, though seldom [in typical Zen Buddhist fashion] did they explain why ... (Parenthesis and italics mine)

In respect of 'eighteen monk boxing', according to Jou Tsung Hwa in his *The Tao of Tai Chi Chuan* (Boston: Tuttle 1980 p.3 & 5):

> ... Ta-mo [Bodhidharma] who encouraged the monks to exercise in the mornings for health, created several systems of exercise: the Yin-Gin Ching or the 'change of tendons', Hsi-Swi Ching or 'the Marrow washing' and eighteen Buddha's hands ... later, Joy-Yuang, a master monk ... began to teach at the temple ... adding his own skills. Thus Shao-lin was developed into seventy-two hands ... The treasures of the Shao-lin Temple were called the five Chuans. Each Chaun was named for the animal best exemplifying its attributes. The Chuans originally only had six postures each ... The original Chuans are: 1. Dragon ... 2. Tiger ... 3. Leopard ... 4. Snake ... 5. Crane ... All the style's names and clans of Chinese martial arts are generated from Shao-lin Chuan, the prototypical Chinese martial art."

Whatever their origins, these unique methods filtered down through the population, allegedly after the burning of the Shao-lin Temple by 1674, and were, as noted, eventually taken to The Ryukyu Islands where they formed the backbone of To-te. I have no need to insist that this is accurate or even true, or that Bodhidharma personally created the Sanchin tradition (there are many versions of Sanchin extant in China today). The 528 CE date of Bodhidharma's residency at the Shao-lin Temple is rather early as a date for the inception of Quan-fa, although, it does not necessarily rule out the foundation of a version of Sanchin (or similar) quan as a holistic exercise dating from that time. I would of course rule out Bodhidharma having created the open hand (Uechi Ryu) Sanchin, for obvious reasons.

Even if Bodhidharma did not *exist* as an individual, and was simply a 'lineage' creation to represent a collective of Chan Buddhist teachers, one fact that emerges from Mr. Mattson's account rings absolutely true: the tradition of the steadfast and persistent practice of Sanchin quan. And even if one doubts or rejects the Shao-lin genesis of Quan-fa, *Sanchin* has been prized, treasured and traditionally taught painstakingly and methodically, with the admonition that it is *primary*, 'numero uno'/number one – important! Do it! Lots!

Whilst my own views regarding the Shao-lin genesis of Chinese Martial Arts have shifted somewhat over the past few years, the notion of Chan monks and nuns practicing pushing hands does seem to be feasible. I last made my views on the possible associations between Karate and the Shao-lin tradition clear in chapter six of my book *Barefoot Zen*. The book was written after several years of committed and regular attendance at a major Buddhist monastery where I was fortunate enough to be taken under the wing of the then abbot – 'Ajahn' Anando – and several senior monks (including Ajahn's Kittisaro and Vajiro), and at a time when I feared Karate was descending 'lock stock and barrel' into the (cage fighting) 'pit'.

Barefoot Zen was heavily oriented towards Karate-related spirituality and personal ennoblement. Several publishers informed me that its basic approach to the problem of trying to resolve Kung Fu and Karate with Buddhism (one of the most passive of religions), was highly original and more credible than the high kicking, wrathful and revengeful 'Kung Fu' monks of modern films and popular imagination. Chapter six and seven of Barefoot Zen explained *how*, within the tenets of Buddhism, monks and nuns could have engaged in what appeared to be Martial Arts. In chapter seven (p.79) I wrote:

> It must have been quite a sight to see the flow of techniques between two [Shao-lin] monks' pushing-hands. When one unbalanced the other or caught him 'out of the moment' (not concentrating), a lay observer could be forgiven for thinking the monks were fighting. They were not. In pushing hands, force is passed from one to another simply with a view to testing a state of mind (psychological balance), physical balance, and reflexes. During practice exponents avoid struggling with force, harmonizing instead with a particular force or series of forces by blending with them, neutralizing them, and returning them ... (Contextual parenthesis)

I wished to suggest, and illustrate, that, for Ming dynasty Shao-lin monks and nuns, the original notion of pushing hands (a kind of 'arms in contact' sparring – not body to body), may well have been a means of objectifying meditation between pairs, and was not intended as a direct means of combat per-se. Using this method, there would be no dichotomy between Buddhist ethics, codes of conduct and philosophy, and the actual physical practice of pushing hands. Non-violent pushing hands could be seen as a useful extension of meditation – an objectification of meditation between pairs, meaning the results of meditation could be *observed*, and the practitioners ability to let go (of force) and be 'empty' could be assessed!

Briefly explained, *you are not your thoughts, thoughts are the product of the mind that has them, not the mind itself.* This information is essential to even the most basic understanding of Buddhist meditation, which aims at gaining serenity through the control (letting go of) useless thoughts and 'mind chatter'. By substituting thoughts (attacking the mind of a seated meditating individual) with 'pushing hands forces' supplied to a standing training partner's arms, a kind of Kinetic meditation between pairs can be achieved, a kind of 'moving Zen', as the person being pushed in a variety of ways, flowed with the forces, and, re-routing them, without struggling, turned them back on the attacker, in the same way that a seated meditating individual returns intrusive thoughts to the void. Because, as I have suggested, this practice could (can) be ethically engaged in by Buddhist monks, I feel this remains a useful hypothesis. Besides, pushing hands has provided a great interactive training platform or 'sparring' method for both Quan-fa and Karate.

I do not here confuse pushing hands with kata application. The kata applications do not require a pushing hands format to work. However, the advantage of pushing hands lies in the opportunity it provides for two skilled (or training) practitioners to interact and produce techniques spontaneously and in a flowing freestyle way. Moreover, practice can be *linked* thereby making it more productive than a stop start practice. For example, if I want to practice a grip escape, I can have my partner stand a few feet away, step up and grip my hand. I can then perform a grip escape. Or I can engage in pushing with a partner and I can repeatedly practice a variety of grip escapes, according to the various ways my partner grabs me! Pushing hands is the sparring method however, not the technique, and pushing hands formats vary from style to style.

Sanchin: Some Esoteric Connections

There are also alleged esoteric associations claimed for Sanchin kata which seemingly indicate certain Buddhist connections and associations – if only culturally – indirectly in the application of numerology, but perhaps more directly in section three which utilises the technique often referred to as Mawashi uke (circular 'receive') or Wa uke (harmony 'receive'). This technique is commensurate with the gesture known in esoteric Buddhism as turning the 'Dharma' wheel, or turning the wheel of the teaching. For those familiar with Chan or Zen statues and icons, one cannot help but notice that section three of Sanchin reflects the actions of fierce guardian deities that guard various gates and are posed in fierce defensive positions to 'ward' those gates or doors.

Mao Yuan-yi, in his 1621 voluminous *Wu-pei chih* (Beijing: Chieh-fang chu-pan-she, 1989) claims that: "*Shao-lin excels at combining hard and soft, and never tries to overcome an opponent with brute force.*"

This would be totally consistent with the traditional 'hard-soft' nature of Sanchin, as a reflection of the Mahayana Chan (Buddhist) 'middle way': neither too hard nor too soft, neither too fast or too slow; doing just what is required, when its required, and never meeting force with force, or giving in.

According to Master Xia Bai Hua,

> ... Sanchin was the basic training form for a number of Fujianese styles [Fujian is the South-western Chinese province from which many original 'Karate kata' came]; primarily those with the 'animals' as the systems base [see Rokushu – an animal system variant/bolt-on to Sanchin]. In the Southern Chinese Shao-lin Temple Ancestors Boxing, Sanchin forms the basis for their breathing method, strength, stance and strategy, and consequently its study is both the preliminary and the advanced training. Sanchin seems to have originated over three hundred years ago and is considered to be a White Crane [Kung Fu] form ... (Parenthesis mine)

The Shao-lin approach to force is to adopt the 'middle way' and to deal with force by *engaging* without *contending*, merging with an attack, without resisting it, and neutralising it by turning the attacker's force *full circle*, back to him. I think this may well be the origin of pushing hands techniques, and the tactics of 'float, sink, swallow and spit-out' (eject). Indeed so many Chinese based quan use the 'Po-pai' or double palm push, that it becomes difficult to believe that they were all discovered or constructed independently, or that they were all associated with weapons.

There are many tell-tale clues connecting the Sanchin tradition with Chan (Zen). For example, as discussed, the circular hand movements found in section three of Sanchin quan and the positions used are almost identical with images depicting 'guardian deities'. In many versions of Sanchin these palms are used as double palm pushes.

Examples of guardian deity statues display the characteristics of fierceness and multiple arms (signs of divinity). In Sanchin quan, the hands turn in a wheel, emulating 'many hands', and terminate in Abhaya and Varada Mudra (see below).

In Japan, Aizen Myoo is said to span the border of physical and intellectual desire; the transition from indulgence to the wish for true knowledge. Traditionally he is fierce but compassionate.

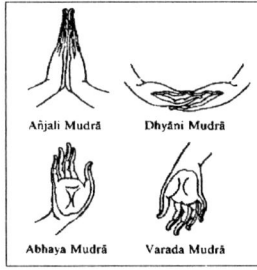
Añjali Mudrā   Dhyāni Mudrā
Abhaya Mudrā   Varada Mudrā

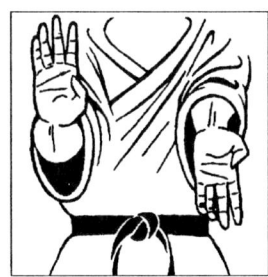

Aizen Myoo

There are many images of the Buddha using 'mudra'. Mudra are ritual arm and hand positions traditionally used in esoteric Buddhism and various Shao-lin quan. Shao-lin Temple Quan-fa may well have been originally utilized as a ritual *physical* enactment of the drama of life and the conflicts involved. In support of this argument saying I would like to quote Patrick McCarthy, who was in turn quoting John Donahue,

> The allure of the martial arts disciplines stems from the fact that they constitute *ritual performances* that *symbolically* deal with the fundamental questions of human existence: mortality; *the quest for control, mystery and power, and the search for identity.* Our sense of mortality is heightened by increased fears of street violence and dissatisfaction with society. The *symbolic* re-creation of danger through the practice of the fighting traditions can provide us with the *illusion* of control over such events ... (Italics mine).

The White Crane Quan-fa School

Sanchin is allegedly an archetypical Crane form, yet there is often confusion between so-called 'Monk Fist' Boxing and 'White Crane'. For instance, it is claimed that the Okinawan, Arakaki Seisho (1840–1818 or 1920), was an expert in *Monk Fist Boxing*, yet he taught 'open handed' Sanchin. I am comfortable with either expression, and I don't think it unwarranted to suggest that the two are similar, or even synonymous despite the weapons association. Names can be used to conceal as well as to reveal.

Perhaps the original White Crane Quan-fa was a product of the Henan Shao-lin Temple. Some Karate researchers dislike this idea because of a so-called 'lack of evidence' but this is to ignore oral tradition (admittedly sometimes unreliable) and the nature of some of the quan themselves. *Conversely, perhaps the old myth of warriors (weapons experts) simply hiding-out in monasteries to avoid detection and persecution, and practicing and teaching weapons sets without the weapons, is true. It would certainly explain much.*

Regardless, White Crane seems to be a development of the Sanchin theme designed to produce a type of animal-imitating 'boxing' that takes several forms, many of which were compiled in the late Qing dynasty (1644–1911) in and around Fuzhou city, Fujian province, China, and on the Island of Taiwan. Now, many cities throughout the world have practitioners of Crane Boxing of one type or another. Stretching the point a bit, it could be claimed that any style using Sanchin is, in some respects, practicing Crane Boxing. Actually, the term 'boxing' as used to denote 'Chinese boxing' or Quan-fa, is a misnomer drawn from an old Victorian term describing the apparent pugilistic Martial Arts of China.

Fujian White Crane – like Uechi Ryu and to some extent Goju Ryu – generally consider that the substance of their art(s) can be seen in the performance of Sanchin kata. Fujianese Crane boxers believe that if you want to view another's art, you should see their Sanchin.

The origin of White Crane Kung Fu is recorded in many sources, but the story seems to vary with the telling. The following tale describes the 'history' of the creation of the world famous 'Yongchun (better known as Wing Chun style – another branch of Crane),' from Yongchun village, Fujian province. In the case of Wing Chun, a Buddhist nun called Ng Mui (Oong Moy) is forced to flee from the Manchu authorities who burn the Shao-lin Temple to the ground in 1644. Ng Mui becomes one of the 'Five Ancestors', legendary progenitors of all Qing dynasty (1644–1911) Quan-fa (Kung Fu).

Whilst living as a recluse, Ng Mui continues to reflect on and to practice the Quan-fa she learned at the Temple. One day, she happens upon a large white crane defending itself from the attentions of a snake and consequently she is inspired to imitate the flexible evasions and defences applied by the crane. Allegedly reworking the existing Shao-lin Kung Fu, she creates the style that will one day bear the name of her famous student Yen Yongchun (Yim Wing Chun).

In another variation on the theme, Fang Qiniang, also from Yongchun village, is devastated by the death of her father at the hands of some ruffians. Fang Qiniang has learned *Monk Fist Boxing* from her father Fang Zonggong, but had not yet mastered the art. Despite this she decides to exact revenge on her father's killers. The revenge motif is a common one in Chinese 'Martial Art' literature (and the films they generated) epitomised by the Fong Sai Yuk 'cycle'. Fong was the archetypal legendary Han (race) avenging hero who gave the Manchu's (a non native dynasty) a run for their money.

Returning to Fang Qiniang – one day she hears a commotion in a bamboo thicket outside her home. Deciding to investigate she discovers two cranes fighting. Their combative tactics intrigue her. Taking up a bamboo pole, she decides to drive them away. But the birds' successfully avoid the pole and foil her efforts, finally flying away at a moment of their own choosing. Contemplating the incident, Fang feels moved to incorporate elements of that which she has witnessed into the Monk Fist Boxing she has learned from her father.

It is not common or popular to consider Sanchin kata and Wing Chun Kung Fu to be related. Sanchin is usually viewed as Karate because it is practiced alongside other 'Karate' kata and practitioners train in a Karate gi (uniform). They refer to what they practice as Karate and train barefoot. Wing Chun is referred to as Kung Fu and its practitioners wear a variety of different uniforms, or no uniform and they generally train in flat-soled Chinese slippers or sports shoes.

I studied Yongchun (Wing Chun Kung Fu) with internationally recognised Chinese masters, received a teaching certificate in 1984, spending a total of some sixteen years practicing before deciding in 1989 to focus on Karate again. Having practiced and researched the closed-fist Sanchin with a student of the late Miyazato Sensei (Jundokan) and two students of Yamaguchi Yoshime (Gogen Yamaguchi), and having studied the open hand Sanchin kata with Uechi Ryu students from the lineage of Uechi Kanei and Tomoyose Ryuyu, I believe that the open handed version was the version once practiced by Higaonna Kanryo. It certainly continued fairly unchanged through the Cho Tzu-ho/Shushiwa/ Uechi Kanbun lineage.

Further, I have no hesitation in suggesting that the 'wooden man' techniques of Wing Chun's final form bear uncanny resemblance to the open handed Sanchin Kata. The ramifications are unfortunately beyond the scope of this book.

Style V's System

In this book I have made an attempt to distinguish between a Karate *style* and a Karate *system*. Indeed, the kata in this book have been fused into a system. It is difficult to create or sustain a system if too many kata are included. One becomes unable to see the wood for the trees, so to speak, and techniques designed to be used reflexively, become unnecessarily duplicated. Using the three kihon kata (or similar) as a system, allows practitioners to avoid duplicating Karate techniques unnecessarily. Regarding actual application, obviously no one is encouraged to go out and practice real civil arrest, anymore than archery enthusiasts are encouraged to shoot people.

Arguably, most (modern) Karate styles are not necessarily 'systems'. By contrast, the conservative (Southern Chinese)

Yongchun style is a 'system'. The term 'system' precludes a haphazard or 'eclectic' compilation of quan or kata. Yongchun and its use of the Chinese single-edged broadsword (used in similar ways to the Sai, but with potentially more deadly results) has three simple but progressive quan and a set of techniques to be performed against a 'wooden man': traditionally a hardwood post made from 'muk toa' wood, a post with three forearm-length poles, two at approximately shoulder height and one at solar plexus height. Such hardwood (unlike for instance pine) could (even) accept the practice strikes of paired broadswords. The 'wooden man' also has a centrally placed 'leg' that protrudes from the bottom quarter of the post. In many respects, the 'wooden man' resembles a person standing in a (Uechi Ryu) Sanchin stance with their arms in the basic open hand Sanchin position.

Contrast Yongchun's three quan and a 'wooden man' drill, with the fifty plus quan of, for example, (modern) Tang Lang (Preying Mantis Kung Fu, which originally only had one quan), or Karate styles that teach anywhere from twelve to *fifty* kata!

Nagamine Shoshin states on page 15 of his *Tales of Okinawa's Great Masters*,

> ... I first became convinced that Shuri-te also evolved from the Chinese boxing native to Fukien [Fujian] province ... *consider the principles of Chinese boxing being haphazardly introduced to one limited area*, subjected to socio-cultural circumstances unlike that of another time and place, and cultivated by men of different insights ... (Parenthesis and italics mine)

This was – in fact – later to be the case, and the foundation for the new and 'eclectic' Karate traditions that haphazardly amassed many (and often unrelated) kata. Nailing my colours firmly to the mast here, I would say that accumulating fifty kata (other than for research purposes) is to miss the point! One should dig a small hole but go very deep. This represents nothing other than the cultivation of a *reliable, compact* and *efficient* set of *conditioned reflexes*! In short, the traditional path is taken by learning and applying *one* to *five* kata (mean average, three), devised in antiquity by the experts and handed down to the present.

In support of the above, I mention Funakoshi Gichin again. He reported that; training every day, a student would learn a new kata approximately every three years, and that *experts would not know more than five* (kata). Just prior to Funakoshi first introducing Karate to mainland Japan, this is probably the number of kata in his repertoire, a fairly typical number of kata for a To-te teacher in the Shuri tradition to practice and teach. The original Naha tradition utilised even less kata. Unfortunately the learning of many kata is now such an ingrained belief system, that it is expected. Few people are prepared to challenge the reasoning and development of this situation, and even fewer recognize that such a situation is only tenable so long as you don't try to *apply* a large number of kata; something that will only lead to muscle memory *confusion*, as I will explain later.

Of course, innumerable kata applications can be committed to memory by rote mechanical means and demonstrated by pre-arrangement. But this does not represent an accessible, 'living', 'vibrant' and spontaneous art – a qualitative art; it merely represents the pursuit of *quantity* as a measure, a matter of how many different ways one can do or *demonstrate* the same thing. This modern attitude and approach to Karate kata is justified by claims that a dozen or more kata are required in order to provide the would-be expert with a comprehensive range of techniques. This is not supported by tradition. The adoption of large numbers of kata is a modern phenomenon.

Miyagi Chojun taught most of his students only two, or occasionally three kata. Even Shinzato Jinnan, arguably Miyagi's favourite pre-war student, knew only three (Sanchin, Sesan and

Tensho). Allegedly Shinzato's Sesan (Seisan) kata was 'near perfect'. Reportedly, when informed it was time to learn the next kata, he said (to Miyagi Chojun): "Ah Sensei, I need just a little more practice on this one" (brackets mine).

Master Uechi Kanbun learned only three kata during his *thirteen* year stay in China, and for many years (until his death in 1948) these were the only three kata taught in Uechi Ryu Karate.

Large numbers of Karate kata have been used to expand and customise Karate 'styles' and to provide more material for ever extending grading or ranking systems. The use of many kata also helps to prevent boredom, especially amongst young students. It has been argued that Karate kata have become as 'empty shells', mere dances with no sensible applications, practiced by teachers and students alike. I repeat: currently, quantity is often stressed over and above quality or depth.

Undoubtedly, many modern Karate-ka are superb 'performers', and modern Japanese Karate has become increasingly 'gymnastic/athletic' in its approach, yet *original* kata consisted of techniques that were all *within the natural range of movement* and relatively accessible (physically) to most individuals. Also, in Quan-fa schools, students spent much time working on (contact reflex) *applications* (see chapter five).

On Okinawa during 1936, Motobu Choki complained to Nagamine Shoshin about the state of kata practiced in Tokyo. Motobu was most likely referring to the kata taught by Funakoshi Gichin. It's common knowledge that there was no love lost between the two men. Motobu claimed that the kata had been carelessly changed in Tokyo. Formerly, on Okinawa, students spent years meticulously learning a single kata or two, whereas Karate tuition in Tokyo encouraged the meaningless but fashionable practice of many kata, devoid of suitable applications.

Motobu further complained that the practice of kata had become reduced to fixed, stiff postures, and that kata had essentially become a dead practice. Indeed, the traditional custom of thoroughly learning and polishing two or three quan until the techniques could be *applied* reflexively (without thinking), although maintained for several hundred years, had already declined by that time.

As I have repeatedly said, modern kata applications often tend to be arbitrary and students and teachers alike regularly interpret them in ways of their own choosing. Frequently these 'applications' deviate so considerably from the kata they are ascribed to that they *invalidate* that kata. Most 'interpretations' of this type centre upon crude blocking and striking techniques, or more recently, undignified headlocks or 'back alley' techniques, that do not take into consideration, let alone include, the Sai or elegant and skilful joint-locking techniques, grip escaping, passing force, yielding techniques, trapping hands and other skilful or subtle measures, as actually outlined in the Chinese quan, inherited by Okinawan To-te, but largely ignored (or not learned) by later practitioners of 'linear' (straight line), simplified modern Karate.

'Conditioned' Reflexes in the 'Empty Hand' Art

One function of empty hand kata is to open and maintain 'neural pathways', in plain language to create specific but limited (or rather *appropriate*) 'muscle memory' – body habits or 'building blocks' that can then be converted to 'conditioned reflexive responses' through training with a partner. Although this approach differs somewhat from, for example, tennis – a sport that places little emphasis on training without a ball or an opponent – a comparison is still useful. More generally, in sport, each discipline has a particular range of techniques that must be cultivated in order to play that sport. In tennis, it can easily be seen that technically it requires a set of basic techniques (overhead service, forehand, backhand, volley and half volley, etc.) supported by a host of improvised variations built on these (relatively few) fundamental techniques, techniques that pertain to the *spontaneous* requirements of the game – getting the ball over the net and keeping the shot in the court, and making that shot a winning one whenever possible!

Many modern traditionally-oriented Martial Artists (by comparison) often pursue too many skills (kata). Current and prevailing attitudes tend to assume that the more solo kata that are studied, the more 'prepared' a practitioner will be in the event of actual combat. This misguided approach is the result of the attitudes taken towards kata (proliferation) since the early 1900s. Prior to that, a system (as opposed to a style), could entirely focus on one kata (the systems manual). Many modern practitioners believe they must spend years collecting and exploring a multitude of techniques (kata), all practiced in quasi shadow-boxing fashion, yet with none truly applicable without pre-arrangement. It is also quite astonishing how theoretical and speculative many kata bunkai are. And this, despite the constant reference made by traditionalists to the vital importance of basics (kihon) in *applied* Karate.

If *basic* techniques break down, overall performance suffers! Continuing with the tennis analogy, if a tennis player gets injured or becomes over-trained, muscle 'memory' can be lost, and the player's game may go a bit 'off'. He may begin and then continue to play a particular shot badly. The more the shot is practiced or played badly, the more a new (contra) habit is formed as a new and useless muscle memory overtakes, for example, the old favourite and winning backhand pass (learning a new and fancy set of shots won't help here). It is the coach's job to recognise this and to help the player to correct it and 'streamline'

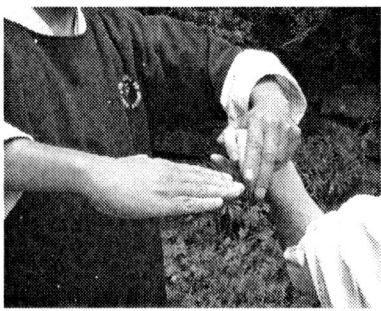

Selected Sanchin applications

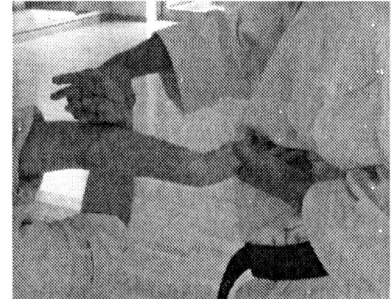
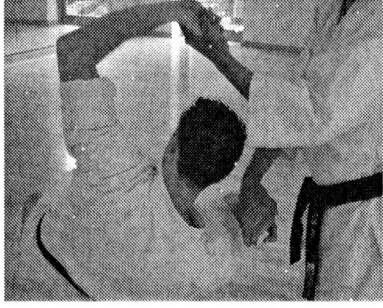

Selected Naihanchin applications

practice, i.e. to get the player to abandon any superfluous habits (old or newly-developing) that create or contribute to the problem of missed or ineffective (basic) shots. This is just one proper reason for the importance of maintaining accuracy of form within kata, based of course on the proper knowledge of its function.

Traditional practice of authentic empty hand kata creates and *maintains*, as I have said, 'neural pathways' – specific body habits – muscle memory. One difficulty, however, lies in determining how much (how many kata) is enough. A simple set of three or so interconnected and progressive kata traditionally provided enough material to methodically lead to maximum practical efficiency. This is another reason why little in the way of (written) theory was provided. In the workaday world of the past, when the various traditions were current and alive, theory and books were not needed!

In the current era, even if one has the time (as in making Karate a lifelong hobby, or being a modern professional instructor) to thoroughly learn to *apply* say twelve (plus) kata, any attempt to apply them *reflexively*, i.e. without pre-arranging, would arguably begin to program conflicting reflexes into the body, thereby confusing muscle memory, particularly if such responses are always drilled in a pre-arranged way, a way that is habitually performed with the luxury of a prior knowledge of what is about to happen! For example (from a sports science perspective), *training too many (rehearsed) varieties of a particular technique does not lead to spontaneity, but to muscle memory confusion* when the certainty of pre-arrangement is removed. One would have to 'think through' the version, as one does in a pre-arranged application. Even if one assumes that *one* version would at least emerge spontaneously, what criteria would determine which one? The usual reason given is – experience. The "I will just 'know'." But that is a naïve, risky and mistaken belief. Proof of this can be observed or experienced in modern 'free-style' sparring, in which, as I have said, one never sees, for example the application of traditional kata bunkai 'set pieces', or 'properly' executed 'traditional' blocks. Instead, one commonly sees just a couple of improvised open-handed 'pat/slap' blocks which, when accompanied by natural distancing easily suffice; that and plenty of dodging, bouncing, shuffling, feints and improvised tactics.

The above is one reason why a large (international) faction of modern Taekwondo (a Korean development of modern Japanese Karate) has utterly abandoned so-called traditional forms (patterns/kata) on the basis that such forms do not reflect the way that sparring, free-fighting or tournament fighting is conducted, particularly as a modern Olympic sport.

Indeed, the repertoire of techniques seen in tournament fighting, whilst varying from person to person, and event to event, is by no means large. The same can be said for Judo, fencing, and other interactive Martial Arts/sports, along with 'cage fighting' and 'Ultimate Fight Challenge' combat.

Without *contact* (plus – as I have said – an understanding and the application of the gate system and 'zoning' inherent in Sanchin kata – the 'tennis court' of Karate), one is reduced to using guesswork and visual reflexes as one often would if using weapons. But, as previously mentioned, weapons have a limitation factor built in. Remove the limitation that a particular weapon places on the user, yet try to employ weapons-based tactics and manoeuvres, and you will surely be subject to error, including deception by feints, and the strong and fast will always have an overwhelming advantage. That is another reason why modern free-style sparring does not resemble so-called 'classical kata' with its full steps and stop-start sharply defined techniques.

Thrust and focus is the hallmark of a weapon strike, not the modern (very effective) flow of Western or Thai style boxing - the modern influences on free-style Karate tactics, not recorded in classical kata, and not part of the original methods. Non-weapon arts based on *visual reflexes* and eye to hand co-ordination, depend upon athleticism, age and strength. Skill diminishes with age as it does for boxers and other athletes. There are no 'old masters' in athletics or sports. Traditionally there have been and are 'old masters' in Karate, Kobudo, and related arts.

For weapon-less arts, reflexes are the key – *contact (touch) reflexes*, not visual reflexes – and in respect of such reflexes, more is not always better, as I will show in chapter five. Sufficient to say for now, many teachers claim that spontaneous (sub-conscious) reflex actions are what count in the practical application of Karate techniques, but they commonly neglect to explain – let alone develop and use – the essential training methods required to make such reflexes work efficiently. They generally fail to distinguish between *contact reflexes* (touch reflexes) and visual reflexes, and do not have training programs or mechanisms in place to develop the essential skills of 'response by touch/contact'! (More on this later)

Even if you are uncertain about what contact reflexes are at this point in the book, *please mark the concept well!*

Training types of reflexes that 'flow-with' and 'stick-to' an attackers limbs, whilst clinging, yielding, making use of his force, trapping down his limbs and subjugating him with a joint locking technique, run contrary to *resisting* him, blocking-him-out, *smashing* him or trying to overwhelm him (at distance) with your own power. These are two *contradictory* approaches. One requires subtlety, 'listening hands' (sticking/pushing hands skill), in short the ability to intercept, read and re-direct force by *touch*. The other requires bluntness, resistance (a rejection of the

Contact reflex

principles above) and the use of *visual reflexes*. The fallacy is to believe that both approaches can be easily combined, or more importantly that both approaches can be attributed to the ancient kata. The former can, the latter can not. Kick boxers and full contact fighters do not practice kata because they do not need to, such offers no advantage.

Quan-fa Blended With 'Te'

Many Okinawan, Japanese, and Western authors conventionally claim that Chinese Quan-fa – the essence and backbone for To-te Jutsu – was allegedly blended with long extant indigenous Okinawan martial techniques (referred to as 'Te') to form Karate, an art they claim was (is) more 'culturally acceptable' to indigenous Okinawans.

It is often maintained that the synthesis that Karate constitutes, improved the allegedly moribund Chinese art of Quan-fa, and strengthened or improved it. The present author questions such claims and points-out that never, in the various assertions made or accounts given, is there any *evidence* provided in respect of dates, personalities or the nature of, or categorisation of the so-called 'indigenous' techniques. Moreover there are no recorded histories, examples or chronologies of (pre Quan-fa) ancient Okinawan 'empty hand' experts, their methods, masters or students. Yet the Okinawans utilise oral tradition and are generally avid recorders of lineage. What I really suspect happened was that Karate pioneers altered *Chinese* forms in conformity with greater ties to, and conformity with, increased Japanese cultural influence after the Meiji restoration of 1868.

In short, and without prejudice, there is little substantial or corroborative evidence to confirm claims that an indigenous, yet ill-defined, Okinawan precursor to To-te, was an equal partner to, or even had a substantial impact upon, imported Chinese Quan-fa much before the nineteenth century. Indeed, I suspect that Chinese Quan-fa set the standard. It was highly prized and clearly sought-out by a number of highly motivated Okinawan Quan-fa enthusiasts during that period.

Admittedly there exists the Okinawan tradition of using 'Tijikun' or 'Seiken', the closed-fist. Tijikun is the Okinawan term for the clenched fist and Seiken or fist/knuckle-sword is a Japanese term. There is also a tradition of training the fist by punching a Makiwara (a padded wooden punching post), but there seems to be little else that is tangible and concrete that constitutes a systematic method of Okinawan empty hand art that preceded Quan-fa.

In summary, there is a paucity of (historical) information concerning indigenous Okinawan *empty hand* arts (excluding *Shima* – Okinawan Sumo) until the importation of Chinese Quan-fa, and the record indicates that was as late as the eighteenth/nineteenth century (although admittedly, Nagamine believed that Wanshu/Enpi kata was practiced in Tomari city Okinawa, as early as 1683).

Ming and Qing (pronounced Ching) dynasty Quan-fa provided the roots and trunk, if not the branches, for/of Okinawan To-te Jutsu and later Karate. It can be said, however, that Karate is genuinely an Okinawan product synthesised largely from Ming and Qing dynasty Quan-fa and ancient Wu-shu (Chinese – to quell a spear), coupled – to a certain extent – with Okinawan *values* and (dominant) Japanese Budo (warrior way) ideals. But please understand (and I stress the point again), that the current dissatisfaction amongst disgruntled and questioning experienced Karate-ka, the world over in respect of applied traditional kata, stems from the fact that combat attitudes (postures, distances and techniques) designed for use with weapons make little sense when used without the required weapons. In short, because of this, the unarmed freestyle (spontaneous) application of (some) traditional kata is highly questionable at best, and virtually impossible at worst.

The original art/science of the empty hand or unarmed art was founded upon common human (and universal) realities, balance, human anatomy and its physiology, leverage, and 'body geometry', etc. Closing the distance, entangling the opponent's arms, controlling his posture and balance and subduing him by means of locking his joints are the primary requirements for effective utilisation of the original empty hand techniques. As I have said, grappling/wrestling is ubiquitous, all cultures have it, and, as previously noted, the success of 'grapplers' has been borne out in the pioneering 'Ultimate Fight Challenge' and other 'total combat' scenarios.

In modern times the grappling nature of, for example, the bedrock Naihanchin kata has been replaced by the promotion of obscure and often (seemingly) bizarre methods and techniques drawn from, for example, Seisan and other Sai or weapon kata, the techniques of which are represented as exotic blocks and equally exotic and mystifying strikes allegedly for use whilst 'unarmed'. It's almost as if modern practitioners believe that the value of the techniques lies in the fact that they appear to be weird and mysterious. The (unadulterated) kata of both the empty hand way and those kata representing the armed (Sai) traditions of civil arrest in Southern China during the Ming dynasty, are in fact highly functional; but the original Seisan kata, for example, is as I have said, of little *practical* use unless the trained user is armed with a pair of Sai and is faced by the user of a sword, pole/staff, spear, or similar weapon.

Without this understanding, many traditional kata become nothing more than exotic techniques from a bygone and seemingly naive era (and for modern Westerners a foreign or alien culture) with no practical application for today – for now! Moreover This is not the case for the empty hand kata outlined in this book.

Ko-do

I have coined the term *Ko-do Ryu*. It refers to the old kata, applications and methods of practice outlined in this book. The term Ko-do was perhaps first used by the late Dr. Jigaro Kano, the founder of Judo (1860–1938), to denote the continuing of 'The Old Way'. Ryu means style, tradition or group, analogous to a family. Kano's Judo was Kodokan Judo, Kodo-kan (old way – hall). Ko-do Ryu therefore (roughly) means The 'Old Way' Style.

The term 'Koryu' could have been used for the practices outlined in this book, but I did not wish to intrude upon those who currently refer to their art as Koryu or 'Old Family' or school, neither did I wish to confuse the respective approaches to ancient Karate. I have also employed the suffix 'Ko' in Roman letters (quite literally Ko), and not Japanese Kanji. '*Ko*' in remembrance of Ko-jo Taitei, the unsung patron of Naha To-te Jutsu to whom I feel many Karate-ka owe a great debt. He will be discussed in chapter three.

Although transplanted to Okinawa mainly between 1800 and 1900, Ko-do To-te (ancient Karate), was born out of Chinese cultural and social standards and based on a civil arrest tradition enriched by Taoist, Buddhist and Confucian moral and spiritual values. Indeed, Ko-do has its theoretical and practical roots in the sophisticated Ming dynasty Chinese culture and ethics. In many respects, the original Ko-do is so ancient that it may have virtually died out in China.

On the Island of Okinawa, originally, Ko-do was not referred to as Quan-fa or Karate (empty hands), but as To-te – Tang or China hand, thus denoting its Chinese origin. Although having been valued and promoted as a method of self defence and physical exercise (particularly for young men living in politically and socially turbulent times), Ko-do To-te also contained (according to one's opinion) either the essence or the remnants of far more direct and practical skills, or profound and holistic practices that perhaps made physically experiential the profound and deep insights of the Shao-lin Temple tradition.

'Upright', both in terms of its physical postures and also in terms of its 'high-brow' ethical values, regrettably, the art has been portrayed as a rather plebeian one. Talk of the old masters as being illiterate can only really refer to the period after the decline and fall of the Ming dynasty and the Shao-lin Temple (1644/5 onward). For instance, when the art reached Okinawa, it was taken up principally by illiterate fishermen and farmers, although it was not necessarily they who developed or modified it.

The source material for Ko-do To-te was efficient, sophisticated, ethical, well-ordered and logical; regrettably, the art then, as now, was sometimes cultivated for the wrong reasons. Nagamine Shoshin had this to say on the matter:

> … in the case of the pre-Meji Okinawans (before 1868), little emphasis was placed on [such] spiritual practices because of harsh political restrictions. To recognize this historical phenomenon is to understand how and why such overemphasis was placed on physical conditioning … (Parenthesis mine)

These are the circumstances under which the image of 'kill or be killed' Karate was most likely generated, an image that some modern enthusiasts seek incorrectly to perpetuate. Karate is not warfare! Similarly its grandparent, Chinese Quan-fa, was not seriously considered as such either.

Here is another quote from Douglas Wile's *Tai Chi Ancestors*, p.5. It pertains to the (late Ming, early Qing) Chinese authorities attitude towards 'Martial Arts':

> Having long been judged irrelevant to mass warfare, that is, useless to the state, martial arts were forced to cling to the margins of society in the form of bodyguard brotherhoods, secret societies, operatic performances, fairground exhibitions, banditry and knight-errantry ... indistinguishable from banditry in the eyes of the state.

As touched upon in the introduction, a misconception that proliferates the spurious connection between To-te (Karate) and battlefield combat is the improper association of Karate with the often romanticized image of the Japanese samurai warrior and the medieval Japanese code of Bushido (Japanese, 'warrior way'). Neither To-te, or Karate, has anything to do with the samurai warriors of ancient Japan, except where modern Japanese teachers have traced their *personal* lineage back to an ancestor who held that social or military rank. As far as Karate is concerned, claimed connections with the Samurai are misguided. It is a cultural imposition to demand that forms originating in China and steeped in Chinese culture, fit the *exclusive* Japanese Samurai code of Bushido. One striking example is the Chinese quan Naihanchin (Chinese, 'internal divided conflict'), which was re-named Tekki. It was claimed that this name better represented the nature of the 'iron clad' Samurai warrior, said to be a feature of the form. This is patently incorrect, as the culture that devised the Naihanchin quan, had no Samurai warriors, nor did the Samurai of Japan practice Naihanchin.

The late Don F. Draeger, a noted Martial Arts practitioner, historian, and author explains in volume two of his *Classical Budo: The Martial Arts and Ways of Japan* (NY: Weatherhill, 1973), p.107, that:

The classical warrior had little use for any system of combat that did not use weapons. This was primarily because the opportunity for unarmed combat was rare, being favoured by neither custom nor circumstances. And the necessities of the time in which he functioned required him to be well armed and trained in the use of deadly weapons. A warrior therefore was never without weapons, even when asleep, and was certainly never without his beloved sword ... For the warrior even to entertain the idea of success in combat, in the sense of killing an opponent; he could attack his foe only when armed. The fact that armour was worn influenced the manner in which a warrior would deal with his foe. Mere sparring tactics of a 'boxing' nature, which must rely for effect upon the natural parts of the body – hand, fist, foot-in delivering *atemi* (blows directed at anatomically weak points) by striking, punching, or kicking, were hopelessly ineffective and would be likely to result in more injury to the attacker than to the intended victim ...

Historically even Samurai grappling 'Yoroi-kumi-uchi' did not imply unarmed combat, and was geared principally towards delivering blows with a short armour-piercing weapon. No classical system of Bu-jutsu required a warrior to be unarmed! Also, as already noted, To-te was never developed to enable an unarmed Okinawan peasant to defend against an armed mainland Satsuma clan Samurai, as has been suggested in the past. The Samurai were efficient, well-trained and well-armed with one of the most efficient and deadly swords ever designed and created! Facing such a sword in the hands of a capable swordsman whilst unarmed would prove fatal (except in Hollywood).

There was undoubtedly a sense of indignation and loss of national pride experienced by the Okinawans when their islands were invaded and occupied by the Satsuma clan, and a weapons ban for all Okinawans was declared. But the Okinawans had already been forbidden to bear arms in an edict issued during the reign of the Okinawan King Sho Shin-O (1477–1526). There was a precedent. Earlier, in China, the hated Mongol invaders successfully established a dynasty there, between 1271 and 1368. They forbade the Chinese Han (race) from owning weapons or even participating in hunting. The Han Chinese people were subject to a curfew, and also restricted in the practice of Martial Arts, religion, and freedom of assembly.

Of the three types of Martial Arts formerly practice by the Han – military, private and theatrical – theatrical Martial Arts (opera style) reached new and unprecedented heights. The Han re-established themselves during the Ming dynasty. But the Manchu's – another non indigenous ethnic group – would impose similar restrictions after the fall of the Ming dynasty in 1644.

I suspect that the original (versions of) kata, illustrated in this book, stem from the middle of the Ming dynasty, the period during which the indigenous Han Chinese had re-established themselves, put the excesses of emperor Hongwu behind them and enjoyed a flowering of art, culture, literature, religion, and Quan-fa. The type of 'Martial Arts' that these kata derive from are not military or theatrical, but civil and private.

Fortunately, early quan were transplanted to Okinawa, but not before Okinawa experienced its own problems. Alas, what happened in Ming dynasty China happened on Okinawa in 1609. It is well known that the small but well-armed and combat-experienced Satsuma Samurai treated the native Okinawans with contempt and brutality, and this may have, in part, fuelled an interest in the empty hand art amongst young Okinawans. However, as already stated, To-te 'proper' does appear on Okinawa much before the end of the eighteenth century and the beginning of the nineteenth century. It was nearly two hundred years after the Satsuma invasion/subjugation of Okinawa that named Okinawans like Teruya Chikudon 'Pechin' Kanga (as Pechin denotes a rank), better known as To-te

Sakugawa, 1782–1862 (some sources claim 1733–1815), are recorded as To-te practitioners.

It is recorded that Uku Giko (1800–1850) taught Naihanchin kata to Matsumora *Kosaku* when the later was young. Matsumora practiced in the master's courtyard learning only Naihanchin for three years, and this may have been as early as 1843. During the first three years of training, Matsumora may well have learned only the first section of Naihanchin known as 'sho'. Originally Naihanchin was one long kata that moved steadily sideways for about thirty feet, and then repeated the techniques in mirror image, thus returning the practitioner to the start. The kata was broken into three parts probably because of the space consideration – especially when To-te (Karate) was practiced secretly in the courtyards of the master's houses. The three parts were considered to be three separate kata, and evidence suggests that each part was studied for three years.

Another Karate luminary from the early period of To-te is Matsumura *Sokon* (1809–1901), author of the Makimono scroll I mentioned earlier. Matsumura learned 'To-te' on Okinawa and 'Quan-fa' (fist art/Kung Fu) in Fuzhou, where he was sent twice as an envoy of the Ryukyu kingdom. Here is an excerpt from his written instructions to a student (c. 1882):

> … an indomitable calmness makes subjugating an adversary effortless. Yet, the proper methods forbid wilful violence …

Ever moral, dignified and based on an intrinsic respect for humanity, Ko-do was characterised by its use of intelligent and highly skilful methods of negating basic physical assaults without the recourse to brutality. Perhaps epitomised by its practical techniques of escaping from being held, gripped, or controlled by an assailant, Ko-do specialised in methods of *restraining* an attacker by seizing (grabbing) an attackers arms, countering any force and locking an attacker's arms to control them – without causing damage!

A definition of Ko-do To-te

Ko-do To-te has two 'limbs' each with three branches. They are as follows:

Limb One

1. Ko-do was not intended for use on a battlefield.

2. Ko-do was not designed to be openly used against a professional warrior or a trained opponent. However, practice with skilled training partners is inevitable and necessary for the development of proficiency.

3. Ko-do was not intended be used in an arena or in a sporting contest.

Limb Two

1. Ko-do creates and maintains (holistic) fitness and acts as a form of recreation.

2. Ko-do facilitates introspection (meditation) and spiritual cultivation (standing or moving Zen).

3. Ko-do facilitates effective confidence, character and 'citizen' building, through training based on rigorous 'ritual combative' experiences, aimed at cultivating and improving the individual, and those with whom s/he associates.

Lao Tzu the famous Chinese sage referred to such as 'the superior man' (man being non gender specific here).

Therefore, to summarize, the value of Ko-do To-te can be classified under the following three headings:

1. As a method of exercise and recreation.
2. As a method of self-discipline and spiritual training.
3. As a method of personal ennoblement and a way to develop and maintain physical prowess.

Hand conditioning and the 'Delayed Death Touch'

Ming and Qing dynasty civil arrest techniques were not created expressly to harm people, or as crafty ways to brutalise our fellow human beings. But, they have often been presented as such. With unsound guidance, people in general and young men in particular, can be attracted to unwholesome ideas and drawn into bizarre practices like pounding and crushing the ends of their fingers, in an attempt to 'harden' them, as advised in the best selling underground Kung Fu 'chap books' of the Chinese 'Ching' and Republican periods.

These cheaply produced and extremely popular books offered pseudo advice on how to obtain 'super powers' and can be viewed as China's equivalent to D.C. comics (lots of pic's). They were (obviously) initially aimed at educated people who could read (but most probably couldn't fight). This group perpetuated and expanded many of the myths and fantasies that are still prevalent in so much Kung Fu to this day. As the Chinese people(s) became increasingly literate however, there were those who actually tried to apply the techniques luridly described in the books. They were generally low status and somewhat gullible seekers after immediate martial prowess, or often street entertainers, such as street peddlers or medicine hawkers. They often used mock combat and 'tricks' to draw crowds they could sell 'medicines' to. Needless to say, instructions in the chap books varied from book to book, with much material expounding little more than circus tricks; for example, iron bar-bending or demonstrations of martial chicanery centring on demonstrating imperviousness to pain and the like. Yet other published methods, often described as 'iron shirt' techniques, encouraged readers to toughen their bodies in various (often grotesque) ways, and even to harden their heads, by banging them, with increasing intensity, against a wall. Thrusting fingertips into a bucket filled initially with dried peas or beans, but later with gravel or similar, also became a firm favourite.

Consequently a cursory familiarity with the open hand Sanchin, for instance, juxtaposed with extremely popular (but misguided) notions of being able to fell an opponent using 'finger jabs', some of which – with training – readers were told, do not even have to make contact, and presto! – a Sai quan, minus the Sai, evolves into methods, claimed by its new promoters to be useful in rendering an opponent unconscious, or even killing him, perhaps even delaying the time of his demise by using the 'delayed death touch'. I am not insinuating here that these claims are made by the Uechi Ryu Karate style which advocates the open hand Sanchin. I merely allude here to the general Qing and Republican appetite for Martial Arts 'magic', 'mystery' and 'super powers'.

The delayed death touch is allegedly a technique that, if delivered during an altercation, will kill the opponent at a remote but pre-determined time of ones own choosing, and not during his fight with you. In Cantonese Chinese, this (legendary) technique is referred to as 'dim mak'. I was once present when the late and great Kung Fu master, Wong Shun Leung told an assembled roomful of Kung Fu students that, fighting in many challenge matches as a young man, he had been delayed death touched so

177

many times that it was a wonder he was still alive. Of course I can not rule out the possibilities of people suffering later from injuries sustained during a fight; for example, from internal haemorrhaging or damage done to a kidney. If a Western boxer tragically dies after a boxing match, no one says, "Oh, he was delayed death punched." Sadly he dies because his brain swells up from being traumatized. I understand that the unpleasant example given here will not appeal to 'delayed death touch' enthusiasts. It's too crude, it's too real and it's too tragic!

My personal feeling about the validity of the delayed death touch, and suchlike, is that it is a slipshod muddle of Quan-fa and traditional Chinese medicine. Popular attempts to integrate these two subjects are conjectural to say the least, largely unproven and represent a kind of underground 'black magic' literature designed to usurp legitimate healing knowledge and re-package it to interested parties as an effective means of causing harm – only to deserving recipients, of course! Moreover it remains a subject that can not be legally or ethically proven. Often full of flaws and errors, the 'delayed death touch' and its association with herbal medicine is also largely spurious and unproven, worse, some of the ingredient quantities suggested in various Qing Martial Art 'remedies' for injuries are positively dangerous, and I have arrived at this conclusion after reviewing some of them with one of the leading Chinese trained herbalists in the UK. Such troublesome associations can only be a nuisance to authentic healers, be they Kung Fu practitioners or otherwise.

More to the point, from the information published in this book, it should be quite clear that none of the kata discussed here (being grappling, grip escaping or Sai kata) could have been designed to deliver 'dim mak' strikes in any case. Besides, quite frankly, you can kill someone with a 'biro' if you've a mind to do it!

Clearly the prerequisite for the use of any weapon is the skill to deliver the blow. A mind/body capable of understanding and developing such skill would be equally able to improvise a weapon should the need arise, which would no longer necessitate the pounding and disfiguring of one's hands. But, the truth is, this would spoil the mystique, not to mention the fun of demonstrating one's imperviousness to pain, or the damage one could do with one's 'bare hands'. Over the years, I have seen some unpleasant consequences for people who have hardened their hands. In respect of callusing ones knuckles, a practice still found in Karate, one of my Karate associate's teachers in Japan, could break a wall-brick with the edge of his hand; yet that hand was so badly damaged by years of reckless abuse, that he could not easily pick up fine objects with it, and he even struggled to pick up a Japanese tea cup!

Callusing one's knuckles (the particular Tijikun or Seiken), whilst definitely an Okinawan tradition, is not, for the most part, a Chinese tradition, yet we are dealing here with Chinese source material (kata). I am not against moderate training with the traditional Okinawan makiwara (a padded striking post) which helps ensure punches are properly focused, for people who practice punching, *but punches directed at a punch bag should definitely be avoided unless one's hands are properly taped. Failure to do so will produce an unpleasant condition known as 'knuckle spread', which is self explanatory.*

In my view, ugly calluses and the means of achieving them are more of a hazard than an asset, and they serve little purpose in the modern world, other than as an advertisement. Curiously, given the era in which he lived, Miyagi Chojun appears to have had callus-free knuckles. If he did, have calluses, they can't be seen in the various photographs in which his hands are clearly visible.

One cannot practice as a craftsman without the appropriate tools. Is this any less true for a 'warrior'? Serious warriors have always gone about their business with *proper* weapons.

Chapter Three
The Development of Naha-te

THIS CHAPTER IS GIVEN to establish the centrality of Sanchin, Seisan and Sanseirui to the entire Naha Karate tradition (and therefore to what would later become Goju Ryu) and also to survey the general creation of Okinawan Karate. It is a broad-spanning chapter with a considerable emphasis on historical 'content and context', included to support many of my findings.

I do not assume that readers will be particularly familiar with the individuals discussed in this chapter. In the material that follows, there are a number of confusing (and for Westerners, tongue-twisting) names and lots of dates, but the devil is in the detail – as they say – and to make a proper case, I've had to critically analyse the dates, the key players, their connections, and their influence on each other, in the development of Naha To-te (and Karate in general). My purpose and intention is to remove what I believe to be a smoke-screen obscuring the true lineage of popular Naha-te, a smoke screen that distorts historical and technical truths connected with that tradition.

Political 'jockeying', designed to support various Karate 'lineages', is at best covertly partisan, and at worst, openly negative and hostile to all but the 'party faithful', but it can also be very revealing and I have included some examples of it in this chapter. I think that researchers who belong to mainstream groups are often apt to 'toe the party line'. No one is perfect. However, as an independent researcher, I have been as dispassionate and non-partisan as possible. Yet I am fully aware that no one is truly independent, and ask readers to judge the facts presented herein, themselves.

Karate Pioneers – Masters Higaonna Kanryo and Uechi Kanbun

There are two *popular* sources for To-te and Karate once designated as Naha-te. They are the Okinawans Higaonna (sometimes recorded as Higashionna) Kanryo (1853–1915), and Uechi Kanbun (1877–1948). Both learned Quan-fa in Qing dynasty Fuzhou, China, during the late nineteenth century, where there appears to have been a tradition of teaching only *one* quan (kata) every three years. This can be supported by the fact that Uechi Kanbun apparently spent three years learning Sanchin kata, three years learning Seisan kata, and three years learning Sanseirui kata. *Higaonna Kanyro* (as I will later propose) learned under similar conformist and somewhat rigorous conditions when he studied Quan-fa on Okinawa and in China – *before Uechi Kanbun was born*. This indicates that a traditional, conservative teaching custom was (still) in place when Uechi Kanbun studied Quan-fa, as late as 1907. There is no substantial evidence to suggest that Chinese Sifu (teacher/s) in Fuzhou taught large numbers of quan when Higaonna Kanyro was studying Quan-fa.

To cite another example of the 'status quo' during that general period, the noted Arakaki Seisho (1840–1918 or 1920) and Nakaima Norisato (1850–1927), from Kumi, Naha (the founder of Ryuei Ryu Karate), travelled to Fuzhou – Nakaima in 1869 and Arakaki before him. Both (originally) learned *Sanchin, Sesan and Sanseirui* – the Sanchin kata being comparable to the Uechi Ryu Sanchin, later reflected in the modified Goju Ryu Sanchin.

In this section, I will contend that the foundation Goju Ryu Karate kata (Sanchin, Seisan/Sesan and Sanseirui/Sanseru) and the three Uechi Ryu Karate kata with the same names have a common origin, and the styles 'championed' by Higaonna Kanryo and Uechi Kanbun derived largely from a *single common source*. I will also contend that the quan (kata) *originally* learned and later taught by *both* teachers were essentially restricted to the following three:

1. *Sanchin* (open handed and with sideways/backwards steps in section three)
2. *Seisan* (Sesan)
3. *Sanseirui* (Sanseru)

I will further contend that both Higaonna Kanyro and Uechi Kanbun (founder of Uechi Ryu Karate) *rigorously* followed an *established* tradition in teaching only *one* kata approximately every three years to students learning To-te (the three kata listed above). This raises several (important) issues. Given that modern Uechi Ryu now has eight kata (five extra kata being 'created' after Uechi Kanbun's death in 1948), where did Goju Ryu's extra kata come from? Claiming lineal decent from Higaonna Kanyro's Naha-te, modern Goju Ryu Karate now includes *twelve* kata.

If a living senior teacher, within a given tradition, makes a series of questionable (historical) claims, he is less likely to be challenged by his students or the group members, both out of respect for and loyalty to that teacher, and that's normal. With regard to the history of Goju Ryu Karate, this has very much been the case. However, like (the often dreaded) investigative journalists, I feel that we should never be afraid to *ask questions*, particularly about things that just plain don't add up. For example, and just for starters, Naha To-te, from the (alleged) Higaonna lineage seems to have inherited/acquired far more kata than was usual for the day, and the assumption – up to the present time – is that these extra kata are ancient and came directly from China. I am not convinced.

Uechi Ryu Karate, and its more popular contemporary, Goju Ryu, are considered to be *two* separate traditions. Yet, my research suggests that the difference or rather divergence is relatively recent. I became suspicious of the recorded lineage of Higaonna's 'Naha-te'. The term 'Ryu Ryu Ko', not a proper name yet used to describe Higaonna's alleged sole teacher didn't make much sense. This anomaly ultimately led me to investigate further, and I felt compelled to question. Part of my initial curiosity focused on the great importance attached to the practice of Sanchin kata in both Karate traditions and in much Fujianese Quan-fa in general, and how the modern and popular (closed-fist) Goju Ryu version differed from the open handed version said to precede it (a detailed analysis of Goju Ryu Sanchin in comparison with Uechi Ryu Sanchin can be found in chapter six).

During the 1980s and 1990s, many prominent international Karate researchers, already in receipt of the basic information that Miyagi Chojun's Karate (or more properly To-te) instructor (Higaonna) had originally learned, practiced, and taught an *open-handed* Sanchin kata, wondered just how that kata had been presented originally. Common questions were:

1. Did the (open) hands in basic Sanchin position slant on a 45° angle (from a palm-up position) like they do in the Uechi Ryu version, or in the Goju Ryu kata Shisochin, or were they (flat) palm up?

2. Was the hand withdrawn in a semicircular (arc) whilst performing section one as it is in Uechi Ryu, or pulled directly back as it is in Goju Ryu?

3. Was the extending hand straightened at the height of shoulder, as it is in Uechi Ryu, or pushed forward at rib height, as it is in Goju Ryu?

4. Were both feet 'in-turned' (toed-in) in the Sanchin stance as they are in some Goju Ryu (or the alternative Goju Kai), or was the back foot kept straight as it is in Uechi Ryu?

Sufficient to say, for now, the Sanchin kata originally practiced by Higaonna was the same as the Sanchin later learned by Uechi Kanbun. The question, 'so what?', springs to mind, yet the 'so what', fails to see the implications; early Naha-Te, 'To-te' or Karate, was, based on my research, founded upon three kata designed for use with 'Sai' weapons! Altering these kata concealed or removed such a connection. Besides, if the fundamental Sanchin has been altered, within the Goju Ryu style, what about the other so called 'Naha-te kata?'

The change made from the open-hand Sanchin to the closed-fist Sanchin, completely and utterly altered the key signature of the kata, away in fact from a weapons kata.

The late Lo Kwang Yu of Preying Mantis Kung Fu   *USA Goju Karate Master Robert Taiani*

The Goju (closed-fist) Sanchin (particularly section two) resembles techniques found in various 'Preying Mantis' Quan-fa forms which possibly served as models for Miyagi's 'reformation' of Sanchin kata, now unquestionably an empty hand kata. In Goju Ryu Karate, Sanchin, Seisan (Sesan) and Sanseirui (Sanseru) have all been altered to reflect the use of the closed-fist, and the function of these kata have all but been excised, making it difficult to use them in the ways originally intended by their creators, i.e. as Sai kata. It readily becomes apparent that this is indeed where the divergence between Quan-fa and modern (Na-ha) Karate really begins; at the point when the quintessential Chinese vision (purpose of the kata – the armed countering of weapons) is revised, discarded, or may have never been learned in the first place, making much early Karate an art based – as I have already said – on the use of weapons kata (techniques) without the weapons.

The Lineage of Higaonna Kanyro

I will deal with Higaonna Kanryo first, and the popular emergence of Naha Karate from his lineage. This is because of the considerable impact his student Miyagi Chojun has had on Karate. Higaonna Kanryo (1853–1915) was the teacher of Miyagi Chojun (founder of Goju Ryu Karate), between (approx) 1902 and 1915. It is from Higaonna Kanryo that Miyagi inherited the Sanchin tradition.

According to Patrick McCarthy, Higaonna Kanryo started his Karate training (aged fourteen – fifteen) in 1867 on Okinawa under Arakaki Seisho. Allegedly, Arakaki was an expert in *Monk Fist Boxing*. Nagamine Shoshin (1907–1997) also states that Higaonna Kanryo trained rigorously under Maya Arakaki (Arakaki Seisho) and quickly became well known around Naha city for his skill. However, the date Nagamine gives for the start of Higaonna's training with Arakaki is 1873, a discrepancy of six years from the 1867 date suggested by Patrick McCarthy. This is worthy of note. *Resolving this inconsistency may help to untangle who taught what to whom, when, and even where.* Moreover it will help to establish the proper lineage and source of the open handed Sanchin kata once practiced by Higaonna Kanryo and preserved in the Uechi Ryu Karate style, generally considered to be a separate tradition from Higaonna's Naha-te and later Miyagi's Goju Ryu. As stated above, *I suggest the two are not separate at all!* A confusion has arisen, due largely to politics and the naming, or failure to properly name, teachers or sources.

Higaonna Morio (no relation to Higaonna Kanryo), in his 'History of Karate Okinawan Goju Ryu' claims that Higaonna Kanryo set sail for Fuzhou to learn Quan-fa in 1867, making the young Higaonna fourteen or fifteen years of age at the time. However, support of this hypothesis obscures the links between Arakaki Seisho and Higaonna Kanryo (and later Kojo Taitei). Also, if Higaonna was resident in China for the fourteen years Higaonna Morio claims he was, Higaonna Kanryo would have *had* to have left for Fuhzou aged only fourteen or fifteen. As I will demonstrate later, there are several glaring inconsistencies that undermine this 'political' history. In reality, it is doubtful that Higaonna Kanryo spent more than eight years associating with the Okinawan and Chinese inhabitants of Fuzhou city in Fujian province, China.

Both Nagamine and McCarthy agree that Arakaki Seisho taught Higaonna Kanryo, but few seem to have seriously considered *how* Higaonna originally practiced and taught Sanchin kata, and the implications of altering the kata for modern consumption. This is an important point.

Higaonna Morio also reports in his 'History of Karate Okinawan Goju Ryu', that: "... Kanryo Higaonna told Chojun Miyagi",

"My teachers name is Ryu Ryu Ko …" But Ryu Ryu Ko is not a proper name. A modern (Western) analogy might be that of referring to someone (in the vernacular) as 'Big Bob', clearly not a proper name that would be useful beyond a local boundary. Ryu Ryu Ko is a person for whom there can be found no proper records, lineages or direct teachers, a situation that has – thus far – disabled non-partisan researchers from comparing the kata of Ryu Ryu Ko's contemporaries (and his teachers kata) with the kata of Goju Ryu. In trying to trace the origins of Goju Ryu kata by using 'in house' Goju Ryu history, the trail mysteriously (and frustratingly) vanishes with Ryu Ryu Ko.

The Mysterious Ryu Ryu Ko

Because Ryu Ryu Ko is not a proper name, there has been much speculation as to exactly who he was. Surely, if one spends ten to fourteen years with an acclaimed teacher (as it is stated by Higaonna Morio that Kanyro did), it would be most unusual not to know Ryu Ryu Ko's proper name, or for *someone* to know *something* about his family, his friends, his status, etc! Particularly as, again according to Higaonna Morio's account, given in *The History of Karate Okinawan Goju Ryu*, that Ryu Ryu Ko, and I quote, was "quite famous," and, "… a great master."

According to Patrick McCarthy, Ryu Ryu Ko was a nickname meaning, to precede – Ko being a suffix that means 'big brother'. However, this is a strange way indeed to refer to one's formal Sifu/teacher. McCarthy bravely equates Ryu Ryu Ko with Xie Zhongxiang (1852–1930) a Fujianese exponent of either White Crane or Monkfist Boxing. Xie would later go on to found 'Whooping Crane Kung Fu'. The dates fit well, Xie being one year older than Higaonna and therefore a figurative 'big brother'.

In comparrison, 'Whooping Crane Kung Fu', bears little direct resemblance to Goju Ryu Karate, and the quan taught by Xie (among them, for the record; Babulien/Happoren and Nipaipo/Nepai) do not seem to have been inherited by Higaonna, a fact evidenced by Kiyoda Juhatsu (1887–1968) – senior to Miyagi under Higaonna – learning the Nipaipo (Nepai) quan from the Chinese tea merchant, Wu Xiangui (Gokenki) (1886–1940), and not from Higaonna. If Higaonna knew Babulien/or Nipaipo, it doesn't appear that he taught these quan to anyone! Moreover, Wu Xiangui (Gokenki) gave instruction in Nipaipo to several Okinawans who would later become prominent figures in Okinawan Martial Arts circles (including Miyagi Chojun). The trained eye can see the influence of Wu Xiangui's Nipaipo in certain Goju Ryu kata, particularly in Goju Sesan and Sanseru kata, but this influence did not come from Higaonna. I suspect that Wu Xiangui was a major influence on Miyagi Chojun in the latter's creation of Goju Ryu Karate (kata).

The Sanchin kata – the key kata of Goju Ryu Karate – resembles the Sanchin kata of Uechi Ryu Karate. It does *not* resemble the (key quan) Babulien/Happoren quan promulgated by Xie Zhongxiang. Elements of (the modified) Sanchin, Sesan and Sanseirui can clearly be seen in contemporary Goju Ryu kata, particularly in the 'advanced' kata Suparinpei!

Who taught Higaonna Kanyro in China and When?

Moreover, Nagamine Shoshin (in conformity with Shimabukuro Kotyu and Funakoshi Gichin) *cites Wai Xianxian as Higaonna Kanryo's teacher.* This is not unreasonable considering that Wai Xianxian was Sifu to Arakaki Seisho and Kojo Taitei, both of whom taught Higaonna on Okinawa in his early years. I can put the case here that Arakaki Seisho, Kojo Taitei, and (by proxy)

Higaonna Kanyro were all students of Wai Xianxian, Wai Xianxian would have been their 'Sifu' (teacher/father). Arakaki Seisho and Kojo Taitei were both senior to Higaonna Kanyro under Wai Xianxian, which would have made them both Higaonna's 'Si-hing' or teacher/brother (big brother), under the same (overall) teacher/father, Wai Xianxian. Kojo Taitei was three years older than Arakaki Seisho, and may have become Higaonna's principle instructor (under Wai Xianxian), thus Kojo Taitei or another Kojo family member (an Okinawan rather than a Chinese) may well have been the mysterious Ryu Ryu Ko, the semi-acknowledged source of Higaonna's Quan-fa/To-te. After all, the training was supported by the Kojo family and conducted in their own kwoon (dojo).

I suggest, given that Higaonna Kanryo was born in 1853 and underwent his *Katagashira* (a boys right of passage into manhood) in January 1867, it seems most likely that he initially undertook the adult pursuit of To-te Jutsu training *at home on Okinawa*, later that year (1867), as McCarthy suggests, learning from both Arakaki Seisho, and after 1870 (when Arakaki Seisho left for Beijing) from Kojo Taitei, who were, as stated, both students of the Chinese Sifu, Wai Xianxian. It seems most likely that Higaonna spent approximately six years (from 1867 to 1873) practicing *on Okinawa* before setting sail for Fuzhou China, aged about twenty, in 1873. Higaonna was definitely – back – on Okinawa by 1881 as I will illustrate.

Karate historians and writers, given their interest is in Karate per se, commonly take it for granted that Higaonna Kanyro's main (or even sole) reason for going to Fuzhou was to pursue and train in Quan-fa/To-te (Karate) and to gain greater knowledge of the art(s). But (with respect), there may well have been a considerable economic reason for Higaonna Kanyro's re-location to, or association with Fuzhou; namely, paid employment and an (albeit limited) opportunity to travel and escape the humdrum and poverty of late nineteenth century Okinawa. We do know that there was considerable economic hardship on Okinawa during that time, and we do know that the hardship impinged on the life of Higaonna Kanyro both before he went to Fuzhou and after his return(s).

Although statistics vary, an indication of the extent of Okinawan emigration can be seen in the numbers who left Okinawa between 1879 (when Okinawa officially became a Japanese prefecture) and 1945. By 1945 it is estimated that over 80,000 Okinawans were living in Japan, out of a population of just something over 500,000. Indeed, Okinawa was Japan's poorest prefecture.

I think it extremely unlikely that Higaonna left Okinawa for Fuzhou aged only fourteen, particularly when most eminent (and non partisan) sources agree that Higaonna Kanryo was approximately twenty years of age when he embarked on his adventure(s) to China (see below). It is based on *what* Higaonna Kanryo learned rather than when or for how long. Sufficient to say, it no coincidence that the Goju Ryu and Uechi Ryu Sanchin kata are related!

Returning to the thorny problem of who taught what to whom in the Naha tradition; as already indicated, Arakaki Seisho, Kojo Taitei (Higaonna's early teachers) and Higashionna Kanryo were almost certainly taught by Wai Xianxian. Arakaki Seisho or Kojo Taitei most likely introduced Higaonna Kanryo to Wai Xianxian. What were the probable kata he taught? Take a guess!

Arakaki Seisho, Kojo Taitei, Nakaima Norisato (a contemporary), Uechi Kanbun (over twenty years later) and to some extent Higaonna Kanryo himself seem to have had one thing in common; they all practiced Sanchin quan – most likely the open hand version taught by Wai Xianxian and most likely studied, if not originally learned, at the *Kojo* kwoon (training hall) in Fuzhou. Rumour has it that Kojo Taitei was a descendant of (one of) the 'Thirty Six (Chinese) Families' that allegedly relocated from Fuzhou to Okinawa in 1392. Whilst I'm not sure about this, it would perhaps go some way to explaining his (greater) acceptance in Fuzhou and the operation of his own kwoon/dojo, apart from the fact that he seemed to have been a rather well-off businessman.

It cannot be assumed that Arakaki Seisho himself learned Quan-fa only in Fuzhou. Funakoshi Gichin states in *Karate – Do Kyohan*, p.8:

> ... Aragaki (Arakaki) ... of Kunenbya [a village in Okinawa], studied with the [Chinese] military attaché Waishinzan [Wai Xianxian] ... (Parenthesis mine)

It seems plausible that Wai Xianxian may have associated with Arakaki Seisho on Okinawa on a professional basis, and most likely taught him Quan-fa there! And as I mentioned earlier, before Arakaki Seisho left for Beijing in 1870, he entrusted his student Higaonna Kanryo to Kojo Taitei. It seems likely that Higaonna continued his studies under Kojo before setting sail for Fuzhou in 1873, thus spending up to five or six years training on Okinawa and possibly learning Seisan kata as well as Sanchin.

Arakaki Seisho spoke fluent Chinese and worked as a translator for the Ryukyu court, a job which took him to Beijing (Peking) in September of 1870, when he was aged thirty. Moreover, this is a man who would have (for professional and other reasons) been more readily accepted in Chinese (Quan-fa) circles than a fourteen year old boy who's father (according to Nagamine Shoshin) did not have enough money to properly educate his children (Kanyro was the fourth of eight children). Nagamine Shoshin, plainly states (*The Essence of Okinawan Karate – Do*, p.42) that, "... the tendency of the time [19th century Okinawa]

was to neglect the education of all but the first born son ...".
(Parenthesis mine)

This is no reflection on the Higaonna family's social standing, but Higaonna Kanryo did not receive an (academic) education, nor did he speak Chinese (until he acquired elements of it by associating with Chinese merchants, seafarers, traders and the like). According to Nagamine, Higaonna was confined to a restrictive lifestyle (at the Ryukyukan) when he did go to China. It may be the case that Arakaki Seisho and Kojo Taitei assisted him with elementary Fujianese words. However, the 'uchi deshi' (live-in student) status often claimed for Higashionna Kanyro is problematic.

In Patrick McCarthy's translation of the *Bubishi* (Wu-pei chih) (Boston & Tokyo: Tuttle 1995) p.37, he has this to say on the subject:

> ... It is not surprising to learn that Kanryo [Higaonna] did not become a live-in student of a *prominent* master, as was previously believed. After all, Kanryo was a young non-Chinese who could not speak, read, or write Chinese. *Chinese gongfu [Kung Fu] masters rarely, if ever accepted outsiders as students, let alone foreigners.* It was not the way things were done during the Qing dynasty (1644–1911) in China. (Parenthesis and italics mine)

Also, Xia Bai Hua (then director – Theoretical Wu Shu Research Institute – North of Beijing) in conversation with Greg Chaplin (*F.A.I.* Volume twelve, number sixty-seven) claims that:

> ... the teachers with whom Okinawans studied were not nationally famous teachers of their day ... this didn't mean that they were not highly proficient ... only that they weren't highly famous.

This supports current views that Higaonna's direct association with a leading Chinese Sifu is questionable. Yet, without doubt,

Ryukyuan visitors to Fuzhou 'banded together', and there were indeed some Quan-fa teachers who would teach them despite the likelihood that most would not. It does seem that Wai Xianxian was one teacher who obliged. However, it must be borne in mind that Higaonna was an Okinawan and not a Chinese. He was a subject of a *Japanese* prefecture that was once a 'tribute' satellite of China, and one must consider the somewhat ambiguous position of the Okinawans and the attitudes to 'outsiders' (virtual xenophobia) prevalent amongst Chinese Sifu in the run-up to the catastrophic war with Japan in 1894 and all the political intrigues that led to the bloody 'Boxer rebellion' of 1900, when misguided Nationalistic Chinese Quan-fa zealots went up against foreign (Western) guns and cannons and were decimated.

It is alleged that *Uechi Kanbun* (1877–1948) also initially trained at the *Kojo* kwoon before becoming a student (or quite possibly a friend) of Zhou Zhihe (Chou tzu-ho). This makes perfect sense because the Kojo kwoon was situated near to the 'Ryukyu Kan' (a kind of hostel for Ryukyuan nationals). The kwoon may well have served as a sort of meeting house for Okinawan migrant workers, traders and travellers to Fuzhou. I think it would be strange for Uechi Kanbun not to have trained there. It seems that most emigrant To-te 'enthusiasts' did. Indeed, the Ryukyuans seemed to have formed a community in Fuzhou that would have been almost a home from home. As in many cases of immigration, the immigrants often head for enclaves of their own people. For most Okinawans, once inside these 'enclaves' they did not venture very far. In many respects, it was quite difficult to do so unless one had an official position or was well-educated, in for example, Confucian classics and Chinese language(s).

It therefore seems highly likely that the lineage (roots) of both Goju Ryu and Uechi Ryu Karate, lay (roughly) in the Quan-fa taught and practiced at the Kojo kwoon, the source of both Higaonna Kanyro's and Uechi Kanbun's kata. Moreover it seems that the patronage of Kojo Taite and his family, coupled with Wai Xianxian's tuition made that possible.

It has been claimed by Higaonna Morio, that Higaonna Kanryo spent fourteen years in China, and for six of them learned only *one* kata. This is quite harsh and unrealistic. It would necessitate him learning *eight* kata in the following eight years, if as is suggested, he stayed in China for fourteen years, and if it is to be accepted that he brought back *nine* kata. Both cases are out of kilter with the Qing dynasty 'three years, one kata' tradition. The teacher would have had to switch from being extremely severe to being exceptionally liberal in matters of passing on quan/kata, and he would have to know that many or more kata himself.

If *nine* quan/kata were taught to Higaonna (an Okinawan and a foreigner), even as the favourite student, where did the ultra-conservative teaching attitude he would later display, come from? Why did he (and later, Uechi Kanbun) teach so few kata and so slowly? Why didn't Hiagaonna teach a *system* – all the kata in sequence, as he himself had (allegedly) been taught? I suppose that for some interested parties, the longer Higaonna is perceived to have been in China, the better, for the 'nine kata from China' hypothesis. The speed and the *way* quan were taught in Qing dynasty Fuzhou should not be confused with the way (number and speed) kata are taught in modern Karate.

Many sources claim that Higaonna Kanryo spent ten years in China. This would make his pace of learning the alleged nine kata, plus various weapons also taught in kata form, and herbal medicine, even more hectic; and once again, contrary to the teaching methods of the day. As noted earlier, the usual explanation for such an anomaly is the cliché of the special schooling provided for a protégé, the 'chosen successor'. But I doubt that the social and political climate of Qing dynasty Fuzhou was egalitarian or a meritocracy! I doubt that an

Okinawan foreigner would have been given the 'mantle of succession' to a Chinese system, or that an outsider would have been allowed to become the Sifu's 'top student'. Yet this hypothesis persists. In *The History of Karate Okinawan Goju Ryu* by Higaonna Morio, p.16, he (Morio) states that:

> ... Kanryo [Higaonna] thus developed great strength and an overall physical balance. Anichi Miyagi [no relation to Miyagi Chojun] told me [Higaonna Morio] that this, combined with his [Kanryo Higaonna's] natural ability, *eventually led him to become Ryu Ryu Ko's top student* ... (Parenthesis and italics mine)

Similar claims are repeated when it comes to Higaonna's alleged 'favourite' student Miyagi Chojun.

There are several problems with much of this. First, the mysterious Ryu Ryu Ko needs to be positively identified (remember, it's generally assumed he was Chinese). Second, why is nothing ever mentioned about Higaonna's sempai (seniors)? He must have had them, unless he arrived in Fuzhou as a senior already! This, of course, is possible but unlikely. I suppose it is more possible for a twenty year old who has already been taught Quan-fa/To-te on Okinawa than it is for a fourteen year old Okinawan Quan-fa hopeful. It is also more likely for an Okinawan 'student' to be favoured by an Okinawan Sensei, if he is favoured at all!

Further, one must consider how Higaonna made a living. After all, he would have needed food, accommodation and clothing. How did he provide for himself? I am not a great supporter of the 'bamboo cutting' he is said to have assisted his master with, as a credible source of income provided by a master who irritatingly (read conveniently) cannot be properly identified. As noted, it has become increasingly clear (from several sources) that Higaonna was not the live-in student of a prominent Fujianese Sifu. Less contentiously; it is clear that he would definitely have had to engage in some financially rewarding work – meaning that it is most unlikely that he could have committed all of his time to Quan-fa practice. Higaonna Kanyro was a sailor by trade. There is no direct evidence of Higaonna staying in Fuzhou for fourteen (or even ten) consecutive years. In fact, to support this hypothesis, he would definitely have had to have left for China no later than 1867 *because he was married on Okinawa before May 15th 1882*, the birth-date of his wife's son (Higaonna was not the biological father of the boy).

I think it highly possible that Higaonna's stay in China did not last for ten consecutive years and that he may well have simply worked (as did his father before him) as a sailor on the large trading ships called 'Shinkosen' that sailed from the Ryuku Islands (for example from the port of Naha) to Fuzhou city, Fujian province, China. Higaonna Kanyro may well have domiciled intermittently at the Ryuku Kan between trips, and practiced Quan-fa there. Irrespective of this hypothesis, it is well known that he was back negotiating Okinawan coastal waters as a 'yanbarusan' (small boat) operative by 1881, eight years at most from his (first) trip to Fuzhou in 1873. The amount of time Higaonna spent learning Quan-fa is, however, of less importance than his reserved and conservative 'three year's one kata' teaching method; that and the traditional (by modern standards, small) number of kata he taught to Kiyoda, Miyagi, and others.

It is alleged in Higaonna Morio's *The History of Karate*, that Higaonna learned Chinese weaponry (the long sword, the short sword, the staff) and that he studied herbal medicine whilst in China, but once again, there is insufficient evidence to support such a claim. Neither is there any evidence that Miyagi Chojun or any other of Higaonna's students ever learned Chinese weaponry or herbal medicine from him. *Indeed, Kiyoda Juhatsu asserted that Miyagi did not learn Chinese weaponry from Higaonna*, and it is totally absent from Goju Ryu Karate, as indeed is any kind of (formal) Kobudo.

In respect of Higaonna having learned herbal medicine, it may be possible (but unlikely) that he was involved in 'medicine hawking' in China; selling medicine on street corners (when not at sea), a popular means of livelihood for Quan-fa students, as Uechi Kanbun would later discover. But such associations with Chinese medicine probably had more to do with the influence of the voguish Martial Arts almanac, the the Wu-pei chih (Bubishi), than anything learned directly in China, or at home on Okinawa (The Wu-pei chih is a fascinating historical document much expanded and skilfully contextualised in the estimable Patrick McCarthy translation).

The (Quan-fa) Wu-pei chih (not to be confused with the voluminous late Ming dynasty treatise on military strategy) was studied with eagerness by several prominent To-te pioneers who attempted to incorporate its medicinal and other stated (unarmed combat) principles into their interpretations of Fujinese quan. Of course, the difficulty I have with the validity of this lies not in the authorship or stated aims and objectives of the various author(s) of the 'articles' that comprise the Wu-pei chih, but with the fact that key Fujianese kata, like the original Sanchin, Sesian, and Sanseirui are (utility) Sai kata that can not be subjected to the theories of an unarmed plebeian art, despite these kata being described variously as Monk Fist, Arahat Boxing, or White Crane Quan-fa. I can only suggest that these and other key forms were eventually altered to conform to ideas expressed in the Wu-pei chi. I certainly think this is the case for Goju Ryu Karate which is quite different in scope and content from the Karate taught by Higaonna Kanyro and Kiyoda Juhatsu.

Regarding the association of Higaonna Kanyro with Arakaki Seisho and Kojo Taitei, Hokama Tetsuhiro, makes an interesting observation in his *History and Traditions of Okinawan Karate* (Masters Publication, Hamilton Ontario Canada, no publication date or copyright):

... His (Higaonna's) martial arts education reportedly began when he was a teenager. He studied with the noted To di [To-te] teacher Arakaki Seisho of Kuma mura. Arakaki was scheduled to travel to Peking [Bejing] for an undetermined stay [?]. In order to ensure Higaonna could continue his martial arts study uninterrupted, Arakaki introduced him to Kojo Taitei. A benevolent benefactor, the wealthy Kojo financed Higaonna's travel to Fuchou [Fuzhou] in 1873. He [Higaonna] remained there for approximately ten years, training with Kojo in his Chinese dojo. He [Higaonna] also studied with other teachers, including Wan Shien Ling [Wan Shin Za/Wai Xianxian?] commonly referred to as Ryu Ryu Ko ... (Parenthesis mine)

I can only assume that the Wan Shien Ling referred to is Wai Xianxian. Further in the same passage, Wan Shien Ling is mentioned as being a shoemaker. I think this is a simple confusion between Wai Xianxian, allegedly a commissioned officer or military attaché, and Xie Zhongxiang, who was reportedly a shoemaker.

In respect of the fourteen years of training claimed by Higaonna Morio for Higaonna Kanryo; if one considers the six years Higaonna Kanryo spent learning from Arakaki Seisho and Kojo Taitei on Okinawa, and combines them with eight years spent as a Sailor on the Shinkosen, during which frequent visits were made to the Kojo kwoon in Fuzhou, then it could indeed be argued that Higaonna Kanryo spent fourteen years (intermittently) studying Quan-fa/To-te.

The important points to establish here are: *What* did Higaonna originally learn? From *whom did he learn it?* – And, what then could we expect him to have taught Miyagi Chojun (and others)? The reason for these questions is simple; if Goju Ryu Karate kata were originally Chinese quan from Fuzhou, learned from *one* teacher (in this case Ryu Ryu Ko), as is claimed, and, if collectively, they formed a tradition, why are there so many of them? If Miyagi Chojun inherited a *tradition* or rather a *system*, (containing an unusually high number of kata) why did he later *add* kata?

This (as I noted earlier) is in contrast to the norms of the period during which the kata were allegedly 'received'. Although I must admit that by the time Miyagi Chojun began training in 1902, the trend had begun to change perhaps as a result of Itosu's influence. Still, from Higaonna's perspective, and certainly during Arakaki Seisho's and Kojo Taitei's formative years, the use of more than three or so quan would be more than just unusual! Indeed, highly unlikely.

Synthesised Kata

In an article by my acquaintance, the excellent Karate historian Graham Noble, in collaboration with Ian McLaren and Professor N. Karasawa (*F.A.I.* No. 50. p.28) in respect of the Shuri-te Karate teacher Itosu Ankho, he states:

> ... I think that for many years he [Itosu] had been collecting and re-structuring and standardising kata ... He left around twenty-five kata to his followers *at a time when a well-known expert might know only three kata.* (Parenthesis and italics mine)

Clearly, the Shuri-te tradition was expanding, so – perhaps the thinking went – why not the Naha-te tradition too?

The origin, or possible genesis of kata in the Goju Ryu tradition, is not usually questioned or examined in any great depth. But there have been relatively recent visits to Fuzhou (China) made by contemporary Goju Ryu Karate-ka, seeking examples of, or sources for, their kata. Yet, even these visits to the 'ancestral land' of Goju Ryu (kata) have yielded largely negative results. Goju Ryu kata can not be found (neither for that matter can Shuri-te kata) in Fuzhou; consequently, many teachers have wistfully consigned this 'problem' to the unknown.

Whilst Sanchin, for Naha, and Naihanchin for Shuri, have a long history, at least on Okinawa (it is a matter of record that both have lineages tracing them back to *named* teachers); several kata practiced in mainstream Goju are problematic from a lineage perspective. Miyagi Chojun seems to be almost the only source for such an 'in house' collective of kata that include: *Saifa, Seiyunchin, Shisochin, Sepai, Kururunfa, Suparinpei and Tensho*. Indeed, these kata do not form part of To-on Ryu, the style of Miyagi's senior, Kiyoda Juhatsu.

Goju Ryu kata generally have a powerful look about them, and although experts can perform the techniques at blinding speed, Goju Ryu kata, in comparison with many Southern Chinese quan, seem a little 'heavy'. Also, Goju Ryu kata, as disseminated by Miyagi Chojun, have postures that are much more 'rooted' and 'fixed' than those used, for example, in the To-on Ryu style which are arguably closer to Higaonna Kanyro's original teachings (i.e. the number of kata and the way they are performed). Moreover, the Higaonna kata were conservatively passed on by Kiyoda. In contrast, Miyagi's innovative modifications to kata, and the emphasis he placed on 'rooted-ness' makes his kata more akin to Itosu's interpretation of Naihanchin (Miyagi had great respect for Naihanchin). That plus Miyagi's eclectic mix of extra kata that make considerable use of the zenkutsu dachi (front leg bent or forward leaning stance) attest to practices influenced by the emerging re-vamped art of Shuri-te Karate, allegedly a separate tradition from the branch of Fujianese Quan-fa that had become known as Naha-te. Indeed, much Fujianese Quan-fa favours various types of triangulated 'ma-po' – 'horse (riding) stances', or the San-jou-ma – the (similar) 'three cornered' stance of some White Crane Quan-fa. Although Goju Ryu kata do of course employ the Sanchin stance.

Tensho (formerly Rokushu) is a much 'lighter' quan/kata and definitely has the look and the feel of Fujianese Quan-fa about it, although 'Tensho' is a synthesis.

Rokushu techniques certainly mirror techniques found in Preying Mantis and White Crane Quan-fa. Tensho has been labelled as a 'high level' Karate kata – an advanced kata. In Goju Ryu Karate (so we are told), Tensho represents the 'Ju' or soft, yielding and pliant half of the art, whilst Sanchin represents the 'Go' or hard part of the art. If this is the case, Miyagi's 'To-te' must already have changed in emphasis from that taught to him by Higaonna, because Higaonna's 'To-te' did not include Tensho, neither (as far as I'm aware) did his principle teachers (Arakaki Seisho and Kojo

Old Sanchin Stance   *Goju Shiko-dachi or*
                        Jigotai dachi

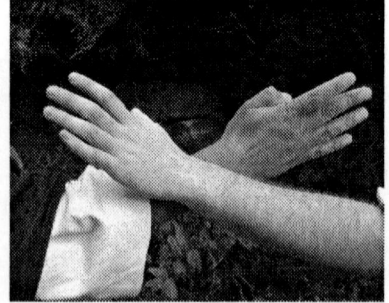

A Tensho grip escape

Kiyoda Juhatsu

Taitei) 'To-te' utilise Tensho. The evidence suggests that Miyagi Chojun was innovating behind the screen of 'tradition', actually a common occurrence by that time, and something that has continued up to the present time.

According to Tasaki Kogyu, a student of both Kiyoda Juhatsu and Miyagi Chojun during the 1920s, there were *three* Suparinpei kata. Suparinpei kata is considered (within Goju Ryu Karate) to be an advanced, if not the most advanced kata. Tasaki Kogyu reports that there once existed three versions of Suparinpei: jo, chu and ge – which I can only assume means, an upper, middle, and lower *version* of the kata. Tasaki claimed that the chu and ge versions have passed out of existence. The fact that they may have existed at all attests to the possibility of variations. On observation, *out of the sixty or so movements performed in Suparinpei, over thirty four are drawn directly (although in somewhat modified form) from the old style Sanchin and Seisan kata.* This is of considerable significance because of the conspicuous connection between techniques (thirty-four movements) found in Suparinpei kata and techniques directly attributable to weapons use! Moreover there are also eleven repetitions of Mawashi uke (Sanchin section three) but all used whilst moving forward in either a Sanchin stance, a cat stance, or whilst turning.

Mawashi Uke in Suparinpei Kata
– modified from Sanchin

Modified Goju Ryu Seisan technique
also found in Suparinpei kata

Original 'old style' Sesian

Sai techniques

It may be that Suparinpei was one of the *first* kata to be synthesised in the Goju tradition as it unfolded, possibly intended to emulate the 'legendary' Peichurin Kata, the final 'one hundred and eight' movements/techniques of a 'grand and *final* kata' (although Suparinpei does not contain one hundred and eight movements/techniques). To some extent, the inclusion of this 'grand kata' mimics the Shuri-te 'Kusanku' kata, considered by Nagamine Shoshin (*The Essence of Okinawan Karate-Do*, p.230) to be:

> The most magnificent and advanced kata of all Matsubaya shi-ryu Karate … (Matsubayashi-ryu is a branch of Shorin [Shao-lin] Ryu or Shuri-te). (Square brackets mine)

Some sources claim that one, Arakaki Seisho taught Peichurin kata, and that it was one of his students (a man from Kuninda named Tomura) who demonstrated the kata at a commemorative event on Okinawa in 1867. Interestingly, Arakaki Seisho demonstrated *Seisan* kata at the same event. Arakaki is puzzlingly linked to other kata; Sochin, Unsu and Niseishi, to name three. But none of these kata is usually practiced within the Naha-te tradition. Altered versions of Sochin, Unsu and Niseishi are currently practiced in Modern Shotokan (and in other styles), but despite Shotokan being an eclectic style, it does not utilise Sanchin or

Sanseirui kata, although it does practice a version of Seisan (Sesan) kata, altered by Itosu and re-named Hangetsu by Funakoshi Gichin.

Modern 'Unsu' kata, now practiced in the Shotokan style, although undoubtedly modified, looks somewhat like 'Hakutsuru', a White Crane quan. It may have been passed on to Mabuni Kenwa by Wu Xiangui (Gokenki), but it's uncertain where Arakaki learned it. I would suggest that he learned it along with other kata, later in life, when the traditional teaching methods had begun to break down.

Irrespective of when the Goju Ryu Suparinpei was created or synthesised, it is distinctive, and in my view bears tell-tale characteristics of an *Okinawan* kata constructed from Chinese techniques, rather than a Chinese quan per-se. Moreover it is unlikely to be the same Suparinpei/Peichurin kata demonstrated on Okinawa in 1867. I have seen a quan from Fuzhou, which is alleged by some sources to be an original version of Suparinpei. It is further alleged that this version should have been inherited by Uechi Ryu as a long lost fourth kata. On observation, the kata under discussion is very different from the Goju Suparinpei, which, as I have already said, is undoubtedly based on, and repeats techniques from, the Goju Ryu Sanchin, Sesan and Sanseirui kata. Moreover, the Goju Ryu Suparinpei reflects the Goju Ryu Sanchin, both in style and structure, and the Goju Sanchin is a comparatively late development.

Initially, transporting important themes and elements from one (empty hand) kata to another, may seem to make sense, but I find no practical reasons for an amalgam of already existing techniques, even with the addition of others. Even considering, for example, that Uechi Sanchin and Sesian kata *start* in the same way, in these kata, the Sanchin theme is *developed* rather than merely repeated. This is important. A repeating theme or motif is usually put into *one* kata (good examples are Rokushu and Naihanchin). One might imagine that there is some inherent advantage in creating differing combinations of the techniques drawn from both kata, but Rokushu and Naihanchin, for example, can not be mixed; one either performs the techniques of one, or the other, depending on whether one is escaping from single arm grips or applying double arm locks/controls to subdue an opponent. Each approach is different and requires a different kata; a straight forward *formulae*. Interestingly, formulae-based kata give less of an impression of being fights against multiple opponents, than amalgamated (modified) kata or Kobudo/weapons kata; probably because they are usually uncomplicated, repetitive and simple or non-spectacular.

Training Reflects the Era

Both Higaonna Kanyro and Uechi Kanbun taught Sanchin as the basis for their *Ryu,* and for that matter, as I have suggested, both seem to have taught *Sanchin* followed by *Seisan* and then *Sanseirui.* According to accounts, Higaonna was a severe 'taskmaster'. Undoubtedly training was difficult in those times. There was a heavy emphasis on physical conditioning, and the modern day equivalent might be going down to the gym for a prolonged but very basic military style aerobics and weight training session. It seems that Uechi Kanbun was also rather strict.

During that period, and mimicking the Chinese tradition started in the later part of the turbulent Qing dynasty (1644–1911), To-te training lacked the usual 'warm up' exercises and 'basics' of modern Karate. According to Nakamoto Seibun (1892–1984), a student of Higaonna Kanryo, there were no preliminary exercises prior to training, which seems to have begun with kata practice. Nakamoto practiced To-te under Higaonna Kanryo from 1910 until 1915 when Higaonna died. Nakamoto then spent a further five years training under the auspices of Miyagi Chojun, finishing in around 1920. During ten years of training, the only kata Nakamoto learned were Sanchin and Sesan (see footnote 5, p.21 in *The History of Karate* by Morio Higaonna).

During the period when Nakamoto trained with Higaonna Kanyro, the Dojo (training hall) system was not yet in place, and group repetition of kata (other than Sanchin) less common. Indeed, as far as I am aware, Ueichi Kanbun gave only individual instruction in Seisan kata, which Mattson records, were not performed on a group basis. Individual effort and training were encouraged, under the watchful eye of the master, who, it seems, often demanded sweat, blood and tears. Sanchin was the basis for all. There were plenty of auxiliary exercises and rudimentary weight lifting too, to strengthen the body. However, this approach to early Naha-te seems to have placed little emphasis on direct kata application. Similar can be said regarding the application of Naihanchin kata in the unfolding Shuri-te tradition. To-on Ryu students were expected to devise applications to kata and present them to Kiyoda for approval or otherwise. Yet, both Sanchin and Naihanchin kata once had specific applications. *These kata were designed for definite reasons, reasons other than those of mere callisthenics* or multiple applications/interpretations. Neither was designed to be 'endurance tests' for young men, even if they were later used as such.

The external, 'hard' aspect of Sanchin 'shime' testing, using fierce slaps and blows to the performer's body, as it is practiced today, probably originated in Qing dynasty China itself, amidst the turbulent backdrop of a disintegrating Chinese society and the desire of angry young men to become strong in order to resist foreign domination. This training was most likely an innovation to suit the times. Ming dynasty Quan-fa was infinitely more sophisticated, and undoubtedly centred around two person drills and the *application* of quan (weapons quan or otherwise).

During the Qing dynasty there was a general loss of the Han (race) pride at the hands of Manchu (non-native) repression and brutality, and the Japanese, German, British French and other interventionists were despised. Xenophobia was the order of the day, and revenge was on the minds of rather a lot of young men. The Qing dynasty edict (mentioned in chapter two) against belligerent young men abandoning productive occupations to spend all day building themselves up, and 'sparring', is interesting, because the 1727 date ascribed to it is only eighty-three years after the fall of the Ming dynasty and only fifty three years or so after the dissolution (burning) of the Shao-lin Temple (by 1674). During this period, secret societies and politically subversive groups arose, often within 'so called' Martial Arts schools.

It is indeed true that some Martial Arts schools were hotbeds of political intrigue and subversive or even criminal activity. It was in such an environment that the later 'Triad' societies evolved in China, and it was for this very reason that many years later, the communist leader Mao Zedong, persecuted Martial Artists and reduced China's traditional arts to the 'official' art, of Wu-Shu – Chinese 'politically correct', philosophically free acrobatic gymnastics that supported communist ideology. Mao took care to ensure that their practical (or any military) potential was strangled. Consequently, Modern Wu-Shu is spectacular but *definitely* not practical (or arguably even very safe for the joints, tendons and ligaments).

In some respects the Okinawans were kindred spirits to the Qing dynasty Chinese. They too had endured centuries of foreign (non indigenous) subjugation at the hands of the mainland Japanese, and had recently become subject to the edicts of the new Meiji 'reformation' (circa 1868) which swiftly abolished the Okinawan monarchy, suppressed Okinawan cultural and political institutions, and introduced even greater strictures from Tokyo. Young men and entire families had to come to terms with Japan's increasing militarization and a draft system that recruited young Okinawans into an army notorious for its ill treatment of conscripts in general, and Okinawans in particular. So the attitudes of politically disgruntled young men practicing Qing dynasty Quan-fa, and the rigorous challenges, attitudes (and sometimes downright dangerous) training routines, found their way quite easily into the arteries of Okinawa's underground, unarmed, dispossessed and disfranchised Bushi (warriors). Thus did To-te truly arrive!

Uechi Kanbun

Uechi Kanbun (1877–1948) travelled from Okinawa to Fuzhou in 1897 to study Quan-fa. Some sources claim that he studied at the central Temple in Fujian province, and that he studied a style called 'Pangai-noon'. Other sources claim that Pangai-noon is not a proper name for a style of Quan-fa, and simply refers to 'bread and butter Kung Fu', taught solely to make money. Regardless of this, Uechi Kanbun was in China between 1897 and 1910 and he seems – for some time – to have associated with Zhou Zhihe, allegedly a 'Tiger' boxer (Chou tzu-ho/Shushiwa, 1878–1926). Zhou Zhihe was one year younger, or at least the same age as Uechi, which is interesting if not a little surprising. Perhaps it helps to corroborate the theory that Uechi Kanbun

Uechi Kanbun

spent his early years in China learning at the Kojo Kwoon, because when he arrived in Fuzhou, Zhou Zhihe was only nineteen years of age; rather youthful for a master. Some sources fix Zhou's birth date at 1874, which would have made him three years older than Uechi. Whichever date is correct, I think the question of whether there was a 'student' and 'master' relationship between the two remains problematic, as does the issue of whether Uechi Kanbun absorbed and transmitted Zhou Zhihe's Quan-fa, or indeed, just what Zhou Zhihe's Quan-fa consisted of.

Considering Uechi Kanbun's sojourn in China, it must be borne in mind that he had no legal way of getting there, and no known sponsor. Indeed, his father had cautioned him that life in China would be difficult. Due to hostile relations between Japan (of which Okinawa was now officially a part) and China, the only way for Kanbun to get to China was to be smuggled out of Okinawa. Consequently he paid ten yen to join a group of young men who boarded a ship bound for Fuzhou.

It is a matter of record that relationships between China and Japan had been poor for centuries. Hoards of Japanese pirates had been endlessly harassing China's South-eastern coast for years (for example when Japan laid siege to Korea in 1592, it took the Chinese until 1598 to repel them). Traditional hostilities exacerbated by the 1894 war between Japan and China ensured Uechi Kanbun's trip was no easy undertaking.

Kanbun reportedly had two reasons for going to China. Firstly his interest in learning Quan-fa, and secondly, absence from Okinawa would mean his avoidance of the Japanese military draft, which although already in practical operation, only became law in 1898. I think it most likely that Uechi acquired Sanchin kata at the Kojo Kwoon during his early stay in Fuzhou. Matsuda Tomosaburo, a young friend of Kanbun's, studied Quan-fa at the same time, but seems to have left after two years or less. Eventually Kanbun met Zhou Zhihe and allegedly studied with him perhaps after leaving the Kojo Kwoon. There seems to have been quite a smoke screen surrounding the Kojo kwoon, its activities and members, because, in the case of Uechi Kanbun, as with Higaonna Kanryo, we can see similar confusion regarding lineage, names of styles and sources, etc.

George Mattson states in *The Way of Karate* p.24:

> In 1900 Mr Uechi, an Okinawan went to southern China and Studied the three foremost styles of kempo [Quan-fa]. He studied for ten years under one of the greatest kempo masters living at that time. At the end of the ten years Mr Uechi took the best *kata* (formal exercises) from the three styles ... he retained the exercise that Bodhidharma developed: the exercise called *sanchin*. From the pangai-noon and the other two styles he adapted the *kata* of *seisan* and *san-juroku* [Sanseirui/Sanseru] (san-shi-liu in Chinese). (Parenthesis mine)

When Mattson wrote this (in the late 1950s/ early 60s), he was less than fifty or so years removed from the actual events, and was probably simply reporting what his teachers had told him. In any case, the above account credits the legendary Bodhidharma (6th century founder of Chan Buddhism), with the creation of (Uechi) Sanchin. Mr Mattson (or his sources) then ascribes the Sesian and Sanseirui kata to the (virtually) unknown 'Pangai Noon' style and to two other completely unnamed styles. If Uechi Kanbun's Sifu was indeed one of the greatest 'kempo' ('Fist art'/Kung Fu) masters alive, his school or style does not seem to have survived, except perhaps the elements (according to the above account) that were incorporated into Uechi Ryu Karate. My personal view regarding this matter remains that it is the three kata, Sanchin, Sesian and Sanseirui that form the only reliable evidence for the stock-in-trade kata taught at the Kojo kwoon/Ryukyu Kan during the mid to late nineteenth century, and it is these kata that form the backbones of both Goju Ryu and Uechi Ryu Karate. Besides, it is now common knowledge that Uechi Kanbun did indeed study at the Kojo kwoon/Ryukyu Kan, although it is unknown for how long.

During his stay in China, Uechi began to sell medicine on street corners – a popular means of livelihood for Quan-Fa students (and it seems masters) at that time. Later, allegedly after obtaining permission to teach Quan-fa, he set up a school in the province of Nansoue in 1907 after ten years of training, only returning to Okinawa in 1910. Actually the dates don't quite add up, but I guess they are near enough. Uechi returned to Okinawa disguised as a Chinese to avoid detection by the authorities, and to avoid the fate of his friend Matsuda who had been imprisoned on his return to Okinawa, eight years earlier. Uechi Kanbun met with and befriended (and according to some sources taught) Wu Xiangui (Gokenki) whilst in China. Wu Xiangui would later have considerable influence upon early Karate pioneers, particularly Miyagi Chojun, Kiyoda Juhatsu, and Mabuni Kenwa.

After an incident in China, in which one of Uechi's students (or Uechi himself) allegedly killed someone in self defence, Kanbun got the blame, and it was this that made him return to Okinawa determined never to teach Quan-fa or even discuss it again; a determination he kept until 1924 when, after moving to Japan, he met a young Okinawan called Tomoyose Ryuyu who suspected Kanbun knew Quan-fa and slowly coaxed him first into discussing it and eventually into teaching it. In about 1926, Kanbun agreed to teach publicly and recruited mostly Okinawan students in Wakiyama prefecture where he taught until 1947.

Uechi Kanbun passed on *three* kata: Open-handed Sanchin, Seisan (Sesan/Seshian) and San-shi-liu (Sanjuroku/Sanseirui). The Sanchin still practiced in Uechi Ryu today is practiced with open hands, takes nine steps, and is practiced with turns. As I have said, it is in fact most likely the Sanchin once practiced by Higaonna Kanyro. It is important to note that Uechi never taught his (more traditional) kata on Okinawa and that when he did eventually begin to teach he did so in Japan. If Uechi Kanbun *had* taught on Okinawa, his kata (learned later than Higaonna's) could have been directly compared with those of the emerging Goju Ryu style, a style which had already – by that time – greatly modified its kata. Such a situation would probably have raised some interesting questions.

Concerning the Origin of Goju-Ryu Kata

At this point I would like to take another look at the conservative attitudes prevalent in China when Higaonna (Miyagi's teacher) and Uechi Kanbun, were learning Quan-fa, and Wai Xianxian was teaching it during the mid-to late-nineteenth century. But this time, I will digress into the controversy surrounding the creation and lineage of the world famous Chinese style of 'Pa Kua Chang' (eight 'trigrams' palm) during the mid nineteenth century. I do so because there are parallels in the disguised lineages of Goju Ryu Karate, and Pa Kua Chang.

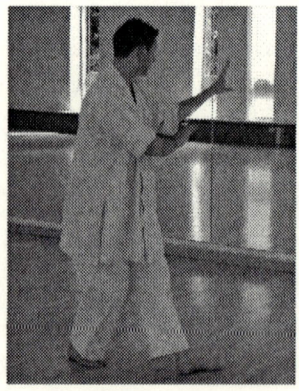

Pa Kua Chang

Without going into too much detail, Pa Kua Chang is considered to be one of China's most important 'internal', 'soft' or flowing Martial Arts, the origin of which allegedly stretches back into the legendary mists of time, a time of Taoist sages and saints. In short, it is often portrayed as being extremely ancient.

In an article by J. Kwong and Ming Lee regarding the genesis of the Pa Kua Chang style (Inside Kung Fu, Burbank CA Nov 1986), the authors note that the Beijing Wu Shu Research Institute investigated 650 cases and conducted over 250 interviews to establish the origins of Pa Kua. Further data collected by the Institute led it to conclude that Pa Kua Chang was created during the mid nineteenth century by Tung Hai Chuan, a native of Hopei province, and an expert in a style of northern Shao-lin Quan-fa that favoured using the palm to deflect and strike. I will quote from the article here,

> ... According to the Beijing Association [Wu Shu Research Institute] Tung [Tung Hai Chuan the founder of Pa Kua] travelled to the provinces south of the Yangtze river and met Taoist priests who practiced a method of moving meditation and chi kung [health exercises] that involved walking in a circle. Tung learned the way of the Taoist moving meditation and then combined those techniques with martial arts movements based on his training in northern Shao-lin. This gave birth to Pa Kua Chang. The art became quite popular in Beijing from 1866–1894 [please bear in mind, Higaonna Kanryo was studying *Sanchin* on Okinawa in and around the time of the first 'exposé' of Pa Kua in Beijing during the 1860s!] ... Because of the conservative nature of China during this period, anything old or traditional was considered good [the prevalent Confucian ethic of the time]. *It was unacceptable for students to deviate from the chosen way. This thinking forced many masters to claim different or untraceable lineages to gain legitimacy for their innovations.* (Parenthesis and italics mine)

This, I suggest, was the route taken first by Higaonna and later by Miyagi. Both were innovators. The same seems to be true regarding Itosu.

According to Higaonna Morio (b. 1939) in his *The History of Karate* (Okinawan Goju Ryu) p.138:

> Our bu [budo/art/, referring expressly here to the kata Saifa, Seyunchin, Shisochin, Sanseru, Sepai, Kururunfa, Sesan and Suparinpei] was brought back *unchanged* from China by Kanryo Higaonna Sensei and, with the exception of Sanchin kata, that is how they are taught today ... (Parenthesis mine)

Miyagi, by his own admission, changed the *fundamental* kata, Sanchin, and reportedly, stated,

> ... through my own research, I created a version of Sanchin where one steps first forward and then backwards.

Miyagi also discarded the original opening of Sanchin kata and used instead the Musubi dachi (heels together) position with the hands crossed (left palm upon the back of the right hand, fingers pointing down) in front of the tanden (lower belly) for the openings of *all* Goju Ryu kata. Strangely this hand positioning is often used in Shuri/Tomari *Naihanchin*, but had not been previously used in Naha-te. Uechi Ryu Karate still opens Sanchin in typical Fujianese style. This alone is evidence of change, however minor, plus the fact that Goju kata betray a connection with Miyagi's/Higaonna's closed-fist Sanchin. As noted earlier, Goju Ryu Sesan and Sanseru start the same way, with closed-fists. Originally the hands were open! These 'alterations' might seem petty to the reader, but they actually indicate the tip of the proverbial iceberg. Uechi Ryu Sanchin, *Seisan* (Sesan) and *Sanseirui* (Sanseru) retain their original Chinese structure which is intimately linked with their practical applications using Sai. Besides, in respect of the persistent assertion by some teachers that the Goju Ryu kata were taken unchanged from China, added to the smoke screen clouding the identity of Ryu Ryu Ko, and the anomaly of too many kata, then there seems to be an insistence that brings to mind the old-fashioned quote, 'Methinks he doth protest too much!' Meaning, due to over-reaction, the accuracy of the claim becomes difficult to accept literally.

I find it fascinating that Miyagi had learned only *two* kata (Sanchin and Seisan) by 1910 – following roughly the usual 'three years, one kata' – after starting his training in 1902/3, and that given that his teacher died in 1915, Miyagi allegedly still learned six or seven other kata in only three years from Higaonna, which is inconsistent with Higaonna's well-known conservative and traditional teaching methods (also, Miyagi missed tuition for two years, between 1910 and 1912). According to George Mattson, Uechi Kanbun displayed a similar conservative tendency and taught (and I quote) 'very slowly'.

I am well aware that kata can be superficially learned at a rapid rate, but accelerated learning seems to be against the norm of the day and against the previous *recorded* track-record of Higaonna Kanryo! For such a thing to happen seems very odd indeed, particularly when other students seem to have learned only the standard three, Sanchin, Seisan (Sesan) and Sanseirui (Sanseru) kata (or less). It has been suggested that Miyagi Chojun was chosen as Higaonna's successor, hence the accelerated learning and favoritism. I know of no records stating such, besides, Miyagi's senior must be considered. For example, it is well known that in 1912, Miyagi's 'senpai' (senior) Kiyoda Juhatsu started to learn a third kata, Sanseirui (which Miyagi did not know at the time) whilst Miyagi was away in Kyushu, mainland Japan. Miyagi was a conscript in the Japanese army between 1910 and 1912, so, not only did he miss two years instruction, but he also missed learning Sanseirui (Sanseru) kata at that time. *Currently there is some controversy over whether Higaonna Kanryo ever personally taught it to him at all.* Matayoshi Shimpo, son of Matayoshi Shinko a student of Wu Xiangui (Gokenki) and a contemporary of Miyagi Chojun's, claimed that Miyagi did not learn Sanseirui (Sanseru) from Higaonna. If correct, this proves to be extremely problematic! If Miyagi did not even learn Sanseirui from Higaonna, how did he manage to learn all the other kata? Where did they come from? Incidentally, Matayoshi Shinko (amongst others) is the source of much Kobudo later inherited by Karate-ka of many styles. I raise this point to support the fact that *Karate kata were (largely) inherited separately from the art(s) of Kobudo.*

It is interesting to note that on page 53 of Morio Higaonna's 'History of Karate' there is a questionable account of Miyagi Chojun's first visit to China during which – it is reported – he met a (perplexingly unnamed) fellow student of Higaonna's to whom he allegedly demonstrated eight kata: Sanchin, Saifa, Seiyunchin, Shisochin, Sepai, Kururunfa, Sesan and Superinpei. If the report is even remotely accurate, the old man who, as Miyagi's senior by far, must have been either very benign, or possibly offended or bored at the length of the demonstration. The inference is that the old man was (genuinely) interested in the protracted demonstration given by the junior and foreign Okinawan, *which must have surely required the participants to at least have engaged in the civility of exchanging names!* The old man supposedly pointed-out that Miyagi had missed-out Sanseru (Sanseirui) kata, to which Miyagi reportedly responded that he had not shown it because it was his least favourite!

Although I'm not the first to suggest that Miyagi Chojun still did not 'know' Sanseirui very well (if at all) at the time of the alleged meeting, I suggest that it is much more likely for the patience (not to mention the respect due to this senior figure) of the old man to be considerably stretched by watching just *two* of the familiar old three kata (Sanchin, Seisan, Sanseirui). If this account holds any veracity, then clearly Sanseirui was not demonstrated for obvious reasons. It has been speculated that Kiyoda Juhatsu taught Sanseirui to Miyagi some time after 1912, but I'm not convinced of this.

Early Miyagi students, like Higa Seko (1898–1966) and Shinzato Jinnan (1901–1945), only seemed to have originally learned (and in the order given) Sanchin, Seisan, and *Rokushu*; Rokushu being the very kata allegedly brought back by Miyagi from the visit in question. Note that Sanseirui is again conspicuous by its absence. In respect of Rokushu, it is my view that Miyagi Chojun synthesised a series of wrist and arm movements that comprised the 'Rokushu' (six variations / varieties) techniques (perhaps not an actual kata) into Tensho kata. These 'exercises' are practiced in To-on Ryu where they follow (in chronological order) Sanchin. Similar techniques can also be seen at the start (and repeated later) of the synthetic (modern) Uechi Ryu kata Konchin, created by Uechi Kanei in 1960.

Perhaps the mention of the other six kata in the account of Miyagi visiting with the unnamed student of 'Ryu Ryu Ko' is an attempt to place these kata earlier in time (history), thus giving them an earlier date than that of their (much later) acquisition/modification or conception. I suspect that the extra kata were sandwiched between Sanchin and Tensho, Miyagi's first synthesis, with the Sesian kata eventually being pushed further back as the Goju Ryu kata grew in number. In Goju Ryu Karate, Sesian kata no longer follows Sanchin. Further evidence for Miyagi having not learned Sanseriui from Higaonna Kanyro can be construed from a question asked, and an answer given, during an interview conducted by Mike Clarke with Higaonna Morio in Tokyo during 1987 (*F.A.I.* No 45 pg 14). The question is in respect of trying to trace Miyagi Chojun's movements during his first visit to China, after Higaonna Kanyro's death (some sources claim he went before Higaonna died).

[Q.] Did anyone remember Miyagi Chojun Sensei?

[A.] No, but this is not surprising because he was there for only a short time. He met with a student of Ryu Ryu Ko Sensei and trained with him studying '*Sanseru*' (Sanseirui). (Parenthesis mine)

Again it is vexing that there is no mention of a name.

Kata were at a premium at that time, and they were withheld until the student was deemed to be 'ready'. As mentioned elsewhere, the usual time-frame for learning a kata was to study one kata for three years – three kata in nine years. How or why did/could Miyagi Chojun have acquired an extra six or seven kata so quickly (between 1912 and 1915)?

The late Toguchi Sekichi, informs us in his book *Okinawan Goju-Ryu*, p.161:

> … The phrase "Three year Sanchin" was heard often at our training sessions.

This indicates that the slow (traditional) teaching method was still in place during the 1930s when Mr Toguchi was learning Karate from both Miyagi Chojun and Higa Seko. Higa was one of Miyagi's eldest and most senior students, being only ten years younger than Miyagi, and a former student of Higaonna Kanyro.

Higa Seko

Yet another question is begging. Why didn't early Naha-te (fledgling Goju Ryu) students see each other's kata (other than Sanchin, which seems to have been the only kata open to everyone)? I suspect they may well have been exposed to other kata (practiced by individuals) but the important point is, perhaps students were inculcated into a belief system that only accepted as valid, kata *directly* taught by the Sensei.

Later, Higa Seko, and others, began to trade kata with each other, much to Miyagi's annoyance, according to some sources. They probably did so to create a common training syllabus. Proving that until this period Goju Ryu was not then the unified system it is currently presented as now. I suggest that Miyagi Chojun was a reformer first and a traditionalist second.

An accusation levelled against the senior and influential Higa Seko was that he did not learn 'certain kata' *directly* from Miyagi Chojun. This is evidence of the belief system that only accepted as valid, kata *directly* taught by the Sensei. But the general application of this belief system renders Miyagi liable to the same charge vis-à-vis his sources for Sanseirui (and other kata). Higa was, as I mentioned, a former student of Kanryo Higaonna (Miyagi's teacher), and had begun to learn Sanchin kata before most of those who would later become Miyagi's senior students were even born! Further, Higa practiced some of the earliest 'versions' of Goju Ryu kata before they were 'standardised' or in some cases totally reformed. Some he probably wasn't on hand to learn because they hadn't been 'refined' (created?). In some 'Higa kata' there were even turns that went in the opposite direction to the 'standard' form. It is claimed that Higa's Suparinpei contained many differences. *Where* why and *how* Higa's kata differ from 'other' Goju Ryu kata is very interesting, and a study of this could probably tell quite a tale!

Brian Frost, the 7th degree black belt National Director for Koei-Kan Karate in the United States, and a former Uchi Deshi (live in student) of Onishi Eizo, records in his book, *Koei-Kan Karate-Do*, (Berkley, California, Frog Ltd. 1998) p.14:

> ... Ruruko [Ryu Ryu Ko] taught Master Higaonna the *five* forms (Kata) that became the foundation of Okinawan Naha-te ... (Parenthesis mine)

It is interesting that only *five* forms are mentioned (see below).

Mr. Frosts' teacher, Onishi Eizo was a prominent student of the well-respected Okinawan Shuri-te stylist, Toyama Kanken (1888–1966 – a contemporary of Miyagi Chojun) and also of Kiyoda Juhatsu, from whom he learned Naha-te, being eventually given permission to found Koei-Kan Karate by both masters. The *five* (Naha) kata enumerated in Frosts' book and in the official Koei-Kan curriculum are: *Sanchin*, *Seisan* and *Sanseirui*, to which are added, *Sepai* and *Suparinpei*. Given the fact that Toyama Kanken's (Naha-te) instructor was Kiyoda Juhatsu who in turn was (as I have said) Miyagi Chojun's *senior* under Higaonna Kanyro, one must ask why the kata, *Saifa*, *Seiyunchin*, *Shisochin*, *Kururunfa* and *Tensho* are absent from the Koei-Kan curriculum? – Or indeed from To-on Ryu, Kiyoda's style (so named by combining the Kanji or characters that make up Higaonna's name). If Toyama had not learned all the kata and had five kata missing, how could he have obtained permission from Kiyoda Juhatsu to found a school?

In fact, it is well known that Kiyoda Juhatsu practiced Sanchin, Sesian and Sanseirui, later acquiring Nipaipo (or *Nepai*, not Sepai) and the ubiquitous Peichurin (rather than Miyagi's Suparinpei), from Wu Xiangui. Kiyoda therefore, did not learn or practice other kata associated with Goju Ryu and allegedly passed-down by Higaonna Kanyro, as some sources insist.

Kata Restructuring Continues

As the art of Karate developed and evolved, some Sensei taught different things to different people at different times, *as their own understanding increased*, or developed. I repeat; ... as the art of Karate developed and evolved, some Sensei taught different things to different people at different times, *as their own understanding increased*, or developed. A Sensei may well have been developing or re-structuring kata, or devising *applications* over a number of years, and taught the things that he/she was interested in and involved in, to whomever he/she happened to be teaching at the time. This was particularly the case when Chinese Quan-fa was haphazardly introduced on Okinawa, before the advent of modern syllabus-based training regimes, and the insistence of subsequent senior teachers that they held the 'keys' to sacrosanct and time-honoured 'traditions'.

Anthony Mirakian (a long time student of the late Yagi Meitoku, one of the most senior Goju masters), was one of the first foreign students to begin Karate training on Okinawa in the early 1950s. This was not long after Miyagi's death. Mirakian personally knew Karate greats such as Uechi *Kanei*, Nagamine Shoshin, Chibana Chosin, and – more importantly for this – discussion, *Higa Seko*. Mirakian was asked in an interview (in *F.A.I.* no 68. 1991), if Miyagi Chojun had made any *changes* to the Naha system that he inherited from Higaonna Kanryo; he replied:

> Yes, Grandmaster Miyagi studied with Grandmaster Kanryo Higaonna ... and upon the masters death went to China for two years to conduct further research into the martial arts. While he was in China he met and befriended the Chinese Go Ken Kin [Wu Xiangui/Gokenki] and travelled around with him to several provinces studying with a number of great Chinese masters. When Chojun Miyagi returned to Okinawa, he decided to take the art of *Naha-te* and expose it to scientific scrutiny. His

approach was very critical and *he disregarded the techniques that did not meet strict scientific standards.* [What standards were these I wonder, and what techniques were 'discarded'?] Chojun Miyagi incorporated many Chinese martial arts techniques which he had learned while in China [in] to the Naha-te system of karate. [He introduced more material, but where did he house it?] He refined the existing kata ... (Parenthesis and italics mine)

Yet these are the kata that – as I have shown – some sources *repeatedly* claim came back from China unchanged and remain unchanged! Moreover Higa was not the only one whose kata were 'different'. Eiko Miyazato (not *Eiichi* Miyazato) initially trained with Miyagi's senior, Kiyoda and stated that there were a number of differences between the teachings of the two Sensei; in particular he noticed that the Sesan (Seisan) kata he learned from the two Sensei were *markedly different.* Goju Sesan (Seisan) is singular and differs considerably from the Seisan of Uechi Ryu Karate, which retains the original Chinese structure. In short, the Goju Ryu version is *heavily* modified. By observing and comparing these kata, and wherever possible understanding the functions, the genesis of Okinawan (Goju Ryu) Karate becomes much clearer.

At a famous meeting between several Karate masters on Okinawa in 1936, Miyagi Chojun was asked a question by a Mr. Oroku Chotei:

> Oroku: "Mr Miyagi, did you go to China with resolve to study Karate (Quan-fa/To-te)?"

> Miyagi: "Although I didn't initially train in China, I went there after recognizing that it was the place I would have to go for more advanced Chuan-fa [Quan-fa] studies." (Parenthesis mine)

It's quite clear from this statement that Miyagi Chojun was still seeking something, and it seems he did not feel he had inherited a complete system or enough 'material'. After visiting China, Miyagi's To-te changed rapidly, and Higa Seko was around to witness it. It was also at that time that Miyagi observed Rokushu quan, allegedly in Fuzhou. He was later to synthesize it into Tensho kata, which he highlighted as co-equal with Sanchin, as noted earlier – Sanchin allegedly being the 'Go' or hard and Tensho the 'Ju' or soft aspect of his emerging style.

As I have already said, Miyagi gave great prominence to Rokushu/Tensho a quan/kata not taught to him by Higaonna, and most likely unknown to Higaonna. This can be supported by his own statements, and those of his prominent students, students such as Yamaguchi Yoshime (1909 to 1989 – aka Yamaguchi Gogen 'The cat'). Yamaguchi considered Sanchin and Tensho to be the 'twin jewels' in the 'crown of Goju Ryu Karate and said so, many times.

According to Higaonna Morio, there was a 'disagreement' between Miyagi and Higa some-where around 1931. Higa was thirty-three years of age, with approximately *twenty years* of Karate experience, and Miyagi was forty-three years old, with around *thirty years* of Karate experience. Allegedly, the 'disagreement' prompted Higa to open his own Dojo, against Miyagi's wishes or without his permission. One wonders what gave Higa the confidence to do such a thing. Hokama Tetsuhiro,

Yamaguchi Gogen

an Okinawan Goju Ryu Shihan (master teacher) claims that Miyagi *authorised* Higa to teach. It is well known that Toguchi Seikichi, a senior Miyagi student, ran a Dojo *under* the auspices of Higa, suggesting that there must have been some kind of 'fluid', if not 'interactive' relationship. In Toguchi's book, *Okinawan Goju-Ryu (The) Fundamentals of Shorei-Kan Karate* (Burbank CA, Ohara: 1975) it is stated in the section entitled 'About the Author' that, "... he studied Karate under Master Chojun Miyagi and his assistant, Mr Seko Higa ..." I note that Miyagi Chojun (Okinawa, 1934, Karate Do Gaisetsu) mentions Higa Seko, as an active To-te/Karate instructor on Okinawa, so one naturally wonders about the degree of estrangement and the severity of any 'disagreement'.

I remind the reader that, reporting claims and counter-claims is not the point here. Examining claims and contrasting them, rather that taking one view at face value (depending upon which faction one belongs to), helps to paint a greater picture of the development of Goju Ryu Karate and the *origins* of its kata, and the relationships between these and other Karate kata, particularly the (extant) original versions.

According to the veteran Goju Ryu Karate teacher Robert Taiani (*F.A.I.* No. 50, 1988, p.43):

> ... Now from what I have been told on Okinawa, it was Master Seiko Higa, a student of Master Miyagi, who developed a system of kata order and also various basic drills ... It was Higa sensei who put it all together ...

One wonders how much input there was from Higa for the genesis of Goju Ryu Karate, in possible *collaboration* with Miyagi Chojun, and what issues led to the later political infighting engaged in by their various students.

My reservations concerning the genesis of Goju Ryu kata are not based on political heresay but on the unlikely *absolute breaking* of tradition that would have been required to allow Higaonna in particular, but Miyagi also (both considered to be traditionalists from traditional backgrounds) to learn so many kata, against the norms of the periods during which they studied. I do not accept the 'chosen student' hypothesis as I have made plain. Besides, the 'chosen student' scenario, no matter how often it is presented, is unethical and can no more be justified than any other prejudices or biases one would expect a true master to be beyond! In short, the 'chosen student' scenario is nothing more than a political tool. How many contemporaneous 'Grandmasters' are there in the various traditions? In Goju Ryu, there were several (not one!), after Miyagi Chojun's death; and fine masters they proved to be too!

Regarding the type of individual training given by Miyagi Chojun, here is a quote from an interview with the late Miyazato Eiichi (1922–1999), a former student of Miyagi's between 1938 and 1953. Miyazato Eiichi was the first head of the Jundokan Karate dojo in the Asato district of Naha Okinawa, where a concentration of pre-World War Two students of Miyagi Chojun, and some new recruits, banded together to continue 'Following in the footsteps of the Father' as it has been claimed the name of the Dojo implies.

Miyazato Eiichi

The interview begins on page 166 of Higaonna Morio's, *The History of Karate Okinawan Goju Ryu.*

> Higaonna: What was Chojun Miyagi Sensei's teaching like?
>
> Miyazato: We didn't have group training, he taught us individually. We all had different years and levels of experience, so he taught us individually …

But it seems that no matter how advanced a student became, he seldom seemed to learn more than 3 (the 'golden number') kata! Moreover, I can hardly find any Miyagi students from the period 1915 to 1945 who knew more than three kata; and those kata seemed to vary. Some examples of the kata taught to senior students follows.

Higa Seko	1898–1966	*Sanchin* (originally learned from Higaonna Kanryo), *Sesan* and *Tensho* (later Seyunchin).
Yagi Meitoku	1912–2003	Sanchin and Suparinpei (Peichurin)
Shinzato Jinnan	1901–1945	*Sanchin, Sesan* and *Tensho*
Kina Seiko	1911–1994	Sanchin and Seiyunchin (originally)

Others include, Furugen Shunshin, who learned Sanchin and Kururunfa and Tomoyose Keie, who learned Sanchin and Sepai only.

Shinzato was considered to be Miyagi's favourite pre-war student, and Higa seems to be one of his first students. It's interesting that Higa and Shinzato, born only three years apart, learned Sanchin, Sesan and Tensho. I would suggest that Miyagi had a soft spot for Tensho (Rokushu) the Quan-fa form he added independently, c. 1917. As noted, Higa was born in 1898 and Shinzato in 1901.

There are many other Miyagi students who learned only two or three kata, but I have compiled the abbreviated list above mainly to show the *variety* of kata being taught and to illustrate that; either the collection of kata that was later to become part of the 'official' Goju Ryu syllabus had not been conceived of at that time, or that such a large number of kata were deemed unnecessary for all but the progenitor/founder/researcher of a Ryu; a full time teacher, a teacher like Miyagi Chojun.

The Myth of the 'Subjective' Allocation of Kata

If the late Goju Ryu grandmaster, Yagi Meitoku (Meibukan), as a student, could jump, from Sanchin (the basic kata) to Superimpei (allegedly the ultimate and most advanced Karate kata, excepting perhaps Tensho) what was the purpose of all the other kata deemed to be? One often-proffered answer to that question is that the 'master' (psychologically?) profiled a student and selected and taught him/her an appropriate kata to supplement Sanchin, which seems to be the only kata common to all (Naha-te) students during the period under discussion. However, this suggests that the To-te (Karate) instructor also had to be a psychologist and measure the student's worth, asses their aptitude, determine their loyalty, calculate their current physical ability (in the case of the young, their future physical, mental and spiritual potential too), establish their character, ascertain their commitment, and so on. The list is endless, and although it has been claimed that this was the 'way things were done back then', the reader will kindly pardon my scepticism concerning the efficacy and morality of such an arbitrary approach to what became for many people a lifetime's interest and study. I rather suspect that this thinking is part of a modern mythology, a mythology that helps to conceal the rapid and relatively late development of Goju Ryu (and other) Karate.

Despite the secrecy in which early Karate was once practiced, the Karate of Miyagi's era was seldom used in actual fighting (except amongst certain troublesome youths). Even Motobu, allegedly the most troublesome Karate 'street-fighter', managed to receive instruction from at least three teachers (including Itosu Ankho) and learned at least three or four (standard) kata, including Naihanchin – his mainstay kata. And although Karate was treated with a certain 'gravitas' it was actually a fledgling art – teachers were 'finding their way' with a newly evolving art and in a newly evolving Okinawan society.

Itosu Ankho and Funakoshi Gichin did not stress or even practice the 'tailoring' of kata to suite the individual, and neither to my knowledge did Higaonna Kanyro or Uechi Kanbun. Such is definitely not a part of contemporary Goju Ryu Karate which now has a progressive syllabus in place. Any *supposition* regarding selective discrimination (in respect of the quan/kata taught), is just that, a supposition, ultimately a falling back on the apparent 'inscrutability' and fickle nature of some Qing dynasty Quan-fa Sifu. An example that helps to question this is the teaching method of Yip Man (1896–1972), the first patriarch of the Southern Chinese Kung Fu system Wing Chun. Although teaching a generation later, Yip Man taught the same quan to each of his students, as did his forbears. I have black and white film footage of him performing them, and they are the same quan taught to me in my own home, over twenty years ago by Yip Chun, his eldest son.

The lack of 'standard', or even reliable, kata applications must have exacerbated the situation, for the developing art of Karate, and within the Naha-te tradition, the 'favourite student' explanation has become the usual and unchallenged justification for different people learning different kata and 'applications' (or no applications) at different times. One rationalization offered in mitigation, is the euphemism that, 'things change', coupled with, Western and therefore non Confucian idea of progress and notions of 'secrets' are of course common and quite popular.

Strands of evidence can be woven together to create a more revealing picture, regarding the proliferation of kata. It is a picture that suggests that, in the absence of satisfactory applications to existing 'old style quan', new kata were synthesised or invented. If you want to know the application to a kata, wouldn't it be convenient if you could ask the person who created it? Or if not, create kata yourself? Lack of proper applications to kata have long been the bane of traditionally minded Karate-ka, and even at Karate's inception on Okinawa, some teachers (and some students too) were clandestinely looking for answers; Miyagi Chojun was definitely among them. It is alleged that after a disappointing visit to a teacher described as having learned the 'secrets' of Chinese boxing at Fuzhou, Miyagi lamented,

> … Once again I am groping my way along an unlit road. (*Okinawan Karate Teachers, styles and secret techniques*, Mark Bishop, London, A&C Black 1989/1991, p.30)

That Miyagi was truly searching for something other than that which he had been taught by Higaonna Kanyro is, in my mind, beyond dispute; but, if one decides to innovate (which tends to present as 'inauthentic'), how does one retain student loyalty (above and beyond the strength of personality) and ensure that one's hard work survives beyond ones own lifetime. How does one achieve this without recourse to the weight and majesty of tradition? The short answer to this question is – One doesn't! Or, one can't! Those who innovate yet present their innovations as traditional probably do so to escape (avoid) appearing to set a dangerous precedent. If you are seen to invent kata (or applications), how do you stop others from inventing kata too, or making unwelcome (further) modifications to existing kata, perhaps even your kata, your hard work? In fact I would suggest this is precisely what has happened. It's nothing new, nothing new at all. Indeed, it happened in China first.

I recognize that this type of thinking is challenging. Martial Artists believe in the masters, in the bygone days, the days of 'yore' – a golden age even. I'm not challenging that, as such, however, in contrast to the more unfathomable kata in the various Karate repertoire's, the kata in this book (perhaps with the exception of Miyagi Sanchin) do not need to 'evolve', they are *fixed formulae* that need never change whilst human anatomy remains consistent. Therefore it is perhaps best to consider them as one would consider the number system – one to ten! No need to evolve that, no need to change it.

Finally, please bear in mind, it seems that within the mainstream Karate 'traditions' a teacher must always have something to teach, sometimes even if the 'student' has over twenty years of experience. This either harks back to Confucian ideals, or suggests that the teacher needs to retain control. My experience suggests that the latter is the case, *particularly* when there is doubt and uncertainty regarding the *applications* to key kata. Such a lack creates an ever-evolving, ever-changing style in terms of *applications* and eventually in terms of ever growing nuances in solo kata; nuances that reflect the newly perceived 'applications' and give rise to another Ryu, often portrayed as traditional but often quite new.

Conserving Innovation

Karate styles or schools are generally stabilised by a 'leader' or a collective of dominant personalities. Given that the senior full-time instructors have both the status and the time to muse over their art, they usually set the standard that others follow, and that is only proper. Inevitably there will be a desire amongst inherently conservative practitioners, to stabilise and conserve an approach to Karate. Hierarchy is all important, and a perceived 'correct' way of doing things is of paramount importance in establishing a (fledgling) art, an art such as Karate, hence the so-called 'traditional styles'. Most 'traditional' Karate styles are relatively late constructions however. In fact, the four major (official) Karate styles in Japan (Shotokan, Wado Ryu, Goju Ryu and Shito Ryu) are all products of the 1920s and 1930s, although some of the kata that form their base are much older.

When Miyagi Chojun began to teach students from the Okinawan Shogyo high school, he had to think again, about what was taught and how. Toguchi Seikichi states on page 16 of his book *Okinawan Goju-Ryu: The Fundamentals of Shorei-Kan Karate*,

> ... Although a master in Goju-Ryu style (Naha-te), Master Miyagi wanted to study karate more completely. [?] He visited the most respected master of Shuri-te, Master Ankho Itosu, and asked for instruction. Master Itosu responded by saying, "You are a top disciple of Master Higashionna [Higaonna] and you have mastered Naha-te techniques. You don't need to study with me. If you watch my techniques you will see what I mean." Master Miyagi persisted, however, and often visited Master Itosu to study Shuri-te. Master Itosu did not teach Master Miyagi physical techniques; rather he taught the theory of techniques ... (Parenthesis mine)

This is quite interesting, because Itosu Ankho died in 1915. As Miyagi Chojun was on Kyushu (mainland Japan) between 1910 and 1912, the alleged visits must have happened either before 1910 or after 1912. If they happened before 1910, then Miyagi Chojun would have been anywhere between fourteen and twenty-two years of age and rather young for a master. If the alleged visits took place between 1912 and 1915, then it could be argued that Itosu's penchant for (re)structuring kata – and collecting/devising greater numbers than historically usual – may have influenced Miyagi. Yet this time period is when, according to some sources, Miyagi would have had to have been 'knuckling down' to learn a (staggering for those days) six or seven kata from Higaonna in the *three* years before Higaonna died, in or around 1915.

I don't doubt that Miyagi Chojun had a huge love of/for Karate and devoted much of his energy to it; however, there were fairly strict student/teacher protocols in those days, and it seems possible that Itosu may have been prepared to discuss kata theory with the young (Higaonna *student*) Miyagi, but not provide instruction per-se. These theories, stemming, as alleged, from the influential Itosu, may well have been contributing factors in the (re)shaping or (re)structuring of Goju Ryu Kata. One must also consider the possible rivalry between Higaonna and Itosu. Senior students of one master visiting the dojo of another master can be problematic, even today.

Probably following the experience of Itosu Ankho, Miyagi *invented* kata for high school student Karate beginners. As I mentioned earlier, he altered Sanchin (the fundamental kata), created at least two other kata and modified Rokushu. But did his creative abilities in kata stretch any further?

After Miyagi's death in 1953, and when the Jundokan Dojo came into existence in 1957, there was a need for uniformity and conformity, so a training syllabus was put in place. As far as I am aware the kata taught were, Gekisai Dai Ichi and Dai Ni,

Sanchin, Saifa, Seiyunchin, Shisochin, Sanseru, Sepai, Kururunfa, Sesan, Suparinpei and finally Tensho. Gekisai Dai Ichi and Dai Ni were created in 1940 by Miyagi Chojun (Goju Ryu) in collaboration with Nagamine Shoshin (Matsubayashi Shorin Ryu). In Matsubayashi Shorin Ryu these kata are referred to as Fukyugata, and there are slight differences (see *The Essence of Okinawan Karate-Do* by Shoshin Nagamine, Rutland Vermont, Tokyo, Tuttle: 1976, p.104.) *However, I repeat, I can find no substantial evidence that Higaonna Kanryo taught anything other than Sanchin, Sesan (Seisan) and Sanseru (Sanseirui) kata!*

A Proposed Okinawan Genesis for Goju Ryu Kata

Having definitely restructured Rokushu to become Tensho kata, and having changed Sanchin kata, did Miyagi – going along with the tide of change begun by Itosu – re-structure many 'new' kata in a radical departure from tradition? Could Miyagi have restructured Sesan and Sanseirui quan to make them conform to the closed-fist Sanchin, and then go on to create/modify, Saifa, Seiyunchin, Shisochin, Sepai, Kururunfa and Suparinpei kata? As I mentioned, he certainly co-created two Gekisai kata and Tensho kata, and he devised a systematic set of warm-up exercises (junbi undo) to complement his vision of a complete art, an Okinawan art.

It has always been *assumed* that the Saifa, Seiyunchin, Shisochin, Sepai, Kururunfa, and Suparinpei kata originated in China. The *names* of these kata can be matched in Chinese. The Kanji (brushed characters) remain the same, only the pronunciations vary, and they translate into both Fuzhou dialect and Mandarin. *However, Chinese quan bearing the same or similar names are entirely different from Goju Ryu kata.* As an aside (or a trivial observation) it's very curious that so many Goju kata (eight out of twelve) begin with 'S', Sanchin, Sesan, Sanseirui, Saifa,

Seiyunchin, Shisochin, Sepai, Suparinpei! Not a common occurrence in any other style, except of course Uechi Ryu with similar roots in the Kojo kwoon/dojo and the three main kata beginning with the 'S' sound.

Whatever the case is, taking a look at the two basic Naha-te Sanchin, Goju Ryu and Uechi Ryu, reveals them to be uncannily similar. It really seems most likely that they share a common origin (Fuzhou Quan-fa taught by Wai Xianxian). So once again I turn my attention to the known Chinese quan; Sanchin, Seisan (Sesan) and Sanseirui (Sanseru) and question the lineage or more properly the genesis of other so called Naha Kata. They're absent from Uechi Ryu and the only possible link they have with China is through Higaonna Kanryo, but I have illustrated that the balance of probability suggests Higaonna is not responsible for the dissemination of the kata Saifa, Seyunchin, Shisochin, Sanseru, Sepai, Kururunfa, Suparinpei, and most definitely not Tensho.

I have raised problematic questions in respect of the genesis of Goju Ryu Karate kata but they are in no way intended to denigrate or malign the reputations of Higaonna Kanryo or Miyagi Chojun – a Sensei who should be considered as a major pioneering influence on the development of Karate. It was he who forged Naha-te into a truly Okinawan empty hand art. Through hard work, self-sacrifice and commitment to ideals, Miyagi created 'strong' Okinawan Karate out of the Chinese Quan-fa from the Qing dynasty and later Republican China.

Perhaps Miyagi Chojun should receive more credit for the codification/organisation of, or even the *construction* (in part) of, Saifa, Seiyunchin, Shisochin, Sepai, Kururunfa, and to some extent Suparinpei kata, than he is currently credited with. Like Funakoshi Gichin of Shuri-te, Miyagi guided the former 'closed door' Chinese Quan-fa through a period of transition when it was simply identified as To-te through to the new and re-defined, internationally recognised art of Karate enjoyed by several millions of people worldwide.

I'm sure some people will be uncomfortable with certain issues being raised here, and some readers will doubtless dislike my conclusions, but as stated earlier, the present author is not bound by political allegiance or 'corporate' loyalty.

There is no doubt that the Goju Ryu style created by Miyagi Chojun (who had made Karate his regular – though largely unpaid – occupation) overshadowed and eclipsed the 'To-on Ryu' created by Kiyoda Juhatsu, whose day job was as the principal of a school. And Miyagi's trips(s) to China, and his independent income, at a time when many Okinawans were extremely poor, undoubtedly gave him extra 'kudos'. However, both Kiyoda and Miyagi originally had the same teacher, and both were also influenced by the Chinese tea merchant Wu Xiangui (Gokenki) from whom, as was mentioned earlier Kyoda learned Nipaipo, a quan/kata actually from the line of Xie Zhongxiang (Ryu Ryu Ko, according to Patrick McCarthy) and it must be remembered that Kiyoda was Miyagi's senior, in a hierarchical structure that was traditionally inflexible.

Miyagi Chojun created his own fame. He produced *many* fine Karate-ka who have in turn produced many other fine Karate-ka. He crafted his reputation by effort and the conception and promotion of nothing less than a truly Okinawan empty hand art, Goju Ryu Karate. His achievements speak for themselves! However, issues of 'tradition' are problematic in respect of much Okinawan and Japanese Karate.

Finally (technically), I view Goju Ryu Sanchin as an empty hand kata, central to the concept of 'Karate'(empty hand), Rokushu as an expansion, a supporting (empty hand) kata, and Naihanchin as the essence of unarmed (grappling) Shuri-te/Shorin Ryu. I regard Uechi Ryu Sanchin, Seisian and Sanseirui kata, as (To-te) Kobodo weapons (Sai) kata, and as I said in chapter one, I view the Shuri-te or Shorin Ryu kata, Passai, Chinto, and Kusanku as Kobudo weapons (Sai) kata not Karate – not 'empty hands'.

To-te – Experimentation and Synthesis

Nagamine Shoshin laments in his *Tales of Okinawa's Greatest Masters*, p.121:

> ... It was purely by chance that such a profound defensive tradition ascended and was handed down in such historical circumstances. Yet on the other hand, under the weight of Satsuma's restriction on religious practices, the tradition failed to incorporate and emphasize spiritual principles.

Whilst I think this may largely be true, it is in direct contrast to Matsumura's (seven) virtues of Bu, quoted in the introduction:

> ... *Bu* prohibits violence, maintains discipline amongst soldiers, keeps control among the civil population, spreads virtue, creates a peaceful heart, helps keep the peace between people and makes folk or a nation prosperous ...

Matsumura was a well educated man with excellent social standing. Employed in the Palace at Shuri and serving no less than three Okinawan kings, Matsumura was probably not a typical exponent of To-te, but, as an acknowledged 'Bushi' he was undoubtedly an important role model.

I repeat a point made in the introduction. The Satsuma subjugation of Okinawa was responsible for the clandestine spread of To-te Jutsu, but not as erroneously believed, so that individuals could fight with or even defend against well-armed well-trained and ruthless Samurai, but so that, given the weapons ban in place, national pride and cultural independence could be maintained, and those with Martial inclinations could at least pursue some kind of physical – albeit unarmed – Martial Arts training, *unknown by, and unknown to their oppressors.*

Please bear in mind that (arguably) Okinawa's first 'Bushi' of note, connected with To-te was Kanga Teruya (To-te Sakugawa) who was born (according to Nagamine Shoshin) in the late eighteenth century (1782). He could not have begun to study To-te until the nineteenth century – say around 1810 – assuming that the earliest age he started training at was fourteen. So, the whole 'tradition' sprang up quite late. Karate (as such) has not – as some writers would have us believe – existed for thousands of years. It's relatively new, even in Okinawa, but *particularly* in Japan. Karate did not start to be propagated in Japan until the 1920s, and even then it met with resistance, for cultural and aesthetic reasons. It wasn't even called Karate at that time but was still referred to as To-te Jutsu. To-te Jutsu did not officially become 'Karate' until 1936/37. To-te was unsystematically introduced from this period, and those with a Martial inclination sought out teachers, and gradually, the art spread. As ever with such an undertaking, there must have been a spirit of danger and adventure, and a sense of fascination with the imported somewhat 'exotic' Chinese Quan-fa. Here is a quote from page 3 (1976 reprint) of *Funakoshi Gichin's Karate – Do Kyohan*, which, although written in 1936, captures the spirit of that early time:

> In Okinawa, a *miraculous* and *mysterious* martial art has come down to us from the past … (Italics mine).

It must be born in mind that Funakoshi was born in 1868/70, and was unquestionably influenced by the political and social unrest of the period during which he studied.

The assumption that Karate was 'old hat' on Okinawa and had been around for centuries is, as I've made clear, incorrect. During the nineteenth century, Okinawan Quan-fa enthusiasts were busy trying to make head or tail out of randomly introduced Chinese Quan-fa (mostly solo kata), and a process of experimentation and synthesis began. But what is not commonly considered – due to romantic images of the 'infallibility' of early To-te and Karate pioneers – is that mistakes were almost certainly made, and excesses committed, particularly when the art entered the twentieth century. It seems, for example, that Naihanchin; a continuous grappling kata, applied against a *single* opponent, was erroneously designated as a 'block punch' kata as the emerging art of To-te began to reflect the rising militarism of the mainland Japanese.

A (partial) quote from Itosu Ankho's ten precepts of To-te (c. 1908) helps to confirm this. In precept eight he states:

> ... To visualise that one is actually engaged on the battlefield during training does much to enhance progression ...

Itosu was one of the main teachers of Naihanchin kata. But remember To-te is a *civil* art not intended for use on a battlefield.

Karate Lineages, Personalities and Puzzles

This section is added to challenge the type of politicking that seeks to benefit from suggesting that a deceased master only passed his 'secrets' on to one student, and one student only – i.e., to master 'X', who, if not the claimant himself, often (conveniently) happens to be the 'claimants' declared teacher.

Times are changing, *modern* Kung Fu/Karate instructors are now influenced by the sheer amount of easily available information on a variety of related arts, and ideas are even borrowed from 'heretical' enemy camps; you know, the styles that 'do it all wrong'. Even with the advent of commercial clubs and 'coaches', the mystique of the 'Master' still persists.

Picture this if you will: it's almost twilight; you are training in To-te/Karate on a breezy Okinawan beach near to an inlet or cove. There is no one else around except the Sensei, your Sensei. He corrects your foot position by pressing against your calf muscle with his roku-shaku bo staff. "Here." he says, gruffly moving your foot. "Hai" (yes) you respond. You are learning the most advanced kata in the Sensei's style. He is the Grandmaster of … such and such style. He's the best. You've been training with him for years. Well that's what it feels like. Actually you've only trained with him a few times over a couple of years, but anyway … once you have learned the kata, you will have a kata, a master, and a lineage! The master has chosen you. He hasn't actually told you so. You just know it … something in his eyes. You are being groomed for … you want to be …

There is of course always the story of the chosen 'disciple' the one person especially selected to learn the true system, fly the flag, bear the torch onwards, etc. I actually trained under a Kung Fu teacher whose famous master publicly made the claim that he was the only one to inherit the true, the real system, and even the master's sons had not been taught the true art. Later I trained with the (late) grandmasters eldest son. I also practiced with another of the grandmasters senior students. Suffice to say, the claim was false.

Interestingly enough, two senior masters that I met and trained with had been responsible for befriending – and in part – training the young 'Bruce Lee', under the auspices of the grandmaster. I suspect that it was the 'golden triangle' of association (the late grandmaster, Bruce Lee, and master so and so) that seems to have prompted a third senior student to claim to be the *only true* inheritor of the *secrets*. Apparently, secrets are good for business.

A wise person doesn't put all of his/her eggs in one basket. I generally treat, with the utmost suspicion – not to mention distain – claims that only one specially chosen 'disciple' inherited a Quan-fa/Karate system (especially when a Sifu/Sensei has many good students to choose from). If an art is valuable, hard-gained and passed-on to that teacher by a sharing soul who inherited or even created a tradition and worked hard within it, and if that art is socially useful and can benefit humankind, is it not an unwise, short-sighted or paranoid Sifu/Sensei that allows his/her so called 'secrets' to die with him, or even risks such by passing them on to only one person, who could, after receiving the final 'secret', get run over by a bus (read rickshaw) on the way home from the dojo or the master's house? – A so called 'master' who takes his 'secrets' to the grave with him is welcome to them!

One hackneyed reason given for this scenario is that an art is too deadly, or the current crop of students is not trustworthy enough to inherit the 'secrets'. This 'smacks' of the 'black magic' syndrome ... my art is so dangerous, so potentially lethal that it could jeopardise the whole of humankind! Now, if we're talking nuclear physics, then ... Besides, it seems to me that these 'dangerous techniques' always seem to find their way into the public domain, in print, or on film, etc. anyway. Titles using the word 'secret' are commonplace. Such secrets are of course no longer secret, if indeed they ever were. Yet people remain interested in the notion of secrets. They have a kind of novelty value which some hope can explain the inexplicable movements in the kata that they practice. There is generally only ever 'talk' about secrets and secret techniques amongst schools that practice kata. Thai boxers and the like rarely talk about secrets. Indeed, most 'secrets' turn out to be a combination of common sense, experience and lots of hard work.

In the case of many kata, the only real secret might have been that certain kata were designed to be used with weapons, but were presented as empty-hand kata instead! Perhaps the 'secret' was well kept but alluded to with admonitions from various teachers, such as: 'Train with me for long enough and you will learn my secrets.'

Of course, barring common access to something, banning it, restricting it, etc, often has the effect of promoting it, enhancing its mystique and making people want it. Thirty years ago, this was the case with the Biu – tze (fling/thrusting fingers), the (so called) deadly third form (quan) of Wing Chun Kung Fu. It was alleged (and in some associations still is) that the form is 'too deadly' to teach to just anyone. To learn that form one had to 'pay through the nose', taking (expensive) private lessons with the master to learn what was openly taught in the previous generations.

Yet another (and more modern) reason for the support of so called 'secret knowledge' is to promote the lineage of the alleged 'chosen one'. Senior students of a deceased master will often jockey for position. Politics is part of the human condition, affected as it is by motive – by what a person wants. So, if someone wishes to become the 'chosen one', what will their election ticket be? Perhaps they are the master's eldest son, or his favourite son. Perhaps they were his longest serving student. Perhaps they lived in the master's house for a while and did his cooking which allowed them to be privy to the 'secrets'. *Perhaps the 'master in-waiting' simply has more students than the other teachers, and therefore brings more revenue into a given association.* Perhaps the grandmaster elect claims to be – or is promoted as – the only one to have received all of the (secret) applications (bunkai) to the kata, or the only one to *learn* all the kata. Perhaps the candidate for grandmaster is the one the master passed his secret scrolls to (without anyone else seeing). Of course, this is all romantic nonsense, but, some people still put great stock in such things.

Another reason for the widespread acceptance of the notion of 'secret' techniques or 'hidden applications' for Karate kata, is cultural, and stems, in part, from (Western) 'Orientalism – a curious 19th century obsession with the 'mystery' of the 'Middle and Far East', and from a (general) confusion of 'function' and purpose, of and for, antique kata. From a contemporary Martial Arts perspective, the confusion between *unarmed* Okinawan To-te Jutsu, an art (of no real military value) based on modified Quan-fa, from China, and the mainland Japanese (Budo) tradition of 'gokui' or 'secret methods', is now apparent.

Gokui became a common phenomenon during the Tokugawa Shogunate (1598–1867) when rival clans sought to protect their methods and strategies in a bid to outmanoeuvre opponents in the frequent skirmishes that occurred during that period. A strong Japanese cultural impact on the Okinawan practitioners of Chinese Quan-fa (kata) designated as To-te and later Karate, created the error of applying notions of 'gokui' to Quan-fa.

This does not mean to imply that some (many in-fact) Chinese Quan-fa teachers were not secretive, however, the true confusion between the gokui – secret methods of the Budo-ka or warrior practitioners and exponents of To-te Jutsu, and later Karate, can be found in the fact that the Budo-ka were protecting methods used in *armed* conflict. The assumption that gokui applied to unarmed fighting or close quarter techniques, commonly referred to as Ju-jutsu (pliant techniques), is fundamentally flawed, as pointed out earlier. Besides, the advent of the gun, and the impact it had on the usefulness (beyond social context) of traditional Martial Arts by the end of the Japanese Shogunate, must also be considered. Also, please bear in mind that it is human nature to find mystery in the unknown. Aspects of (for example)

Funakoshi's '*miraculous* and *mysterious* martial art' (Karate) were designated as secret simply because they were not understood!

Trial and Error

There was, and remains, a continual process of 'trial and error' as far as To-te and Karate are concerned; not just in form, but most importantly in *function*, and this is nothing new. For example, anyone who trained in Karate during the early to late 1970s will have (because the essential and original functions of authentic kata remained largely unknown) experienced an almost total lack of sensible kata applications, and further experienced the 'gung ho' attitudes towards dangerous old-fashioned 'rugby style' warm-ups. These warm-ups included the unsafe hyper-extension of joints that have led to serious health consequences for some now senior Sensei. Often, brutal and dangerous training masqueraded as 'real Karate'. I personally suffered from innumerable split lips, bruised shins, cheeks, black eyes, two broken fingers, a broken nose and a nasty case of septicaemia, which, no doubt as a result of my opponent's lack of personal hygiene, required me to be hospitalised, after being 'clawed at' (breaking the skin), in a roughhouse dojo free-for-all. Those of us involved at that time thought we were supposed to become tough fighters, and we were influenced by fictitious tales connecting our practice with the Samurai code of conduct, ethics and values, improperly ascribed to the Karate training of the day. Personally, that aspect of the Martial Arts used to get me down, and still no-one really seemed to know what the kata did.

In Goju Ryu Karate, Sanchin kata practice was often so 'overdone' that practitioners suffered from hypertension and piles! And Shuri Karate, altered in Japan, advocated knee-damaging low stances and kicking techniques that alas for many instructors have led to serious knee and hip injuries, sometimes even leading to hip replacements! Hernias became common too. All the foolish and dangerous exercises and attitudes practiced at that time were a combination of experimentation, excitement at the novelty of Karate, the importation of improperly associated and misunderstood modern Japanese military attitudes (some of which were cultivated during the Russo Japanese and Sino Japanese wars at the beginning of the twentieth century), youth, hot-headedness, lack of experience, and large doses of bravado! – All in all, a great recipe for error and injury.

Kata were generally though to be, and misleadingly taught as, preparations for fights against multiple opponents. Again in the words of the late Nakayama Masatoshi, the first Chief instructor of the Japan Karate Association:

> Imaginary enemies surround the Karate-ka as he executes the four fundamental movements of the kata: uke (blocking) tsuki (punching) uchi (striking) and keri (kicking).

Funakoshi Gichin, one of Nakayama's teachers, studied Naihanchin (the bedrock kata of Shuri-te) under Itosu for ten years. He too ascribed ballistic block, punch, strike, applications to them in his book 'Karate – Do Kyohan'. Yet, in the present book, it is made absolutely plain that *Naihanchin is a Chinese grappling quan/kata*. As you are by now aware, *the fundamental Shuri kata, bedrock of the entire Shuri tradition, is a civil arrest method devised to subjugate a single opponent! There is not one block, punch or strike in the whole kata!* From a visual perspective, it looks 'solid' but oddly steps sideways. In comparison with other Shuri kata it could perhaps (mistakenly) seem a little dull. That is why, today, in many Karate schools, little regard is given to Naihanchin, other than as a stepping stone to the coveted black belt. In the Shotokan style of the Japan Karate Association, Tekki shodan (part one of Naihanchin) has to be studied to obtain the rank of 3rd Kyu brown belt.

As I have suggested, the applications to Naihanchin kata were omitted (deliberately or otherwise) by the Chinese teachers, and modern applications, stressing combat against multiple opponents, make no more sense as a means to fight multiple opponents than trying to use Sanchin or Rokushu for the same purpose!

Chapter Four
The Development of Shuri-te

SHURI KARATE IS GENERALLY regarded to be the oldest type of Karate on Okinawa, although I'm not sure how accurate or useful this classification is. Shuri-te gave rise to the modern popular styles of Shotokan and Wado Ryu, as well as contributing significantly to a host of other eclectic styles. From an early time, there was a kind of inherent 'snobbery' associated with Shuri city and with pre-eminent Shuri families who, after all, resided in the royal capital. For men of that time, it was a distinct social advantage to have been born in Shuri, to have married a Shuri woman and to have been educated in Shuri, and if you could associate yourself with, or connect yourself to the royal household at Shuri castle, so much the better. So, Shuri-te was the 'up market' 'Te' but actually no more important or technically superior to the Naha-te. As mentioned in the introduction, Tomari-te seems to have been absorbed into Shuri-te by the late nineteenth century. Indeed, I could suggest that the kata Wanshu (Enpi), Rohai (Meikyo), and Wanhkan, seem to be three of the few traceable Tomari kata, except perhaps Naihanchin; with the Naihanchin kata, as I mentioned earlier, being practiced on Okinawa (in Tomari and Shuri) perhaps as early as 1810, if not earlier. Other mainstay Shuri-te kata were mentioned in chapter one

To-te Sakugawa

To-te Sakugawa

Okinawa's first To-te 'Bushi' (China-hand 'warrior') of note, was Kanga Teruya who changed his name to *Sakugawa* when he was in his thirties, according to some sources, and when he was in his fifties according to others. *Sakugawa* was born (as claimed by Nagamine Shoshin) in the late eighteenth century (1782). Often credited with instructing the famous Matsumura Sokon (b. 1809) but there being little evidence to support the supposition, Sakugawa's technical contribution to Karate remains problematic. He is, however, generally associated with early Shuri-te and the kata 'Kusanku'

Accounts differ as to Sakugawa's exact occupation. Some sources suggest that he was expected to become an important statesman, and sent by the Rykyuan kingdom to China for 'grooming' when he was in his thirties. Career wise, that seems quite late in life, and one wonders what he did beforehand.

Other sources suggest that Sakugawa was a kind of security officer for a merchant shipping line. Most sources suggest that Sakugawa began his To-te training under a man named Takahara, a mapmaker and astronomer from the village of Akata. This is not unreasonable given that Sakugawa was born in-between Akata and Torihori villages, and seems to have been connected with the Okinawan mercantile trade, but, no one really knows who Takahara was or what he taught.

It is often claimed that Sakagawa met and studied with a Chinese military attaché named 'Kusanku' from whom he learned 'Kempo' (another term for Quan-fa or To-te). The Shuri-te kata 'Kusanku' is said to be the result of that interaction. Whether Sakugawa was taught an actual quan, or whether he synthesised separate Quan-fa techniques into new 'kata', no one knows. No one knows precisely who Kusanku was either. Not only are the various dates confusing, but the lineages are fragmented and scattered.

Stephen Chan, a Martial Arts expert and former *Traditional Karate* magazine columnist, commented on the following excerpt from an obscure document translated from French into English and pertaining to the so called, 'Twenty-four Ancient Kata', and their transmission to Okinawa (attributed to the July/Aug 1988 edition of *Traditional Karate*, UK):

> The third method of transmission was through Chinese military attaches posted to the Island. Thus in 1683 an important diplomatic mission went to Okinawa for six months. There were several military attaches, some of whom were Kung Fu experts. One of them, Wanshu, taught a kata to the native population that still bears his name [Wanshu is the original name of the Shotokan kata 'Empi']. (Parenthesis mine)

Stephen's comment on the origins of Shuri-te and Tomari-te kata are as follows:

> ... I have to be honest here, for I also traded on this story. It may be true and it may not. Wanshu, Kushanku and Chinto may have been diplomats or they may have been freelance messengers between the Okinawan and Chinese authorities, maybe even pirates. They probably existed in one form or another, but it is not necessarily the case that they knew good Kung Fu. If they were true diplomats they probably did. If they

were pirates or lowly messengers ... don't believe too hard that we've all come down from something great and noble ... I think we should practice kata to appreciate the refined movements of the last two centuries. That is the only time span we can be sure about ... we should experiment, sit at the feet of their [the dead master's] descendents, and try to appreciate the hidden intent of these masters. But kata is not something that is sacred. We know too little about it, and what we do know has changed too much for us to worship." (Parenthesis mine)

Piracy was rife in the South China seas at that time, and shipping had problems with corruption, as did the overland carrying of goods by wagon. Travelling parties could be set upon by teams of rival or even collaborating bandits who each operated out of allotted territories. Each gang had its own fiercely protected 'patch', and unless the bandits had been previously 'bought off' the wagon trains were plundered, sometimes even by the accompanying guards!

Ships were similarly targeted by pirates. If the shippers paid a 'tax' they would most likely be left alone (extortion). Business is business. The piracy of the period was not just simple opportunism. Information was required. Information on both outgoing and incoming vessels, their passengers, cargoes, defence capabilities and so on. Like anything useful, such 'intelligence' could be traded, and you can be sure someone was a trader. The image of a few 'scurvy cutthroats' endlessly sailing around looking for a boat to rob is misguided. Piracy was an industry with extensive networks, employees and resources.

Just to give you some idea of the scale of piracy in the south and east China seas during the seventeenth and eighteenth centuries, the port of Xiamen in Fujian, was overtaken by an army led by one Zheng Chenggong, who was allied with a defunct Ming dynasty prince. Zheng's father was said to have run away and married a Japanese woman – Zheng's mother. Apparently

Zheng's father returned to China as a pirate, raiding the Gaundong and Fujian coasts and even taking possession of Xiamen, a major seaport and commercial centre and place of refuge for Ming rulers fleeing from the Manchu's. From here, Ming armies fought their way north under the leadership of the pirate general Zheng Chenggong. Now this occurred before the Manchu's could get the region of Fujian under control, however, it is the numbers of men and resources, and their links to piracy that are astounding!

Zheng had under his control 8,000 war junks, 240,000 men at arms, and all the pirates who infested the coastal waters at that time – a combined force estimated at 800,000! Zheng Chenggong was much more than a mere pirate, but pirate numbers (junks and men) massively boosted his 'army', and it seems the family business (piracy) had provided well for him.

The 17th century Chinese writer Gu Yanwu stated that taxes levied against only 20–30 percent of goods shipped by sea paid for half of the states expenditure at the end of the 16th century. Enormous amounts of goods were being shipped, piracy was uncontrollable, and towards the end of the Ming dynasty, considerable damage was being inflicted on China's economy by *Japanese* pirates and by official inactivity in respect of huge rises in smuggling and contraband.

There is a curious tale given independently by both Anthony Mirakian and George Mattson. Mattson recounts the tale told to him by Uechi Kanei, who in turn was quoting his father Uechi Kanbun who trained in Fuzhou. The tale involves Higaonna Kanyro's teacher the elusive 'Ryu Ryu Ko' who was, allegedly, tested three times to become (the equivalent of) a knight. He failed twice, at the ages of thirty-seven and fifty. Supposedly, on his seventy-third birthday, he once again went before the 'emperor' asking to be tested. Using the strength he had gained from his Sanchin training, he carried a rock weighing (at least) four hundred pounds and passed the test.

253

Contrast this tale with the reported historical tale regarding the pirate warlord Zeng Chenggong after the fall of the Ming and inception of the Qing dynasties. Allegedly, Zeng Chenggong used a stone lion weighing up to six hundred pounds to test the strength of his soldiers. Those strong enough to lift and carry the stone were enlisted in the advance guard of the army.

Tales of strength and valour were passed on from the (native) Ming dynasty to bolster young (Han race) anti-Qing men, and encourage them to engage in martial arts and rebellion. It seems that the 'stone lion tale' found its way all the way down to include the teacher of an Okinawan Quan-fa student, teaching in Fuzhou during the late nineteenth century!

Returning to the mercantile trade between Okinawa and Fujian, and to the Karate personality To-te Sakugawa; outward bound on a tribute vessel to Fuzhou, the ship he was travelling on was besieged by pirates. During a fierce fight, in which Sakugawa used a roku-shaku bo (six foot staff) to combat the pirates who had boarded the ship (so the story goes), he put up a fine performance, but eventually ended up overboard, along with some pirates. Picked up by a Fujianese naval patrol boat on manoeuvres, he was taken to Fuzhou, charged with piracy, found guilty and packed off to Beijing for sentencing. Piracy had escalated at an alarming rate, and as a result he received the allotted death sentence. Fortunately he obtained a reprieve after allegedly refusing to eat the condemned man's last meal and being given an opportunity to explain himself.

This tale is certainly curious, and one wonders why it was not possible for Sakugawa to explain himself in Fuzhou. If he was an ambassador, as has been suggested, someone surely could have been called to vouch for him. There must have been some point of contact with the Chinese authorities there, some counterpart or professional colleague in Fuzhou, particularly as that is where his ship was bound for in the first place! Clearly no one knew him in Beijing, but no one was expected to know him there, so perhaps that helped.

I suspect that Sakugawa was a kind of ships security officer. I'm not suggesting he was a pirate, but, he may very well have known a man or two who was …

Whilst on the theme of piracy, the Okinawan Karate kata Chinto was allegedly named after a Kung Fu expert who happened to be 'washed ashore' on Okinawa. What kind of occupation risks getting washed ashore? Perhaps I'm just seeing pirates everywhere! But seriously, both Kung Fu and Karate have always been loosely connected with underworld activity. Even to this day, Kung Fu, in Hong Kong, for example, is deeply associated with the Triad societies, and various types of 'underworld' syndicates. Similarly, Karate in Japan has 'Yakuza' (gang) connections. I do not mean to imply that the average Kung Fu or Karate practitioner is associated with such activities, but just to reveal the long standing associations.

Shuri-te Kata and Dancing

To-te Sakugawa is credited by Nagamine with revising old village 'Meikata', folk dances that were used at village festivals. Finding Shuri-te kata somewhat puzzling, I once speculated that there might be a connection between Meikata and Shuri-te Karate kata. Unfortunately my speculation – part of the usual process of investigation and research – was pirated by individuals with their own agenda and an incomplete knowledge of my research or knowledge of the subject proper. A little knowledge is a dangerous thing, so it is said. Because they could not make the kata Kusanku work in any direct and practical way, they stated that the kata must be a two armed grappling/dance with a religious background; all in all, quite a jumble of my ideas – spirituality and nobility in kata, cultural relativity, etc. They have however let themselves off the hook in respect of fighting by declaring that their 'system' is not for fighting but for dancing and for fun. But, Shuri-te Kata quite clearly contain something far more practical than ritual 'Cha-cha', for fun.

By comparing contemporary and well-preserved Okinawan dances with antique Shuri-te Karate kata, it is easy to see that Kusanku is not a dance, neither for that matter is it for grappling, another avenue I was bound to and indeed did begin to explore in 1991. Meikata contain movements only vaguely if at all connected with Karate, and links between Meikata and Shuri-te Karate kata are tenuous.

Evidence for Sakugawa's contribution to Shuri-te Kata is scarce. Shuri-te Karate is, at first glance, different in look and in feel from Naha-te, but Nagamine Shoshin believed (even before World War Two!), that Shuri-te also developed out of Fujianese Quan-fa.

The key to the construction of Shuri-te kata is the use of the Sai, or, in a couple of cases (involving kata once practiced in Tomari-te), the use of 'Tonfa' (a wooden arm protector used in pairs that can be swiveled by means of their handles). The distances, types of techniques, foot placements and turns illustrated in Shuri Kata, can most effectively be utilised with a pair of Sai.

Whilst the Shuri tradition unfolded, Naihanchin, the 'old kata' that moves through a simple straight line, became less prominent. It certainly has less visual appeal, particularly for audiences at demonstrations or kata competitions.

Shuto (Sword Hand Block)

Shuto with Sai

Application

Shuri-te Kata – Sai and Tonfa

Excluding Naihanchin, if Shuri kata were designed to be used empty handed, why, for instance, should three or four successive 'knife hand blocks' (also called 'sword hand blocks), be executed whilst stepping forward? In a 'block strike scenario' *this would necessitate an opponent stepping back to attack*, which is impossible! Nor can these movements be *practically* explained in a grappling format. Yet these techniques are a signature theme of Kusanku, the most advanced Shuri-te kata. Until recently, these techniques were indeed considered to be knife hand blocks, as recorded by Funakoshi and others, but now 'interpretations' abound. They include seizing an opponent's wrist with one hand and 'chopping' the neck with the other, to explain the former 'knife' or 'sword hand' block, however a clenched fist would denote the gripping hand more effectively in the solo kata if indeed a grip and 'chop' were the intention here.

Let us consider instead, these techniques being applied with a pair of Sai. Besides countering a sword, a major use of the Sai was in countering the attack of the pole/staff (originally synonymous with the spear). The main task the user of a pole has to undertake is to maintain the advantage of greater distance and maximise the ability to inflict damage from that distance! In contrast, the Sai user must close this distance down, engaging the pole and sticking with it to neutralise its distance advantage. When the pole user thrusts the pole out, it must be quickly removed to prevent the Sai user from trapping it or punishing the holding hand. I suspect that the origin of the successive so called 'sword' or 'knife hand' blocks lies in tactics applied to close down the long distance and make adequate contact with the pole, engaging it with the aim of deflecting it and punishing (striking) the opponents hand/arm from above. Repeated attempts might have to be made. Similar repetitive sequences of technique occur in Seisan kata, and the purpose of Seisan kata, in my view, should be clear to readers by now.

Finally, referring back to Nagamine's suspicion that both Shuri-te and Naha-te Kata derive from Fujianese Quan-fa, we could consider the front foot 'floating' cat stance, common to Sanseriui, Passai, Chinto, and Kusanku, perhaps indicates that there may indeed be a connection between Shuri-te and Naha-te kata. I suggest the cat stance, in both cases, is used to facilitate a swift front leg kick, aimed either at the opponent's gripping hands or at his weapon, after having trapped the weapon down, using Sai.

Returning to the subject of the attempts to explain the knife hand block(s) as unarmed techniques; as with other ambiguous Karate techniques, there are currently myriad theories regarding vital point or nerve point attacks that represent attempts to arrive at workable utilitarian applications. However, as noted, it is always tricky to explain the repetition of the same technique three times in terms of chronological application! Such problems tend to be less difficult in kata performed through a simple straight line (i.e. Naihanchin), although they too have been subject to the misleading multiple opponent interpretations!

Kusanku, like Seisan, is a key Sai kata and has nothing at all to do with barehanded blocks and strikes, and nothing whatsoever to do with grappling. As in the case of Seisan kata, I understand the implications of what I say here, and am fully aware of the large numbers of Karate students who practice versions of this kata, and the teachers and students alike who have tried for many years to apply its techniques minus the Sai. I do not imply or attach any criticism to them, or to individuals seeking the meaning to the kata via, for instance, block strike ballistic interpretations, Admittedly, I do favour less the various current 'nerve strike' theories, and bottom of my list, by way of application for antique kata, is the ill-conceived belief that kata is a form of (religious) grappling/dancing with little or no practical use. Unfortunately, we can now find such irresponsible, sweeping reductionisms currently being 'revealed' in cyberspace, where – in my view – they belong.

The Inspiration of Master Matsumura and Itosu

Bushi Matsumura Sokon (b. 1809) is commonly hailed as the first concrete character in Shuri-te Karate. Although, once again, it is unclear who taught him, what he was taught, and what *he* taught in turn. Funakoshi Gichin claimed that Matsumura was taught by a military attaché called 'Iwah', but Nagamine wrote that there is no information on who Matsumura's teachers were.

It is not the case that all so called Shuri-te (or Shorin/Shao-lin, as some Shuri Karate would later be called) is traceable to Matsumura. In reality, it is uncertain which kata are associated with him. Matsumura had several students, and from the kata they *taught* it might become possible to take a guess at which kata Matsumura taught.

In respect of the development of To-te and modern Karate, the most notable of Matsumura's students were Azato (Ankho) Yasutsune and Itosu (Ankho) Yasutsune who both shared the same given name and the same nickname (Ankho) and were responsible for teaching Funakoshi Gichin. Indeed, much modern Karate can be traced back to Itosu, who was very active and energetic in promoting Karate. Itosu, who was born in Shuri in 1832, came from a relatively high ranking family. Becoming highly literate in both Chinese and Japanese literature, and a fine calligrapher, he obtained a secretarial post at the royal palace.

I think that Itosu, although widely believed to be a student of Sokon Matsumura, actually learned from several instructors, including a contemporary of Matsumura named Nagahama. The lineages are very unclear. Funakoshi wrote that Azato learned from Matsumura and Itosu from Gusukuma, who in turn learned from a Southern Chinese who 'drifted ashore'. The lack of a proper name for this latter individual is somewhat irritating if not a little suspect. Initially, Itosu taught To-te secretly and to a selected few students, including Funakoshi Gichin. But by the beginning of the twentieth century, the veil of secrecy was lifted and Karate began to be taught openly, eventually being taught at Okinawan high schools. Itosu devised the five Pinan (Heian) kata for this purpose (as I mentioned in chapter one).

Itosu was responsible for a 'sea change' in the way To-te was perceived, practiced, and taught. There were tremendous political, social and cultural upheavals during his lifetime. For example, the Samurai tradition was abolished and the men of Samurai class were forbidden to wear swords. They were further ordered to remove their 'topknots', the traditional Samurai hairstyle. The Okinawan king was deposed, the Okinawan nobles were dispossessed and the whole Japanese/Okinawan social structure went through a brutal upheaval. I think that Itosu responded by looking to future generations, and by breaking with tradition and broadening the curriculum of To-te, making the soon-to-emerge art of Karate into less of a functional form and more into a recreational or callisthenic activity to be widely disseminated in schools.

It is well-known that Itosu's To-te was originally very conservative and well-grounded in Naihanchin kata, which in his earlier career he seems to have promoted with the utmost enthusiasm. Remember, Funakoshi Gichin spent ten years studying solely these kata. Later, Itosu attempted to develop a 'collective' style of 'Karate', with many kata. He collected and restructured a number of kata over the years, and eventually accumulated over twenty five (as I noted earlier). No one knows where all these kata came from, but there was certainly a proliferation of them during his career.

This was revolutionary for the day, and created a new 'tradition', a kata craze even, and kata would eventually become almost a form of currency amongst Karate enthusiasts. Undoubtedly, Funakoshi later followed suite, detailing *nineteen* kata in his 1936 book *Karate – Do Kyohan*, even though, on page 38, he (conservatively) states:

> In the past, it was expected that about three years were required to learn a single kata, and it was usual that even an expert of considerable skill would only know three or at the most five kata. Thus in short, it was felt that a superficial understanding of many kata was of little use ... I too studied for ten years to really learn the three Tekki [Naihanchin] forms. (Parenthesis mine)

This statement seems at odds with the presentation of nineteen kata in Karate – Do Kyohan – Particularly when *four* kata were, as I have suggested, Funakoshi's own creations! Besides, the traditional 'three years, one kata' time-frame, would mean the mastery of nineteen kata would take fifty-seven years! Contrast that with Itosu's own words from his ten lessons of To-te:

> (Rule number 3) "If you train one or two hours everyday, your body will change after three or four years – you will get to the core of Karate." (Some translations simply read "master Karate.")

The late Uechi Ryu grandmaster *Uechi Kanei*, in George Mattson's, *Uechi Ryu Karate Do*, (Brockton MA, Peabody 1974) p.309, states, when asked about the number of kata in Uechi Ryu:

We could form hundreds of kata, but for what purpose [?] All is in the three kata. [Sanchin, Seisan, Sanseirui]. *Shorin Ryu has nearly fifty kata, but most were created by Anku [Ankho] Itosu.* They were created for the same reason that I created five kata for study between the main three; to hold the students interest while they develop their minds. (Parenthesis and italics mine)

It should be borne in mind that Itosu was engaged in popularising Karate, particularly, it seems, for young people. Graham Noble (quoting the Karate master Hiroshi Kinjo, writing in *Karate-do monthly*) recounts in *F.A.I.* No. 50. p.28):

It was in 1908 that Itosu Sensei formulated modern karate. In short, the fact Itosu Sensei established a modern form of karate-do points to the co-existence at that time of old karate and modern karate. I should add kempo (i.e. Chinese based styles – ed.) so there were three styles of karate co-existing. Sensei Itosu taught at the Okinawan prefecture school for teachers and it was modern karate he taught there, not the old style ... most of the people thought he was teaching the old style, and this misunderstanding exists even today. This is a serious misunderstanding ...

Kenwa Mabuni (1889–1957) a later student of Itosu and the founder of Shito Ryu Karate, was (perhaps having been influenced by Itosu) an avid collector of kata and amassed the Shuri-te Kata and the kata of Miyagi Chojun, some fifty kata in all. Mabuni gave the following anecdote (from 'The History of Japanese Karate: Masters of the Shorin-ryu.' *F.A.I.* No. 50. p.28):

Mabuni: "... One of my servants Morihiro Matayoshi once taught me kib-dachi-no kata. [Naihanchin]. It was different from the kata I learned from Itosu Sensei, so one day I showed him the kata that Matayoshi had taught me. He said it was the original form of the kata he had studied, and that he had improved it following his own research." (Parenthesis mine)

This reference is about Naihanchin kata. Kibadachi is the Japanese mainland name for the straddle leg or 'horse stance' used throughout the kata.

Chibana Chosin (1887–1969) studied Karate with Itosu from a young age until Itosu's death in 1915/16. Chibana claimed that Itosu originally learned Naihanchin from an un-named Chinese living in Tomari, and later re-structured the (three) kata. No one can be sure what these 'improvements' were, but there doesn't seem to be very much evidence that the intended grappling application of Naihanchin was understood! In fact, I'm convinced that it was not understood at all. Motobu Choki seems to have been uninterested in the kata boom and seems to have stuck to Naihanchin (and probably Pasai).

As I have already suggested, warfare, plague epidemics in China, the massive displacement of peoples, food shortage and other social upheavals, particularly at the close of the Ming dynasty, undoubtedly had a hand in burying a tradition or approach in which quan had *definite meanings*.

Without the keys to unlock the (not always obvious) applications, there appeared to be teachers ready to step in and fill the gaps left in knowledge with their own ideas. Sometimes these teachers were not Chinese, couldn't speak read or write Chinese and learned their quan for instance on Okinawa, where, as I have suggested, Chinese methods were subjected to revision, using ideas taken from mainland Japanese Budo and the social and cultural values and attitudes associated with it.

These 'reinterpretations' did not always fit well with the *technical material* (intrinsic applications) actually contained in the quan. This is particularly the case in respect of engagement distances and the (later) widespread non-use of the Sai in the case of kata intended for use with such, or the failure to understand the nature

264

of kata methodically delineating grappling or counter-grappling techniques. *Thus, in respect of Shuri-te (Shorin Ryu) kata, it is my view that the Pinan kata of Itosu, were created for very different reasons than the Naihanchin kata, and that the Pinan (Heian) represents the new Karate and the Naihanchin represents the old.*

I recall the attempts I made during the late 1980s, to investigate the possibility of pushing hands and or grappling as a key to kata. It really began to develop (rather fittingly perhaps) with a cursory investigation of (Goju Ryu) Sesan. Somewhat frustrated with the kata, one day, around the spring of 1990, I said to a young black belt practitioner, "Just grab my wrists will you?" My wrists were positioned in the clenched fist 'Juji uke' X block position that preceded the final movement in the kata. He did so, and when I performed the final movement which astoundingly separated and divided his limbs, almost throwing him halfway across the room, I thought, "That's interesting!" Of course it didn't work on the stocky builder who was building an extension to the house I lived in and just happened to be a Goju Ryu dan grade. But it certainly got me thinking, and during that period, I also began serious investigation into the Tekki/Naihanchin' series of three kata, at first concentrating on simultaneous blocks, strikes, and foot sweeps done in a Kung Fu type format. But I couldn't explain the order of the kata, or find sensible applications (without duplication) for the techniques in all three kata. Later, I was shocked (but elated) to make the discovery I did. I first (superficially) learned Tekki in the early 1970s and personally became interested in Naihanchin in 1979 after noticing the differences between the Shotokan 'Tekki' kata and the original Naihanchin kata from which it was adapted.

With considerable commitment from Dave Franks, one of my fellow researchers who noticed a similarity between the principles being proposed and Shotokan's Tekki nidan kata (actually as it happened, an incorrect and altered part), I began to consider that

Tekki/Naihanchin might be a form of grappling. Indeed Tekki, or at least in its original Naihanchin version, was a grappling kata. Seisan, though, as I would later find out, was, in its original version, something entirely different. I published early (incomplete) results with Charles E. Tuttle (Japan) as *Zen Shaolin Karate* (My publisher's choice of title).

Whilst exploring these and other kata during the early 1990s I suggested that the knife hand block and follow-up 'nukite' (spear hand strike) found in Pinan Shodan (Hein nidan), might be an escape from a double 'crossed arm' grappling situation. But this was incorrect.

Recognising that the discovery of the exact Shuri-te kata applications would be more challenging than merely assuming they were a repeat – with variations – on the Naihanchin theme (grappling), a supposition I had earlier made, in collaboration with one of my colleagues, I was fortunate enough to harbour a third, much stronger hypothesis – that which is published here.

Research certainly has its dangers, particularly when people take it piecemeal and disappear with bits and pieces without being party to the final results. I soon realised that my poor view (read virtual rejection) of conventional Karate organisations had backfired. Having been advised time and time again by my peers, I finally succumbed, accepted a lesson from big brother, 'corporate Karate', battened down the hatches and formed Ko-do Ryu Karate and Kobudo along tried and tested conventional lines to protect, promote, and disseminate, some rather important discoveries.

Chapter Five
Contact Reflexes

ORIGINAL WEAPONLESS QUAN were designed to be used via a process known as 'contact reflex'. Contact reflexes are the reflexes of touch rather than vision. Contact reflexes are primary reflexes. They are faster than visual reflexes, so, proper responses in the applications are triggered by contact not by vision. This goes against modern perceptions of martial arts and 'self defence' in which opponents are generally perceived to engage in combat separated by a considerable space – a gap, which can only be engaged with visually at first. Authentic quan are intensely concerned with what happens *after contact!*

The initial movement – prior to making contact – is of course a matter of concern for the defender. No-one has concrete failsafe answers, but using the original approach, there will be a general melding-with or blending-with an attack. This process is described under the heading 'Uke'. As I mentioned before, this procedure could even extend to preventing an opponent from drawing a weapon (thereby stopping an escalation of conflict) and pacifying or subduing him, without recourse to weapons-use, and the associated dangers of these.

Given that contact reflexes are primary reflexes, the reflexes of touch rather than vision, responses to attacks don't have to be thought-through or planned provided all defences (bar the initial one) are undertaken whilst in contact with the opponent. A visual reflex on the other hand is a much more complicated and time consuming process. First the eyes see; then they send a message to the brain which identifies what has been seen. The brain then initiates a response (nervous impulse) that finally starts the muscles responding. In (modern) Karate, successfully utilizing visual reflexes depends on good eye-hand coordination, natural athletic ability, and tactics. These abilities are of less importance when one uses contact reflexes.

Compared with other physical faculties that can decline by up to ninety percent with age, touch reflexes are amongst the last of our faculties to diminish. This, coupled with the use of kata that operate only within the natural range of movement, means that a high degree of skill in application can be developed and maintained into old age – hence the 'old Karate master'.

One vehicle traditionally used to train contact or touch reflexes is pushing-hands.

Pushing-hands

Dr. Yang Jwing Ming, a prolific author on Chinese Kung Fu, states in 'The Rational of Chinese Boxing' *F.A.I.* 68 Vol. 12, No. 2), p.48:

> In China every style has pushing-hands ... It doesn't matter which style. Firstly you have to get in touch with each other to learn sensitivity [How to feel-out responses]. (Parenthesis mine)

Pushing-hands developed as a contact medium through which to express (apply) techniques spontaneously and without pre-arranging. Pushing-hands practice was created to develop good defensive skills and is closely tied to 'listening techniques'. Listening techniques are dependent on the sense of touch. Therefore, pushing-hands skills are dependent on *contact reflexes*, (only supported by visual reflexes and the senses of distance, timing and rhythm). Pushing-hands drills are used to read or determine an opponent's strengths and weaknesses and also to determine the nature and direction of any attack.

> Be as a dragonfly that perches on the top of a stick raised to strike it. (Chinese Proverb)

Pushing-hands is much more than the mere auxiliary 'exercise' that it has unfortunately become in much modern Karate. However, the situation is far better now than it was in the mid-to-late 1980s. During that period, I remember encountering resistance when trying to re-introduce pushing-hands to Karate-ka.

> "Pushing-hands practice is a part of Kung Fu or Tai Chi Ch'uan," they complained. "Not Karate."

> "That's not Karate," one prominent Japanese Sensei said about my schools' performance one day.

According to Miyagi Chojun, 'Kakie' (pushing-hands) *is* the Kumi-te (meeting hands/sparring) of Goju Ryu Karate. Miyagi's view is certainly adhered-to in Ko-do Ryu Karate. Moreover, pushing-hands formed the backbone or 'platform' for the use of Ming dynasty (empty hands) Quan-fa; meaning, there is a clear precedent for the use of pushing hands in Karate and in To-te, the ancestor of Karate. This can be borne out by the practices of Miyagi Chojun, Uechi Kanei and Nagamine Shoshin, who were all 'au-fait' with a (basic) drill known as 'ko-te-ki-te' or 'rubbing arms', and basic pushing-hands, referred to in the Okinawan dialect as 'Kakie', yet gleaned from Ming and Qing dynasty Fujianese, Chinese sources.

At the time of writing, I have had the pleasure of contributing to a general revival (amounting almost to a renaissance) of pushing-hands. And many Karate-ka in Europe and the US have become involved. The well-ordered Ko-do Ryu pushing hands methods have now been widely adopted and disseminated (sometimes by other groups and under different banners), but they remain very distinctive, and are the result of a process of structuring I introduced after finding Karate Kakie (push hands) to be somewhat neglected, relegated to a mere auxiliary exercise or drill; quite unsophisticated in comparison with more comprehensive methods. What distinguishes the Ko-do Ryu method of pushing hands is its systematic *methodical* use of the gate system described below.

Over the last few years, senior international Karate teachers have raised their game considerably when it comes to pushing hands. Certainly, pushing hands now enjoys greater exposure, happily with more emphasis being placed on using it to express techniques from kata. As the records (and their own students' reports) show, this was not commonplace twenty, or even ten years ago.

Another useful contribution to structuring pushing hands and increasing its efficiency, rests in the Ko-do Ryu method of *defining the roles of the 'players'*. This cuts down unnecessary and unproductive competitiveness, a competitiveness that would otherwise impede progress. Without a clear understanding of what one is supposed to be doing, pushing-hands practice can degenerate into a crude wrestling match, particularly when 'listening techniques' break down, and the urge to dominate, or win takes over. Both domination and winning are incompatible with pushing hands, a reciprocal, non-competitive technique executed in pairs.

How to Practice Pushing Hands

In all contact manoeuvres, especially pushing hands, keep the amount of force used, reasonable. Generally, keep all 'presses' and pushes forward or across the midline and within the box made by the Sanchin 'fortress' – the basic Sanchin arm positions from section one of the kata. In basic pushing hands, press smoothly towards your training partner's centre and avoid jerky or abrupt actions. Originate all pushes from the 'frame' of the stance; that is, push from the ground, and when you receive the force back from your training partner, yield by adjusting your body, either by turning at the waist when required to, or by smoothly transferring the force to your other arm. Try to keep the pressure even. The Chinese refer to this as 'silk reeling' because, in order to make fine strong silk, the tension (pressure) must be kept even when 'reeling' it in. If the pressure is not kept smooth and even, lumpy, unattractive and weak silk is produced.

The consistency required to practice good quality pushing hands can be suggested by the smooth action required to skilfully operate a yo-yo; it's a kind of smooth 'kinetic' bounce with no jerky interruptions as partners control each other's corner, and use the 'third hand' when corner control is lost.

The Third Hand

The 'third hand' is a strategic manoeuvre used to gain positional advantage – to 'cross' an opponent, positioning to his outside 'corner'– or to strategically turn positional disadvantage into advantage, with reference to the 'corner'. The corner refers to being at one side of a training partner or opponent, and being able to use both arms whilst your opponent has his lead arm trapped, pinned, or otherwise disadvantaged while his free hand is too far away (being on the other side of his midline) to be used without turning, which would of course alert you because you would feel it. This is a classical Chinese tactic long used to avoid frontal opposition and gain a distinct positional advantage. The third arm technique allows either practitioner to quickly 'reverse' a lost corner position, regain a lost corner, and keep both hands in use. The third hand is the essence of the so called 'middle level forearm block'.

The continuous action of 'pushing hands' is the sensible medium through which to express the techniques from traditional (weapon-less) Quan-fa and To-te forms, automatically, by touch and without thinking. Remember, through pushing hands you can feel what is going on and react instantly because contact reflexes are in play.

Linking Pushing Hands with Kata Application

Initially, Ko-do Ryu pushing-hands practice (not grappling) designates one of two players as being the 'driver', the initiator of all the action. The other person then becomes the 'driven' or the receiver of force. Pushing hands practice can later become a much more mutual practice. Whilst mutuality may form a part of the pushing hands drills, so called 'boxing' exchanges (punches and

The Third Hand

Pushing hands sequence

blocks) should remain driver led. Mutuality is not consistent with the pro-active nature of civil arrest techniques (unless pairs are 'drilling'), so, grappling applications are practiced by one person at a time, although the roles may change.

Rokushu grip escapes are not necessarily anti-Chin-Na techniques, they are intended only to counter ordinary restricting grips, the sort of grip an untrained person might apply to stop someone 'going about their business'. So, generally speaking, practice is best conducted with only one person 'driving' the techniques.

Whilst repetition is part of learning to push hands, movements must never become routine. To which I would add that pushing-hands is the most advanced method of testing Sanchin ability. It is the only interactive 'litmus test' of Sanchin' in action! The popular Goju and Uechi Ryu 'shime' (testing), where a student's Sanchin posture and techniques are physically 'corrected' and

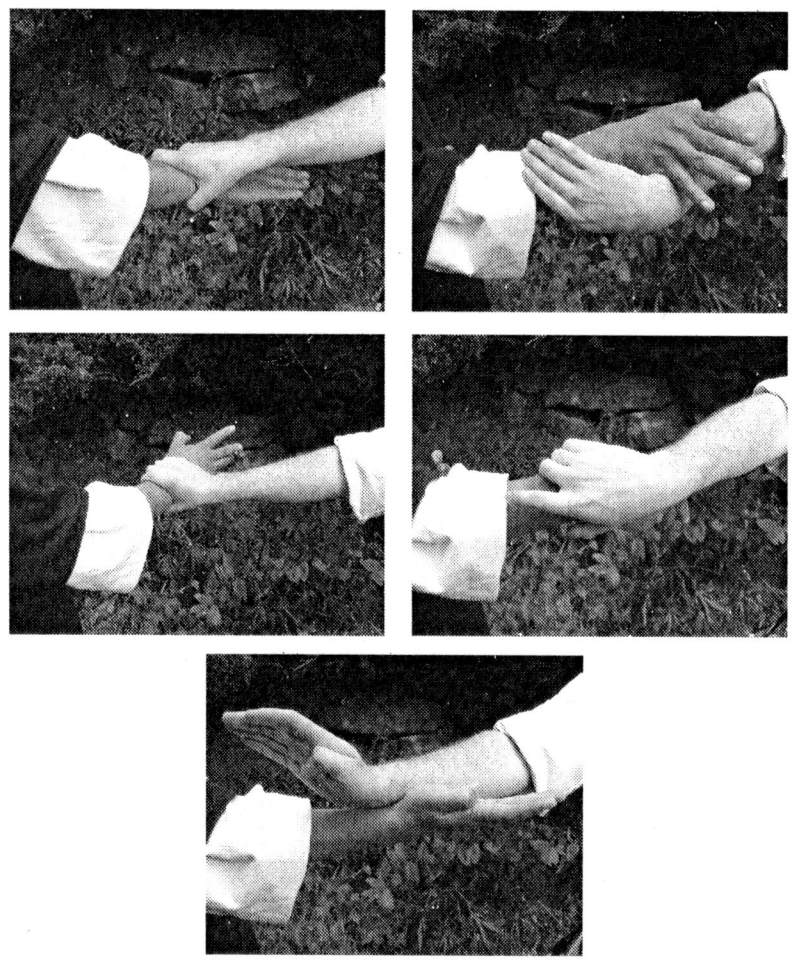

Rokushu grip escape examples

tested by the teacher, is only the most *basic* type of Sanchin testing. Further, it was overemphasised in Qing dynasty Fuzhou and later on Okinawa where, in comparison with Chinese methods, only *rudimentary* pushing hands skills have been passed down, with greater emphasis being placed on the fierce slapping of the performers shoulders, thighs and other muscle groups, as the Karate-ka performs Sanchin kata.

In this context, it is a little odd that the open hand (Uechi) Sanchin was (is) actually a weapons kata! Perhaps politically motivated parties 'commandeered' weapons Sanchin and other Kata for new (perceived weapon-less) purposes at that time. On a more sinister note, whilst I think it's quite unlikely, though not entirely impossible, early To-te students could simply have been duped!

Another quote from Stephen Chan's insightful commentary on Angus Watson's, translation (detailing the origins of Karate kata), will illustrate that I'm not alone in considering this. Although *Mr. Chan* is not questioning Naha-te here, he does air a parallel doubt regarding Shuri and Tomari Karate by saying that, if the early teachers were pirates rather than diplomats, then they probably had only rudimentary Kung Fu knowledge or ability, and,

> … the origin of Shuri and Tomari kata may have lain in a joke. We don't really know. Don't believe that we've all come down from something great and noble …

This quote is further evidence for the doubt and confusion regarding the authenticity of received Karate and the widespread confusion regarding the applications to its kata. Yet despite this situation, I feel that embracing the notion of the Sai being a basis for the development and construction of the antique Karate kata does go some way to rectifying this problem. Of course, one question regarding kata in general springs to mind, particularly when considering the confusion surrounding Sanchin, mentioned above, because no one can easily and definitively answer the question of which came first, the empty hands or the weapons versions. However, my guess is along the lines of 'fingers were invented before forks' (or more appropriately 'chopsticks').

Uke

The term Uke is commonly misused to replace or stand in for the English word 'block'. Uke does not mean to block, obstruct or oppose. It means, 'to receive'. Obviously, the term 'to receive' (a punch) has connotations of allowing it to hit you. Properly considered, Uke refers to the *person* being struck, pushed, or experiencing whatever force is directed at him.

The following example pertains to pushing hands (and Sanchin boxing. See Miyagi Sanchin as a 'Boxing' kata, chapter six). To block or dodge a force, and then counter-attack, is to waste the energy or force of the attack and to expose oneself to a counterattack. *It is, in terms of efficiency, far more useful to 'absorb' and re-direct an attacking force.* One is therefore not trying to 'fight' and 'give as-good-as-one gets'. One is, in fact, trying to give *exactly* what one gets, returning the attackers force without losing any. This (Buddhist based) philosophy is quite beautiful. Crudely put, there is a person giving force, and a person receiving it. The defender realises that he must not allow the attacker to hit him, and being a good sort of person, really, he also recognises that the incoming force doesn't belong to him. Not wanting to take something that doesn't belong to him, he makes sure he scoops up/collects every last little ounce of that force and kindly gives it right back to the attacker, immediately! No hard feelings, he smiles.

The difference between 'dead blocks', followed by equally as 'dead' counter-attacks, can be partially explained in the following two analogies. First, absorbing and returning a force can be likened to a springy branch that when walked into, 'springs' back into place and wreaks a bit of havoc for the person behind.

Springy force is needed, it's a force that is stored and released rather than generated. Second, imagine taking a small piece of paper and crumpling it up into a ball. Putting it on a flat table, you press your forefinger against your thumb and flick the ball of paper across the room. Imagine trying again, only this time just using the index finger alone. You don't involve your thumb to hold the forefinger back. Obviously the force is weedy by comparison.

The first instance represents stored force, the second, generated. In training, the stored force is first borrowed from the opponent, so this is referred to as 'borrowing force'. A supplied force is 'let go of'/ released, and one becomes empty of that force, in similar fashion to Chan Buddhist notions of being 'empty', or of 'letting go'. This, I believe, is a possible justification for a Shaolin Temple based Ming dynasty Quan-fa.

Please remember: *Pushing hands responses are mutual and reciprocal, but they should not be confused with the pro-active nature of Chin-Na.* Pushing hands and 'borrowing force' are best understood in terms of the 'gate system'.

The Gate System

The gate system is a central element in the proper understanding and practical operation of the principles and 'waza' (technique[s]) inherent in Sanchin kata. Indeed only a practical understanding of the gate system will allow one to fully understand the potential applications of the kata. The gate system is illustrated in the basic Sanchin arm positions assumed in section one of the kata where one stands with one leg advanced in the Sanchin stance.

Human beings naturally have two legs and two arms. The legs are strongest, and are used for weight-bearing and walking, etc. The arms are more 'flexible' and the hands, in comparison to the feet, are extremely dexterous. There are 27 joints in each hand! There are three major joints in the arm; the wrist, the elbow and the shoulder. The shoulder is closest to the spine. The spine is central to the control of posture, balance, and centre of gravity. These *facts* are unalterable, and the gate system reflects them.

Successful utilisation of the gate system requires a comprehensive understanding of three categories:

1. Levels (height)
2. Angles (direction a limb travels in relative to the opponents position)
3. Ranges (distances)

1. There are three horizontal 'levels': upper, middle and lower. They are situated as follows: Upper, from the top of the head to shoulders: Middle, from the shoulders to hips: Lower, from the hips to the ground.

2. There are three vertical 'doors' or angles (defined by the double Sanchin arms) through which an attack can enter. These doors consist of the 'centre' and two shoulder lines. Simply put, they comprise two 'outside gates' and one inside gate. These are the lines that must be fully mastered and kept shut by angling, re-positioning and the use of tight, efficient, economical hand-techniques.

3. There are three 'guards' which control the distance. These 'guards' are defined by the three joints of the human arm: the wrist, elbow, and shoulder. Proper control of the wrist controls the elbow, which in turn controls the shoulder and eventually an opponent's posture.

A clear understanding of the 'gate system' allows for the systematic and comprehensive use of 'applied' Sanchin which I will introduce in chapter six, after first explaining more about the practice of the solo kata.

Chapter Six
Practical Sanchin

THE FOLLOWING ANALYSIS surmises how, and in what ways, Miyagi Chojun modified the Sanchin kata taught to him by Higaonna Kanyro. Although it must be borne in mind that what Miyagi actually inherited was an altered (re-structured) Sai/weapon kata, his modification was influenced by sources other than his (formal and acknowledged) teacher. Moreover, Miyagi Chojun produced (along with Tensho/Rokushu) the only 'smooth action' 'soft/hard' non-ballistic kata in the Karate repertoire. I think major influences upon Miyagi's modifications to Sanchin and Rokushu were Wu Xiangui (Gokenki) or other Fujianese associates, members of the Karate Kenkyu club established by Miyagi and other master teachers of Karate during the 1920s (this group included Wu Xiangui).

I'm sure that ideas expressed in the Wu-pei chih (Bubishi) also strongly influenced Miyagi Chojun, whom I suspect, desired to bring Hiagaonna's Sanchin more in line with the Sanchin quan of other Fujianese styles or methods – like, for example the Sam chien (Sanchin) of Ngo Cho or 'Five Ancestors' (Kung Fu) – and add an element of 'Chi Gung' (training the vital spirit) to Sanchin, by slowing the kata down, 'rooting' and 'grounding' it out, and linking it to a deliberate breath pattern. Incidentally, in 'Five ancestors Kung Fu', the Sam chien is considered to be the nucleus of the art – sound familiar? Here is a quote from an article by Alexander Co, (California, *Inside Kung Fu*, April 1985, K48325):

… The essence of ngo cho kuen lies in the sam chien, which means three wars, as it does in Okinawa. Deceptive in that the form *looks* simple, behind sam chien stands the core, the nucleus from which all ngo cho techniques are derived. Indeed, the sam chien is recognized as the most basic – and the most advanced – form of ngo cho …

Incidentally, Wu Xiangui, Miyagi's friend, associated with at least one 'Ngo Cho practitioner. Also, it would be prudent at this point to consider Fujianese quan like the so called 'Incense Shop Lohan quan' or incense shop monkfist that (although more complex) does resemble Miyagi Sanchin in the use of clenched fists, the use of the Sanchin guard (fortress), the chambering method of the hand, and to some extent the 'ma po' three-cornered foothold or foot placement (stance).

Analysis of the Technical Construction of Miyagi Chojun's Sanchin

After analysing the number of repetitions of techniques in the three sections into which Miyagi Sanchin remains divided (which is still in keeping with the Uechi and Higaonna versions); listed here are the key differences between these versions, and their significance.

1. Comparing Miyagi Sanchin with the versions that preceded it; perhaps the first thing to note is the complete removal of the two turns used in the version taught to Miyagi by Higaonna, and the two turns in the Uechi version that chronologically preceded the Higaonna modification.

2. The second point to note is the clenching of the fists during section one of Miyagi's version, which, although present in the Higaonna version and in various similar Chinese quan, is absent

in the open handed version from which Higaonna and Miyagi Sanchin were derived.

3. Third, is the smooth and non-ballistic movement of Miyagi's closed-fist version as opposed to the rapid 'nukite' thrust of the Uechi version; that and the removal in the Miyagi version of the semi-circle used when withdrawing the arm during section one (it is this smooth heavy/sticky feeling used in Goju Ryu Sanchin that makes it so compatible with pushing hands).

4. Fourth, is that the alleged 'nukite', spear-hand strike, found in section one of Uechi Sanchin is thrust swiftly out at shoulder height and in line with the shoulder of the thrusting hand, making it off-centre or off-target as a strike, which makes for a strange way to practice striking at an opponents face or trunk. Even pre-supposing the use of an oblique or lateral angle, normal Karate punches are delivered along ones own midline and focussed in the centre.

5. In the Miyagi version, this technique is performed slowly at rib height and with the fist clenched. Some practitioners (Students of Toguchi Sekichi for example) practice a more centred 'push-punch', however, practitioners of both versions generally extend the (striking) arm along a line that remains constant with the side of the body.

6. Uechi Sanchin (usually) starts with a left-leg half-step being used to establish the Sanchin stance. Thereafter, *three full steps* are taken before the first of two turns occur. In contrast, Miyagi Sanchin start with a *right leg* half-step, and thereafter only takes two full steps forward, finally executing two full steps back with accompanying techniques, before closing the kata with a half step up/back to the start position.

7. The twelve (sometimes demonstrated as eleven) repetitions of waza in section one of the Uechi Sanchin, are reduced to seven in Miyagi Sanchin. Two repetitions are performed, however, with the same leg forward as the extending hand, not in the more orthodox opposite-hand opposite-leg format. There does not seem to be a (Sanchin) precedent for this, although a similar hand-leg arrangement can be found in Uechi *Seisan*, but the hands are open – one palm up and one palm down.

Uechi Sanchin stresses the repetition of the techniques used in section one of the kata, and facilitates their repetitions by including two turns in the kata. This is done because section one of this Sai kata stresses the fundamental technique of Sai manipulation – the skill to flip/change the Sai from pommel-back to pommel-forward position, and the basic 'pommel strike', the basic Sai action. One can easily imagine this being a cyclical, 'looped' drill that was possibly repeated for as long as the instructor requested or the student chose, before moving on to section two.

The balance of techniques, in terms of repetition, for Uechi, Higaonna, and Miyagi Sanchin kata is as follows:

Uechi Sanchin
Three sections that should logically produce *twelve* repetitions of section one's waza (but often portrayed as eleven), three repetitions of section two's waza, and *three* of section three's waza; eighteen repetitions in all.

Embusen (floor plan of steps):
Half step, *three full steps forward*, turn; *three full steps forward*, turn; *three full steps forward*, three steps to the sides and back, half step to close.

Miyagi Sanchin
Three sections; seven repetitions of section one's waza, three of section two's waza and *two* of section three's waza; twelve repetitions in all (thirteen movements in total, counting the closing half step). I strongly suspect that Miyagi simply removed the turns, and practiced the techniques as though the two turns had already been completed. He further added a second repetition of the waza executed with the same leg forward as the extending hand. Therefore, the first section of Miyagi Sanchin requires the practice of three waza, each following a step, and four executed whilst standing still.

Embusen:
Half step forward, *two* full steps forward, two full steps backwards, half step to close.

Higaonna Sanchin
On Okinawa and in Japan there exists a closed fist version of Sanchin complete with two turns, and this version is often referred to as Higaonna Sanchin. Also, some schools practice a closed fist version of Sanchin in which the returning hand in section one is brought back in a semi-circle in similar fashion to Uechi Ryu Sanchin. This may have been how the kata was initially performed after the open hand version was changed to use the fist. Higaonna Sanchin presents in three sections with eleven repetitions of section one waza being used. Only one repetition of the extended fist position executed with the same leg forward as the extending hand is used, then three repetitions of section two waza are practiced and *one* mawashi uke comprising section three (Toguchi version). Higaonna Sanchin also includes two turns in the kata before the kata is ended, marginally (half a pace) behind the starting point. This was, quite possibly, the version learned by Miyagi in 1902.

Embusen:
Half step forward, *two* full steps forward, turn, *three full steps forward*, turn; *three full steps forward*, one step back, half step to close.

In summary, I suspect that Miyagi simply removed the turns, but included seven waza in section one of his adaptation and two mawashi uke techniques in section three. It would, after all, be a rather short kata without the turns and accompanying repetitions. I further suspect that Miyagi included the two repetitions of waza performed with the same leg forward as the extending hand, to maintain a minimum number of seven waza and thus avoid using the turns, extra steps, or adding unnecessary complications. Finally, it must be borne in mind that there were several prominent students of Miyagi Chojun who espoused different Sanchin kata: Higa Seko, Toguchi Sekichi, and Yamaguchi Gogen, to name just three. Toguchi, for example, seems to have favoured a Sanchin kata that followed the Higaonna format described above.

The small amount of floor space required to practice Miyagi Sanchin is another reason for its popularity. I have had many letters from people all over the world who enjoyed my previously published work on Sanchin kata. Amongst them were people who live in restricted spaces (correctional institutions in the USA, for example) and use Sanchin kata as a means of physical and mental exercise. Yet others say they enjoy the fact that they can practice in a small office or workspace, including stressed executives, bankers, medical doctors and academics. I even had one communication from a janitor who practiced Sanchin in a broom closet!

Ko-do Ryu Sanchin – Solo Kata

Unlike most schools that practice Sanchin, Ko-do Ryu performs the kata on both sides of the body. That which is practiced on the right, is also practiced equally on the left, including the openings and closings of the kata. Also, the breathing pattern used in Ko-do Ryu Sanchin differs somewhat from that used in, for example, Goju Ryu.

Within Ko-do Ryu, Sanchin is practiced in a 'softer' (more relaxed) way than is often seen, for example, in some Goju Ryu. This is done to avoid hypertension (high blood pressure), haemorrhoids (piles), and other complaints listed by several prominent Karate authors as being common amongst certain Goju Ryu practitioners (those who practice with too much 'Go'/hard, and not enough 'Ju'/soft). For example, in his book *Okinawan Karate Teachers, styles and secret techniques* (London: A&C Black 1989, p.39) Mark Bishop, an extremely experienced Karate-ka and a historian who spent many years living on Okinawa and trained directly under Miyazato Eiichi of the Jundokan, wrote in a sub-section entitled, 'Goju Ryu and Health':

> During the course of my research I met quite a few karate teachers who berated Goju-ryu for its general hardness and warned me to discontinue the training (which I eventually did) or face high blood pressure related illnesses and a premature death. These critics gained much of their visual evidence from watching unskilled practitioners doing dynamic-tension demonstrations of Sanchin … whilst being punched and kicked by an associate and issuing a loud and guttural 'hiss' … The result of the exertion on the heart, blood vessels and internal organs is not considered by the critics to be good for the health … but the fact that premature deaths through illness associated with high blood pressure are common among Goju-ryu practitioners cannot be disputed …

Bishop goes on to suggest that haemorrhoids and other health conditions are the result of the practice of a 'crowd pleasing', 'body building', 'dynamic tension' type of Sanchin. It is clear from his assertion (not to mention the records) that Sanchin kata, like virtually anything else, can be abused. However, it is the present author's belief that, if approached sensibly, and never 'overdone' – during, for example, a demonstration designed to attract students – Miyagi Sanchin is a fine holistic exercise and a worthy foundation upon which to build Karate.

Sanchin Solo Kata

Sanchin quan is divided into three sections.

Section 1. One limb (arm) is moved independently of and from the other(s), and the arms are involved singly and perform separate roles. This section utilises only closed fists.

Section 2. Two limbs (both arms) are moved simultaneously performing the same roles. This section utilises open hands and closed fists.

Section 3. Three limbs (two arms and a leg) are moved simultaneously but independently, performing different roles. This section utilises only open hands.

This template (paradigm) contains the essential skills of physical co-ordination required to be effective in any Martial Art. It is the foundation/basic kata of Ko-do Ryu.

Skill acquired from section one allows independent action (operation) of the arms, for example one to trap/block-with, the other to strike. Skills acquired from section two allow the simultaneous use of both hands to trap, intercept or 'tie-up' limbs during, for example, pushing hands. And skills acquired in section three epitomize the concept of 'float, sink, swallow and spit/push', the underlying tactic of the whole kata, and a concept drawn directly from unarmed Chinese Quan-fa. The co-ordination and 'muscle memory' to effectively utilize this technique (designed to 'draw the opponent in', unbalance him and 'expel' him, pushing him off-balance) can be most clearly seen in section three of Sanchin.

The Sanchin Kata sequence

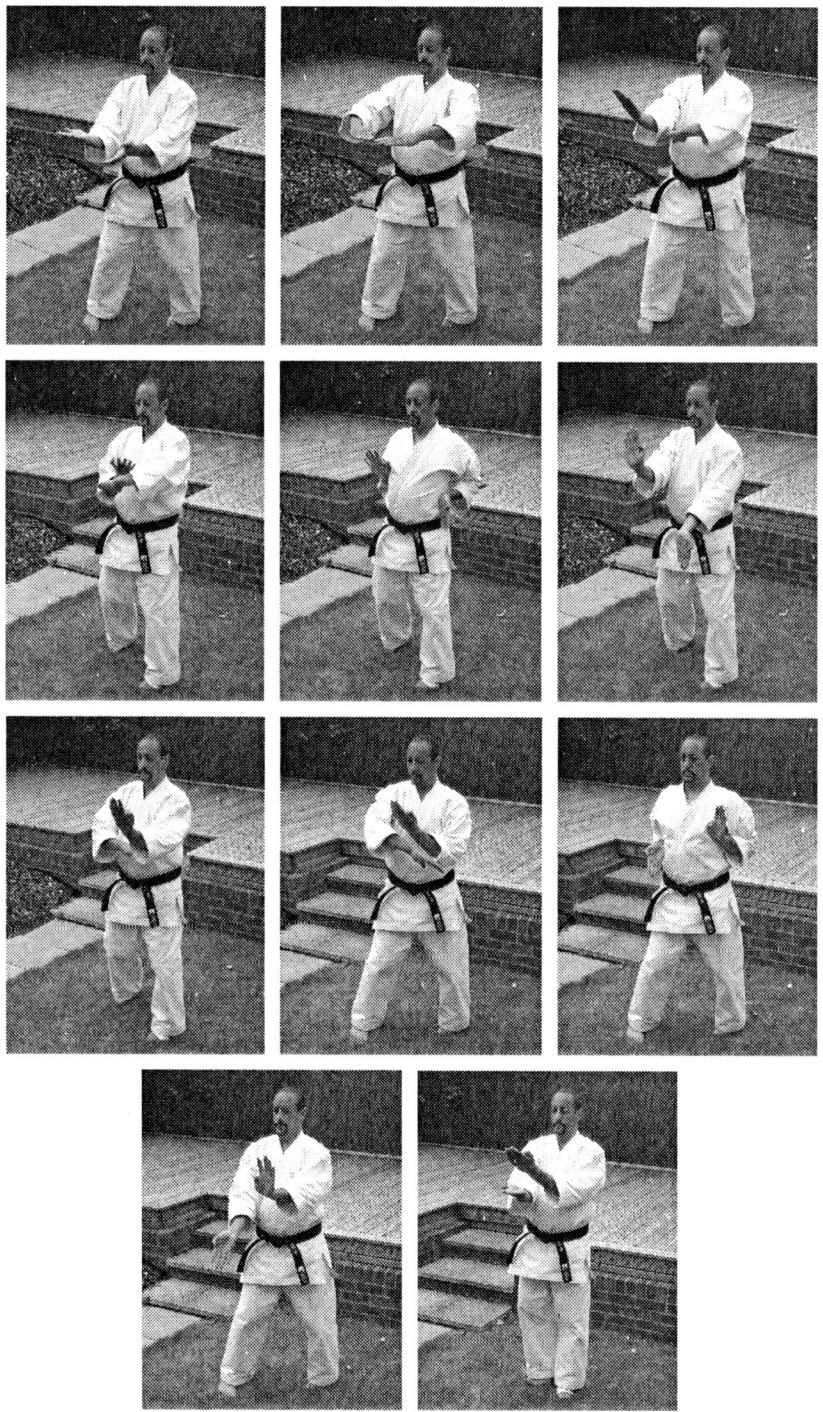

*repeat on
opposite side*

Sanchin Breathing

Ko-do Ryu Sanchin is often performed using an ancient and specific breathing pattern known variously as 'Pot bellied' breathing or 'Pranayama'; meaning to restrain the breath. The emphasis is on control of the out-breath during which the belly is encouraged to 'pot' upon inhalation and to flatten upon exhalation. The abdomen should be fully tensed on completion of each exhalation. Traditionally, only beginners need to 'show' their breathing or breathe noisily, simply so that the teacher can check it. Thereafter (generally) breathing should not be shown or sounded.

Sanchin Section One – Breathing Rate

Sanchin is perhaps best performed to a constant and synchronised rhythm of one 'beat' to breathe in and four 'beats' to breathe out. Thus, four times as long is spent exhaling as is spent inhaling. To learn this, simply count 'one' whilst retracting an arm and breathing in, and 'two' and 'three' whilst stepping forward and breathing out, and 'four' upon arrival and consolidation of the 'Sanchin fortress' as I shall name the double arm Sanchin position.

On completion of the third and final right foot placement and upon assumption of the Sanchin fortress, and on the count of four, tense the abdomen by 'rolling' it back and up, pressing with the diaphragm to expel the maximum amount of air. Then, retract the left hand to the side of the body as you breathe in. Press the arm forward as you begin to breathe out. Continue breathing out, somewhat extending the breath here (in lieu of another step). Then, standing still, repeat the movements another four times without stepping, measuring the breathing, taking care to prolong the out breath to be four times as long as the in breath. On completion of the required repetitions of section one waza, instead of making the 'Sanchin fortress', turn the right hand over to make one half of the 'diamond' position ('cranes wing'), bring the left hand up from its extended position to form the second half of the 'diamond' ('cranes wings'), and control the breath so that the final fourth 'beat' coincides with the change of the arms to the double 'diamond' ('cranes wings') position.

Section Two – Breathing

Retract both arms as you breathe in. This counts as one beat. Begin to extend the arms first with the hands (palms up) over a two ... three count, consolidating the final diamond shape with the fourth beat and full expulsion of air.

Section Three – Breathing
Withdraw your hands in two semi-circles, complete inhaling.
This counts for one beat. Press your hands forward and exhale
over a two and three count (beat) consolidating the out-breath by
tensing the diaphragm and consolidating the position on the
fourth beat.

The Purpose of Sanchin Breathing

The (yoga) Ishopanishad informs us that (to achieve the goals of
yoga) physical movements alone are not helpful in themselves,
nor does concentration alone bring success (Ishopanishad 9 and
11, from the translation found in *Chakras: Energy Centres of
Transformation* by Harish Johari (Rochester, VT: Inner traditions,
1987)). One who combines concentration with physical
control achieves success. This idea is also found in the spiritual
cultivation traditionally associated with many types of
unarmed Quan.

The purpose of Sanchin breathing is to coordinate the breath
with physical movement. In line with this dictum, *Sanchin is a
whole body and mind exercise.* The feet press and strongly grip the
floor. The 'frame' made by the stance exercise the ankles, calves,
knees (quadriceps), thighs and buttocks. Avoiding undue tension,
the shoulders should be kept down and the armpits locked,
providing exercise for the deltoids (shoulders), the Lattisimus
dorsi (muscles at the side of the body), the pectorals (chest
muscles) and all the muscle groups of the back. The chest is
opened up and the ribcage stretched during section three
of Sanchin.

Next to be considered are the extensive muscle groups controlling
the diaphragm. They are exercised by breath control. One may
also consider the facial grimace (mouth stretched) sometimes

used during Sanchin, as an emulation of various guardian deities traditionally associated with both Chinese and Japanese Martial Arts. This 'grimace' can be used as an aid to controlling and exercising the muscles and glands in the neck. However, too much tension must be strictly avoided.

During Sanchin kata, the breath is carefully regulated through 'tension diaphragmatic breathing'. The lungs work under a negative pressure, therefore the urge to breathe-in, whilst controllable to a certain degree, is largely reflexive. Normal breathing usually takes care of itself. Tension diaphragmatic breathing places emphasis on the out breath. The breath should be regulated but not held. Breath has a direct relationship to concentration. Tension diaphragmatic breathing is designed to super-oxygenate the practitioner's brain, without causing light-headedness.

Physiologically, tension diaphragmatic breathing stimulates the nerves within the muscles called proprioceptors, which in turn induce a state of alertness in the posterior hypothalamus of the brain, making one fully awake whilst one's brain waves change from a beta to an alpha frequency. Associated with Chinese concepts of the 'Tao' or 'Way' (of things), Chinese Taoist philosophy had an enormous if somewhat indirect influence on social attitudes, values and spiritual and physical culture. The practice of Sanchin does indeed provide the necessary tools for the practitioner to experience a direct relationship with the 'Tao'. This is accomplished by the intense cultivation of posture in combination with breath.

Everything has a vibration, a rhythm, and a cycle, including the human body and the breath. The normal breath rate for an adult engaged in light activity is approximately eighteen breaths per minute. Yoga teaches that at this breathing rate we are the most focused on the external world and fully subject to the domination of thought, emotion, and the stresses and strains of everyday life. During heavy concentration, the breath rate drops to about nine breaths per minute. If one is tired, protracted concentration may then easily become sleepiness, which occurs as a result of the reduced oxygen intake.

Normal breath volume for an adult is approximately 5000 ml of air per breath. During Sanchin kata, the breath rate can be reduced to 7.5 breaths (or even less) per minute, but the air intake per breath is increased from 500 to 1200 ml of air or more. The result is a significant increase in concentration due to the improved oxygenation of the brain. This is not hyperventilation because although the rate of air intake is increased, the breath *rate* is actually lowered.

Another effect of this type of breathing is the altered state of consciousness it induces, which occurs as a result of being put in synchronization with powerful natural cycles. There is a 1 to 4 ratio between the breath and pulse rates, 18 breaths are taken for every 72 pulses. Comparing the human respiration and circulatory systems with that of the solar system yields some interesting facts. The Earth rotates one degree every four minutes. It is useful here to view these minutes as *pulses* rather than arbitrarily conceived time periods. It would appear that the human breath and circulatory rates match the clocking mechanism that controls the Earth's rotation around its axis. By practicing Sanchin kata and carefully applying the 1:4 ratio outlined above, it becomes possible to harmonize with the Tao. 'Being at one with nature' and the Tao becomes a physical reality rather than a mystical or poetic metaphor. Finally, connecting Sanchin with breathing, one should understand the following important point. In matters of concentration, it is not the will-power that controls thought drift, but rather the mechanism of the breath (all systems shut down without oxygen). For effective Sanchin breathing, it is important to breathe using the diaphragm and upon exhaling to tighten the abdomen in order to harness the considerable muscle power of the diaphragm.

Applied Sanchin

Applied Sanchin Kata centres around the three sections into which the kata is divided. These three sections can be (should be) applied between 'pairs' (in 'shime testing' and pushing hands) as a means of 'practically' applying the theories and concepts inherent in the solo kata, rather than individuals (or groups) merely endlessly training in the solo routine (as beneficial as that may be).

Due to the re-constructed and non specific (applications) nature of Miyagi Chojun's Sanchin, it is impossible (unlike with more conventional kata) to give only a single set of applications. This is due to the universal nature of the simple or basic techniques in this foundation (core *modern* Karate) kata and their similarity to movements (shapes) found in other (specific) kata – Naihanchin for example. So, one should consider looking instead at the 'body geometry' used in Sanchin kata; the triangles, semi circles and circles – and what I would call 'strong' points. Even if Miyagi Sanchin was unwittingly evolved from a modified weapons kata, it should not be disparaged. As a basic *synthesis* its technical construction does yield up a (simplified) version of a Fujianese Quan-fa (boxing type) form, without the bewildering complexity commonly seen in many such Quan. Simplicity is often difficult to attain as human aspirations often lead to intricacy or embellishment. The very (Zen-like) simplicity of Miyagi Sanchin is one of its greatest strengths. Moreover, it must be borne in mind that Miyagi was closer to the times of the Fujianese Quan-fa boxers than we are, and (if Rokushu/Tensho kata is anything to go by) he was quite an insightful reformer.

Of course, anything can be claimed as an *application* for Sanchin, and I must admit that my declaration that function dictated form, and that a true kata has a specific set of applications and not multiple layers of applications, can not be asserted where Miyagi Sanchin is concerned. There are two basic reasons for this:

1. The minimalism of Miyagi Sanchin
2. Its evolution from a weapons kata

However, the basic structure of the kata has led me, after many years of effort and commitment to it, to be able to bring to life the legend or mythology that states,

> Sanchin is the beginner's kata but it is also the most advanced kata and is therefore the beginning and the end of Karate.

Strangely, without gaining comprehensive knowledge of the applications of Rokushu and Naihanchin, probing Sanchin, with the same degree of depth, would have proved to be much more difficult. All in all quite a 'chicken and egg' paradox! Conceptually, Sanchin can indeed successfully and profitably be considered as a 'building block' kata.

Miyagi Sanchin can therefore most usefully be viewed as a structural paradigm, a skeleton on which to build; a catalogue providing the strongest fundamental positions of leverage for the human body. Indeed the kata is powerful and comprehensive, yet quite beautiful in its minimalism. Toguchi Seikichi had this to say about Sanchin in general (Okinawan Goju-Ryu, p.161):

> ... We can be proud of Sanchin. It is unique to karate and does not exist in any other Japanese martial art. I feel that it should be regarded not only as part of the Goju-Ryu system but as a precious resource of Okinawan Karate-Do ... It [Sanchin] can and should be practiced frequently. (Parenthesis mine)

Sanchin and Efficiency

The human touch-reflex system will operate most efficiently if structures (and shapes) with which it is familiar are constantly used. What I mean by this is, *the closer, for example, a wrist lock resembles a structure in Sanchin kata, the better a well-trained body (one trained in Sanchin) will recall it and use it. The 'neural pathway' (muscle memory) will be well travelled, and a good body-habit formed by constant solo kata practice, supported by application that deviates as little as possible from the solo kata.* This is important because the kata itself provides, precisely the catalogue of moves pertinent to such applications. This way of practicing strengthens kata and application which become mutually supportive. This remains one of the single most important points regarding kata.

It is, however, extremely important that readers do not confuse the genesis of Miyagi's Sanchin with older kata, or think that all kata, those that do indeed have one specific set of applications, can be viewed in the same way as Miyagi Sanchin. As I have indicated, Miyagi Sanchin is somewhat unique. George Mattson, quoting Uechi Kanei, the late senior master of Uechi in, *Uechiryu Karate Do* (p.88) states,

> ... the famous Chogan [Chojun] Myagi [Miyagi] after studying many years from Higashionna, [Higaonna Kanyro] created the now popular Goju Ryu method of performing Sanchin ... Goju Sanchin ... has to be classified as an exercise, whereas Uechi Sanchin still remains a Kata ... (Parenthesis mine)

I agree with this to the extent that Uechi Sanchin is a specific and systematic treatment of basic Sai techniques whereas Miyagi Sanchin is abstract. Further, it is probable that Miyagi Chojun, like his teacher before him, did not know that the old open-handed Sanchin (from which the modern Sanchin was probably developed) was a weapons kata. Of course, Miyagi may well have known, but, on the balance of probability I doubt it.

Miyagi Sanchin as Chin-Na

The structure of Miyagi Sanchin conveniently yields a complete series of Chin-Na techniques ('kansetsu waza' in Japanese). All of the basic methods of effecting (frontal) wrist locks can be covered by the positions in the kata. What's incredible is the uncanny accuracy with which they fit!

The twisting of the wrist is the primary tactic used in Chin-Na. Due to the nature of human skeletal construction, Chin-Na effectively restrains an opponent, and the techniques can be logically and systematically classified into classes or categories of movement. The most basic are; the wrist can only be twisted to turn the elbow out or to turn the elbow in, and only two types of grip can be used to do this; the sword grip and the scabbard grip.

The Sword Grip

The sword grip refers to the way one grips a sword. Despite the similarities with the sword grip proper, once again, the term used applies to the directional relationship between the hands and arms of two people facing each other.

The Scabbard Grip

The scabbard grip refers to the way one holds a sword scabbard, or more accurately, the directional relationship between the hand and the scabbard, or between two grapplers.

Furthermore, the following techniques marked with an asterisk (*) are found in Naihanchin where they are used as one half of double-handed techniques designed to 'tumble' or throw an opponent. Note: All Naihanchin techniques are 'crossed arm'.

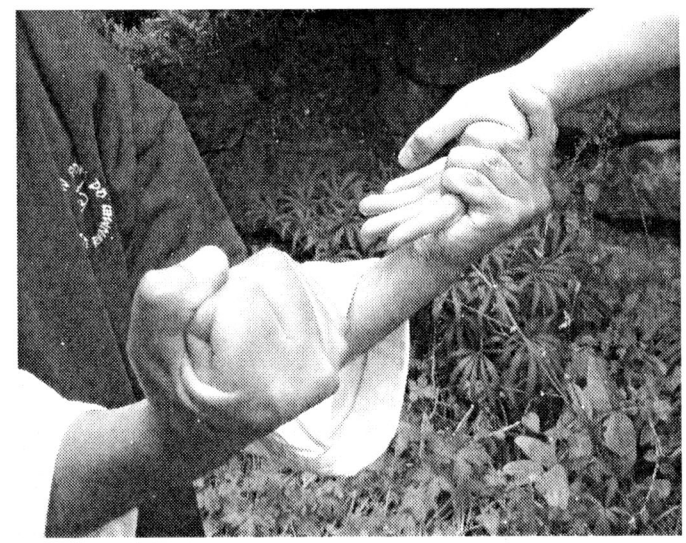

The Sword Grip

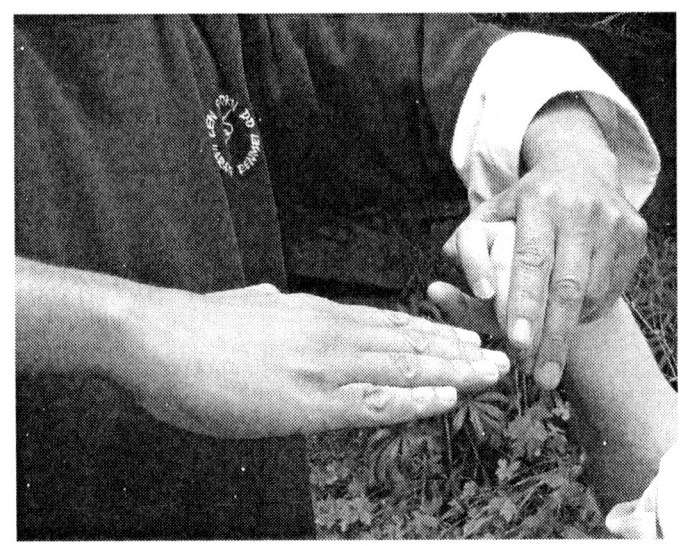

The Scabbard Grip

Section One
There are two distinct (practical) 'sword grip' Chin-Na techniques that can be gleaned from section one of Sanchin. They are both 'crossed arm' (right hand to right hand, for example).

1. Crossed side twisting from the outside of the opponent's wrist, locking his elbow out * (Fig. A).

2. Crossed side twisting from underneath the opponent's wrist/palm up hand, locking his elbow in * (Fig. B).

Section one techniques comprise two 'inside gate' techniques.

Section Two
There are two distinct 'scabbard grip' Chin-Na techniques that can be gleaned from section two. They are both 'crossed arm'.

1. The application of a scabbard grip that locks the opponent's elbow in * (Fig. C).

2. The application of a scabbard grip that locks the opponent's elbow out (Fig. D).

Section two techniques comprise one 'outside gate' technique and one 'inside gate' technique.

Fig. A. crossed side twisting   *Fig. B. crossed side twisting*

Fig. C. Scabbard grip

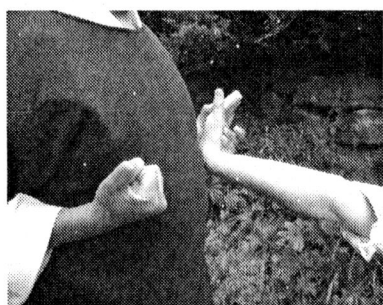

Fig. D. Scabbard grip

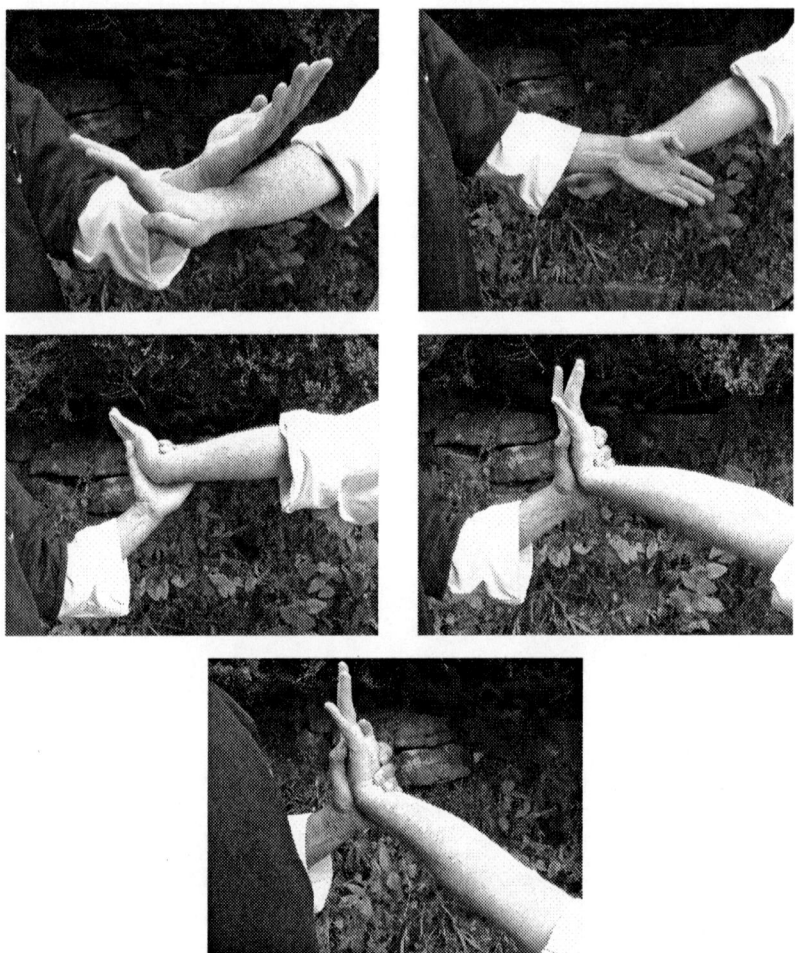

Fig. E. 'Scabbard technique'

Section Three
There are two techniques that can be gleaned from section three, one 'sword grip' and one 'scabbard' grip.

1. The application of one 'scabbard technique' (Fig. E).

2. The application of one 'sword grip' technique (Fig. F).

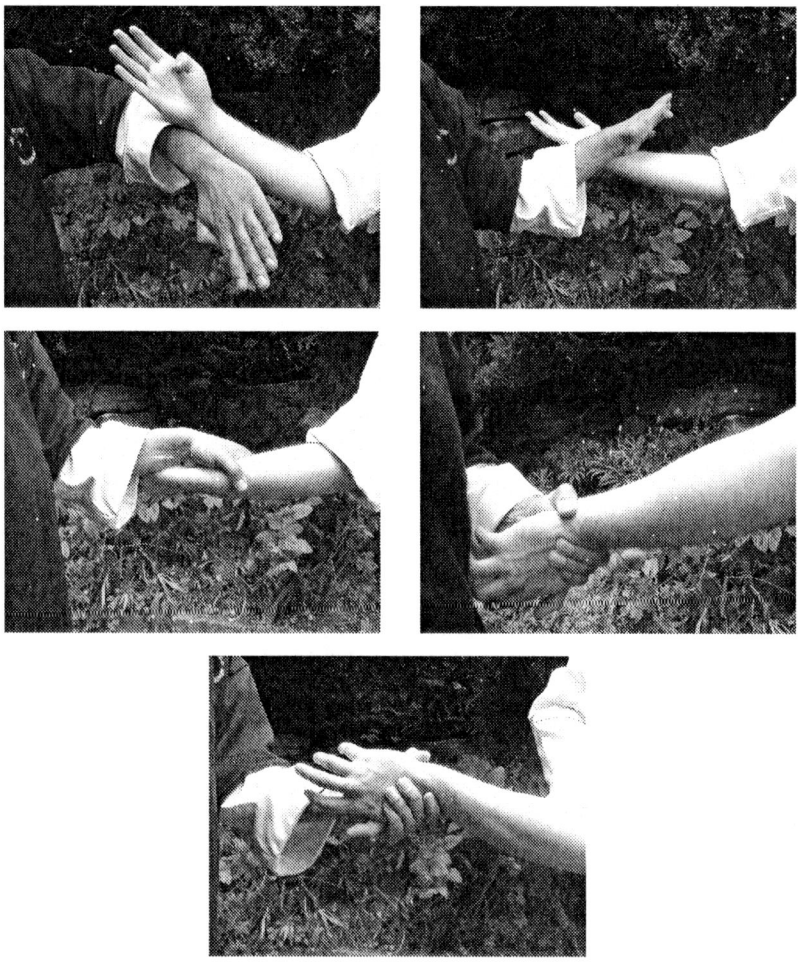

Fig. F. 'Sword technique'

The Chin-Na techniques in section three allow the application of *two* (same-sided) 'deflections' to the outside of an opponents arm, one elbow up and the other elbow down – both resulting in a sword and scabbard grip Chin-Na respectively. Please note, they are both 'same-sided' grips (left arm to right arm, for example).

Miyagi Sanchin as a 'Boxing' Kata

Sanchin, in common with other methods founded in Chinese Quan-fa, can most successfully be used in the free-flow of pushing hands, in which its techniques can be successfully used in a structured 'game of boxing'. But the idea here is not to engage in a free for all, or to emulate Western boxing.

The Sanchin 'boxing game' is played in similar fashion to pushing hands, with one noticeable difference. The force is collected and stored with one hand, and transferred to the other, giving a kind of 'end game' appearance to using the gate system and the pushing hands positions. Thus, Sanchin Boxing is a positive way of gaining a conclusive advantage over an opponent employing the 'third hand'. The emphasis in Sanchin Boxing is on using the Sanchin fortress; the so called 'middle level block' position, and the fore-fist thrust, in combination to attack; and the triangular position from section two in collaboration with a fore-fist thrust, to defend. The double palm push/jolt from section three may also be used. Sanchin boxing techniques rely upon using a stored force rather than a self-generated force. Moreover, they are not as dependent on fast twitch (athletic) muscle fibre activity because they are 'push punches', operated smoothly and under load. In short, the 'punches' represent a release of stored force, and the defences against them re-absorb and re-direct that force.

Typically, in Sanchin boxing, the driver will open up with a push/block, triggering his opponent to respond with his own middle level passing/block followed by a fore-fist thrust counter. It is this counter that the driver is inviting and wants to work with. He has, in effect, asked for the attack, carefully setting up the right conditions in the pushing hands to practice against this attack. It is a contact reflex request not a visual or verbally asked-for attack. 'Asking' for an attack in this way prevents pushing hands from deteriorating into a practice that merely generates a constant sense of apprehension or sporadic 'flinching' when one's opponent suddenly opens up with a punch.

'Tijikun' or 'Seiken', the well-known Okinawan penchant for using a basic fore-fist punch, sits very well with the technical construction of Miyagi Chojun's Sanchin. The (slowly practiced) 'fore-fist thrust' is anatomically one of the strongest methods of and for delivering a short (body blow) provided the thrusting arm is never fully extended. Keeping the elbow in and down, and never completely extending the arm during a thrust, allows one to deliver powerful blows yet protects the elbow joint(s) from damage. Moreover, a short swift blow to, for example, the solar plexus will definitely facilitate the application of a 'Chin-Na' technique in cases of resistance. This idea is an old idea ('distracting' an awkward opponent prior to restraining him). Whilst I previously rejected this idea, historical investigation into the use and application of Chin-Na has changed my view.

It is important to note that there is no jodan (upper level or face) punch in Sanchin. Ethically this does make sense, and despite the potential effect of a punch to the head, one risks damage to the fist. Besides, punching to the head is frowned upon by the authorities, even today. One could consider the ethics of Sai use in which striking to the body is discouraged (the opponent must be rendered up in reasonable condition). Thus, as in the use of the Sai, striking ('punching') the arms is a good option. One may consider directing a strong fist attack towards the bicep of an attacker, automatically bringing an arm down, thereby discouraging that attacker and taking the fight out of him.

Sanchin Boxing: Method 1

Sanchin Boxing

Method One
Method one is analogous to the first pushing hands *change*.

1. From pushing hands, 'A', on the right, using a clenched-fist backhand (blocking) action with his front (contact) arm, 'presses' 'B's' contact arm across and towards the shoulder of his rear arm to trigger 'B's' punch.

312

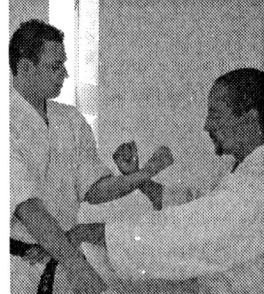

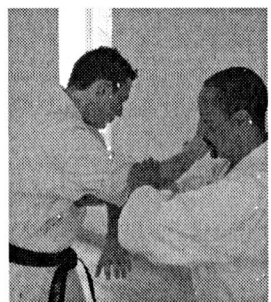

Sanchin Boxing: Method 1

2. 'B' 'borrows' 'A's' force by using a middle level forearm block/passing technique. 'B' then transfers the borrowed force into a punch, leaving the blocking hand in the basic Sanchin arm position – 'inside gate' – thus trapping 'A's' pushing arm.

3. 'A', using the triangulated position from section two of Sanchin kata, deflects 'B's' attack, taking care to 'jam' 'B's' punch at the elbow and not at the wrist which could provoke an undesirable response (a back-fist strike for example).

4. 'A' then 'wraps-up' 'B's' attacking arm with his contact (blocking) hand, by circling, lifting and pressing to the outside of 'B's' arm, trapping it whilst simultaneously delivering a short, focused fore-fist punch. The punch easily breaches 'B's' blocking (Sanchin) arm which is weak from the side.

Sanchin Boxing: Method 2

Method Two

Method two is analogous to the second pushing hands change, and simply repeats the techniques of method one on the opposite side of the body but from the same pushing hands start side (position).

1. 'A', using a clenched-fist *forehand* (blocking) action with his *rear* hand, 'presses' 'B's' contact arm across and towards the shoulder of his rear arm to trigger 'B's' punch.

2. Once again, 'B' 'borrows' 'A's' force by using a middle-level forearm block/passing technique, passing the force to the 'outside gate' this time. 'B' then transfers the borrowed force into a punch, leaving the blocking hand in the basic Sanchin arm position, thus trapping 'A's' pushing arm.

3. 'A', using the triangulated position from section two of Sanchin kata, deflects 'B's' attack, once again taking care to 'jam' 'B's' punch at the elbow and not at the wrist. 'A' simultaneously removes his trapped hand from an 'outside gate' position to an 'inside gate' position.

4. In similar fashion to method one, 'A' then 'wraps-up' 'B's' attacking arm with his contact (blocking) hand, by circling to the outside and trapping the arm whilst simultaneously delivering a short, focused fore-fist punch with a hand that has already breached 'B's' Sanchin position.

Sanchin Boxing: Method 3

Method Three

Method three is analogous to the third pushing hands *change*.

1. 'A', using a clenched-fist middle-level backhand (blocking) action with his *rear* hand (in effect the third hand), 'presses' 'B's' *rear* arm across and towards the shoulder of his front (pushing) arm to trigger 'B's' punch.

Sanchin Boxing: Method 3

2. 'B' 'borrows' 'A's' force by using a middle level forearm block/passing technique. 'B' then transfers the borrowed force into a punch, leaving the blocking hand in the basic Sanchin arm position, thus trapping 'A's' pushing arm.

3. 'A', using the triangulated position from section two of Sanchin kata, deflects 'B's' attack, once again taking care to 'jam' 'B's' punch at the elbow and not at the wrist. 'A' then 'passes' the force from one arm to the other, using the same triangulated position.

4. 'A' then circles his lead hand in, around and underneath 'B's' punching arm and simultaneously slaps/presses or pushes 'B's' punching arm and his guard arm to expel 'B'. This technique is a form of repulsion/expulsion using the type of energy known amongst Chinese stylists as 'Fa-jing'. This technique is also known as 'turning the Dharma wheel'. It is one of the most fundamental of all Shao-lin Quan-fa techniques, and is found in many Shao-lin based styles, including Yongchun in which it is referred to as Po Pai (a double palm push), and is used in the 'wooden man' exercise. Variations on Po Pai can also be seen in Chukka Shao-lin (Phoenix eye Kung Fu), Babulien (Happoren) quan, Hung Gar and Hung Kuen Kung fu, besides many other (Southern) Shao-lin based Kung Fu styles, too numerous to list. The function of Po Pai is that of, 'float', 'sink', 'swallow' and 'spit' (out).

Chapter Seven
Rokushu (Tensho)

Rokushu Capsule History

DECIPHERING THE APPLICATIONS to Rokushu ('six variations' or varieties, better known as Tensho, 'rotating palms'), was no easy matter. Having seen a number of peculiar (not to mention bizarre) applications of this kata over the years, and having heard quite a lot of mysticism being espoused regarding the development of 'secret' or 'higher-level Karate power' gained from the practice of this 'top' kata, it was quite shocking to discover that Rokushu was, in effect, a simple series of grip escapes! The natural control or grasping of the arms developed by the Chinese, and used to 'shut off' the opponent's arms (control them) during pushing hands, necessitated the development of counter strategies, grip reversals and grip escapes, which is precisely what the Rokushu applications facilitate.

Although Tensho was supposedly synthesised from a quan called Rokushu, no one is sure how. All that the practitioner can be certain about is that *none of the vital six techniques of Rokushu are missing from Tensho*. I think that Rokushu, if not designed to be *incorporated* with(in) Sanchin, fits it with uncanny accuracy, and is, as the name suggests, six variations or varieties on the Sanchin theme, accessible to anyone who has a firm grasp of Sanchin.

It is curious that no one seems to know from whom Miyagi learned this hitherto enigmatic kata. It is not recorded that he learned it from Higaonna. Historically, all that is really known about Rokushu is that Miyagi Chojun allegedly observed a quan of that name in Fuzhou, supposedly sometime after the death of Higaonna. According to Higaonna Morio, Miyagi was twenty-seven years of age at the time. It is further alleged that he spent from 1917 to 1921 carrying out the research that culminated in Tensho kata, although it's not really known what that research consisted of. According to Kogyu Tasaki, Tensho kata continued to be referred to as Rokushu (Rokkishu) as late as 1929.

Steve Rowe, a leading British Karate Sensei, author, experienced Martial Artist and columnist for various Martial Arts magazines (and a personal acquaintance), happened to be attending a delegation of various Chinese and other Martial Artists in the early 1990s, when he was asked to demonstrate Karate. He elected to perform Tensho, stood up and did so. At the conclusion of Steve's demonstration, an elderly Chinese Sifu was heard to say,

> "That was White Crane. I thought he was going to demonstrate Karate!"

Indeed, although there is very little evidence or proof regarding the origin of Tensho/Rokushu, similar techniques can clearly be seen in both Preying Mantis and White Crane quan. Fortunately, the applications of Rokushu are easy to see and learn, and therefore the qualities of the form speak for themselves. The successful application of Rokushu does, however, require a degree of familiarity with basic Sanchin arm positioning, and the ability to assume and use a good Sanchin stance.

Examining Goju Ryu Karate kata, it can be noted that Sanchin and Tensho kata are the only two kata to begin and end in exactly the same way. This is curios, to say the least. Cutting to the chase here, Rokushu is, I argue, simply a 'bolt-on' series of six variations on the Sanchin theme.

'Function Dictates Form' is the appellation definitely worth remembering with respect to Rokushu. This kata really 'does do what it says in the title'. Rokushu means six varieties or variations – on the Sanchin theme. It is a famous form allegedly with its origins in China. Referred to as Tensho in Goju Ryu, remember, it is considered to be one of the twin jewels in the crown of Goju Ryu Karate, the other being Sanchin.

Returning to the theme of Sanchin and Tensho kata being the only two kata (within Goju Ryu) to begin and end in exactly the same way, strong evidence suggests that the Rokushu kata has profoundly influenced the development of Goju Ryu Karate. That evidence comes in the understanding that all the (subsequent) kata were sandwiched in between Sanchin and Rokushu/Tensho. I think the influence of Rokushu/Tensho can be seen in Goju Seisan and Suparinpei kata, where the characteristic bent wrist, 'standing dragon' techniques are repeated.

Within Rokushu, the symmetrical and simultaneous performance of each of the six techniques (the third time they are repeated) does not have a direct application; it merely represents an opportunity to identify and correct left/right bias and inconsistencies. Beginners have a tendency to advance the shoulder of the 'working hand' further forward than the dormant hand/shoulder, thus making them unequal or 'body biased'. In application, this will reduce the effectiveness of the techniques and compromise the practitioner's posture and balance.

Analysis of the Technical Construction
of Miyagi Chojun's Tensho (Rokushu)

Goju Ryu Tensho kata, whilst possibly reflecting the technical substance of the Rokushu Quan from which it was allegedly constructed, remains a kata that breaks the golden rule which insists an authentic kata finishes at the same spot on which it was started. Goju Ryu Tensho does not. In fact, it finishes one and a half steps behind its starting point. This is because of its sequencing. After practicing five of the six essential techniques on the right, and again on the left, it finally practices all *six* techniques together in a third section using both hands simultaneously. This section includes the so-far absent crane wing, which is then repeated twice, each time, however, being accompanied by a full step backwards. By the time two 'Mawashi uke' techniques are added, accompanied by a further two steps backwards, the practitioner ends the kata a full one and a half steps *behind* the starting point. Goju Ryu practitioners do not usually repeat the kata in mirror image.

Ko-do Ryu Rokushu

Ko-do Ryu *Rokushu*, in contrast to the Goju version, simply includes the crane wing technique at each stage; once for the right hand, once for the left, and once using both hands together. Ko-do Ryu Rokushu is also practiced in mirror image, and (like Sanchin) finishes at the same spot on which it was started. Ko-do Ryu Rokushu is often performed a little more rapidly than Goju Ryu Tensho.

*Ko-do Ryu
Rokushu*

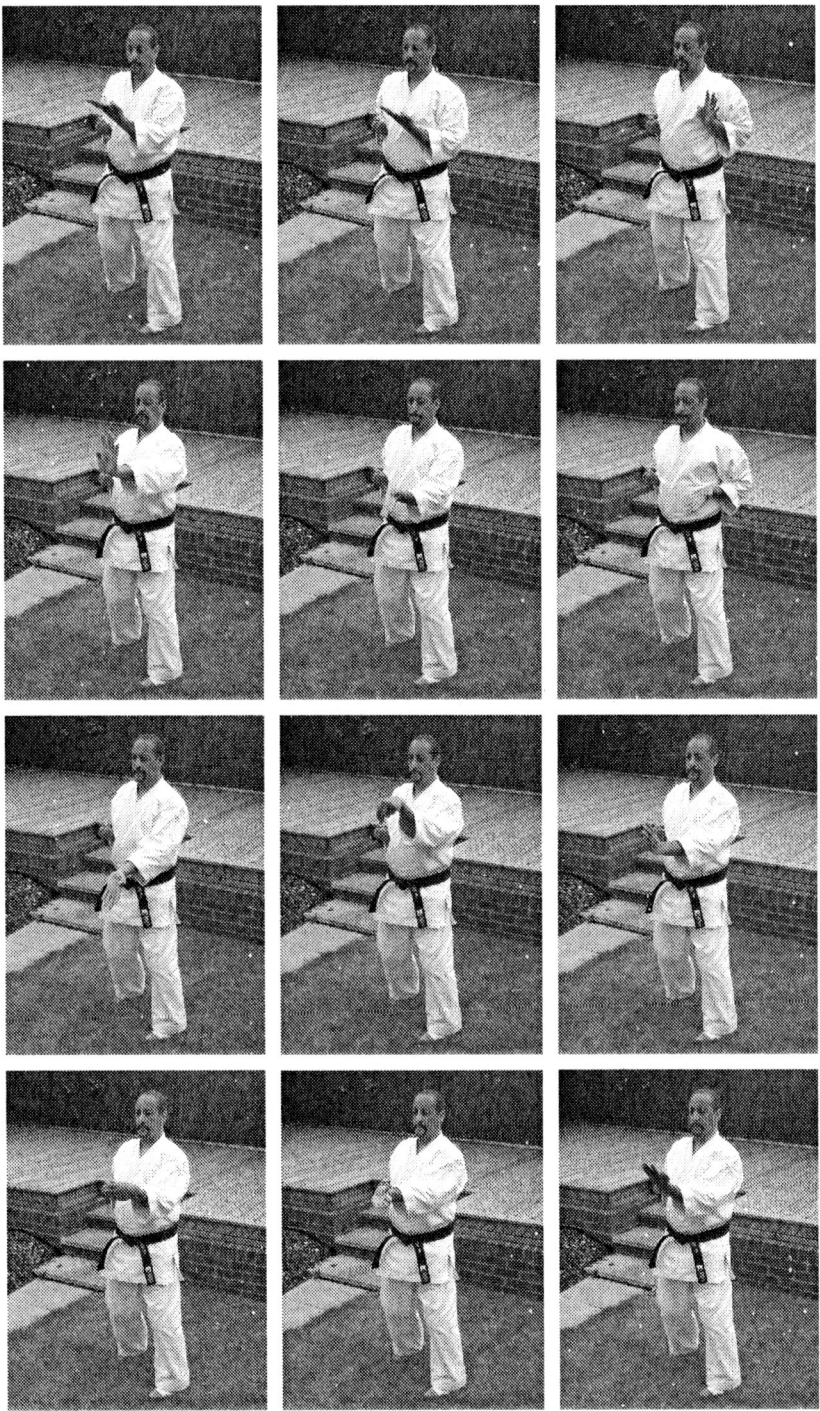

*repeat on
other side*

Applied Rokushu

In the application of Rokushu, there are three elements to each 'grip release' technique:

1. Establishing a rooted stance,
2. Establishing a strong arm position,
3. Effecting the release of a grip.

They are intended for use between standing practitioners.

Rokushu's Six Grip Release Techniques

Rokushu's 'grip release' techniques, in the order in which they occur in the kata, are known in Ko-do Ryu as

1. Snake
2. Tiger
3. Leopard
4. Standing-dragon
5. Laying-dragon
6. Crane's wing

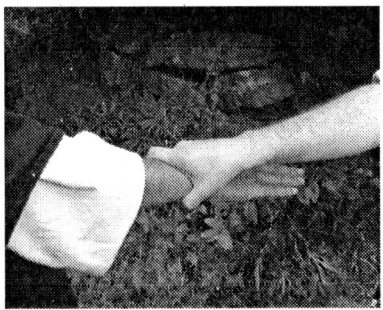 

Snake

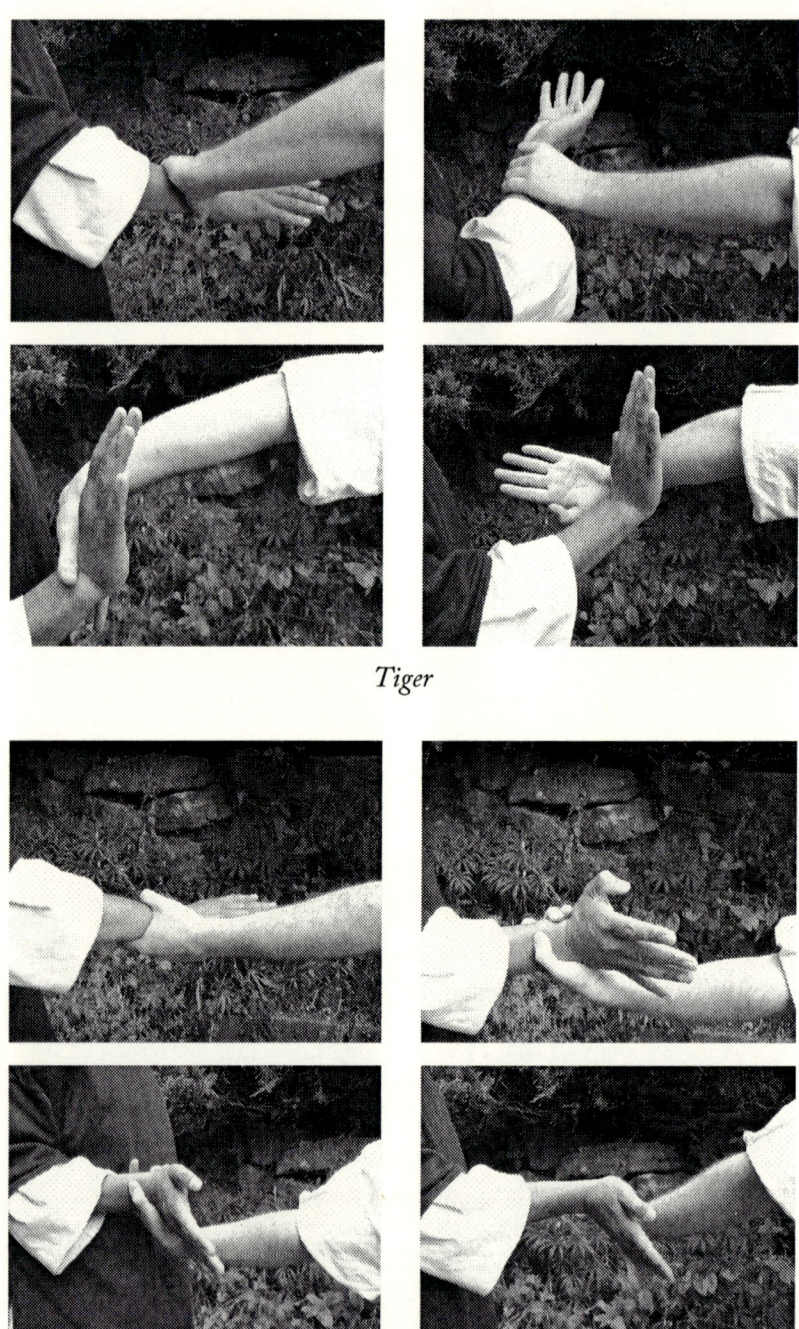

Tiger

Leopard

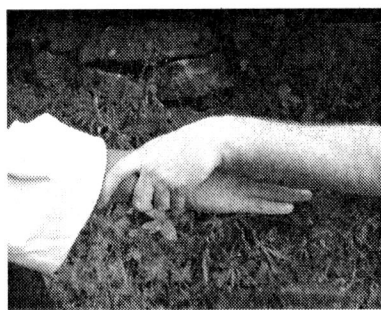

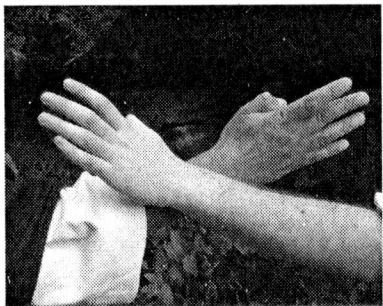

Standing–dragon

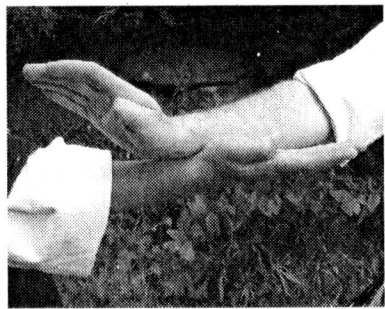

Laying–dragon

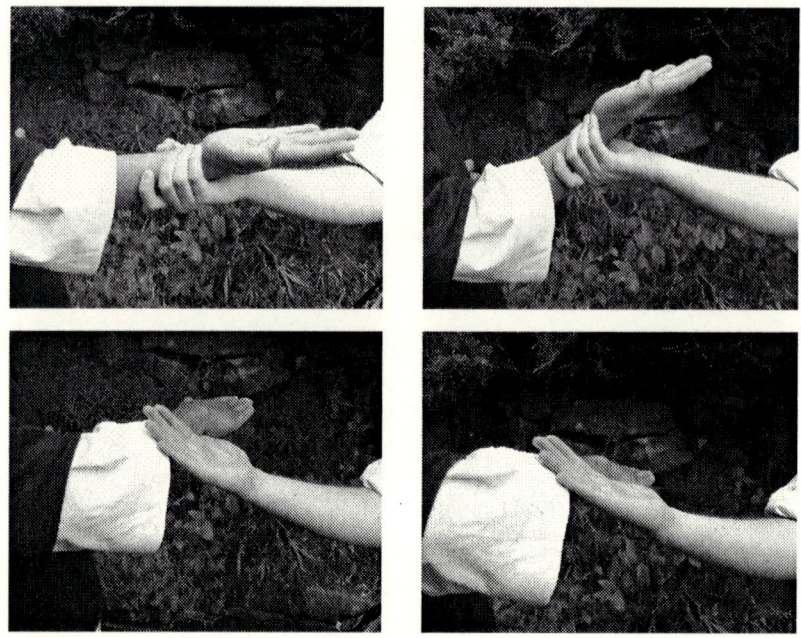

Crane's-wing

Note on escaping from double (parallel-arm) grips

Any attempt to disengage from a double grip by using a symmetrical double grip escape (the double standing dragon for instance), will not work against a determined gripper, who, in tightening his shoulders, plays off one shoulder against the other, naturally making a 'frame' that can not be broken without recourse to unprincipled brutality on the part of the defender.

To escape from a double arm grip, the combination of the Tiger and Leopard techniques can be used. The turning of the circle (of both arms) should be small in the combined technique. The hands should not cross the midline in application. Also, careful attention must be paid to first 'dividing' the opponent's two grips (seen in the preparation movement for Mawashi uke). This 'dividing' of a double grip at the end of Rokushu kata is important because it prevents the opponent from making a 'frame' across his two (equal) shoulders. This 'application' appears to be uncannily similar to 'Po Pai' the double push (and strengthens Ko-do Ryu as a system).

For Ko-do Ryu Karate practitioners, the principle of 'dividing' a double grip, drawn from the combined Tiger and Leopard Rokushu techniques, heralds the next kata in the system, Naihanchin, which translates as 'divided conflict'. The 'rule of thumb' for Naihanchin is that the opponent's strength must be kept divided – split in two different directions.

Chapter Eight
Naihanchin/Tekki (Dai Po Chin)

Capsule History

WHEN REFERRING TO Naihanchin kata and applications below, I refer to the whole kata, which was, my research reveals, later broken into three parts (Naihanchin shodan, nidan and sandan), probably for ease of teaching and possibly because of the large amount of space the original version requires for practice. In this book (and on film) I will present the aspects of the more widespread three kata version, but concentrate more on the (original) joined-up version.

Naihanchin is known variously as Naihanchi, Naifanchi, Nai Fuan Chin, and Dai Po Chin. In all respects the common translation of Naihanchin as 'surreptitious steps' is tolerable, but, for reasons I will explain later, I favour the translation, 'Internal' (nai or nei) 'divided' (fa, fan, fuan) 'conflict' (chin), that is, 'Internal divided conflict'.

The 'f', used in *Naifuanchin*, would be silent and the additional vowel sound (u) is problematic, so I prefer to use the more straightforward phonetic 'Naihanchin'. This kata is commonly referred to in Shotokan and Shotokai Karate as 'Tekki', which as I made clear in chapter two, is a wholly inappropriate term, although Funakoshi may have been influenced by the fact that Itosu, whose actual given name was Yasatsune, was nicknamed 'Ankho' or iron horse, a name reportedly stemming from his enthusiasm for, and practice of, Naihanchin, as well as his ability to root himself firmly in Naihanchin stance.

Naihanchin has long and erroneously been presented as a ballistic (block/strike) kata. This goes back *at least* to Itosu. Even if Itosu had known the applications, he certainly didn't teach them to Funakoshi or others – because, as stated earlier, Funakoshi (and others) have taught Naihanchin (a catalogue of gripping, subduing, twisting, locking and tumbling techniques) as a series of blocks and strikes. They even published Naihanchin as such. The common applications are generally limited to a multiple opponent scenario with assailants who attack using bizarre and mechanical (read choreographed) 'stop start' attacks launched from strange (again read choreographed) distances.

The Japan Karate Association, following the advice of the late Nakayama Masatoshi, represented the 'Tekki' as a choreographed combative sequence applied against several (orderly) attackers, who politely and patiently queue up and wait their turn to attack the defender who, oddly, never moves backwards or forwards, but only moves sideways and employs few of the customary Karate defences, turns or manoeuvres, and frequently 'blocks' without counterattacking.

Indeed, Naihanchin steps solely sideways, but this phenomenon has given rise to absurd suggestions that the kata represents combat on a long narrow boat, in a Chinese 'paddy field', in a narrow alley way with one's back to a wall, or on a narrow ledge or precipice. Without wishing to be polemical, these notions are severely misguided and naive! Further, they have their origins in romantic notions of combat, not in the painstaking investigation of the kata application once blocking and striking are ruled out.

This is the crux of the matter. Institutionalised Karate-thinking has insisted for years that Naihanchin is a 'block strike' kata, and until recently nothing else has been considered. When I released my early findings in print, over a decade ago, and when I proudly went to press with what was unquestionably a major breakthrough, I was initially treated with derision. How could this man (not even Japanese or Okinawan) make such claims – they shouted. Is he saying that he is right and established Karate (beliefs) mistaken?

(Again) Here is what Patrick McCarthy had to say (cited in *Barefoot Zen*, N. J. Johnson, York Beach Maine 2000, p.177–178):

> I was fascinated to experience his (Johnson's) theory and application of Naifuanchin ... If one was to consider it for what it most likely is, a two man grappling-hands exercise without worrying about politics, uniform, name, etc. then I believe that Nathan's theory would be widely recognised. In fact I bet that if an Okinawan master had come forward and introduced that which Nathan has already done, he'd probably have been hailed from the highest sources.

Even now, some fifteen years after the initial discovery of the purpose of Naihanchin, I am still shocked to consider that much (Shuri) Karate and modern ballistic Karate was unwittingly built upon a kata (system) of grappling and subjugation techniques from China! Perhaps it is the blind following of inflexible ersatz tradition that creates such situations and may be one of the 'down-sides' or cultural negatives associated with the Orient that is seldom discussed in Karate history.

I am not motivated by self-promotion, as the many people who practice with me and have taken my seminars know well, but my determination and enthusiasm for what remains an important discovery, deserving of far more recognition that it currently enjoys, compels me to state openly:

In respect of Naihanchin, even the 'experts' got it wrong, and they continue to!

For the record, I will make it plain just what Naihanchin kata and its application by providing a complete definition, in two parts:

1. *Naihanchin kata is the solo representation of a pro-active collective of crossed-arm grappling and restraining techniques meticulously designed and engineered to arrest and subdue a single opponent with whom contact is never lost.*

2. *When applied, Naihanchin facilitates the non-brutal process of effectively negating the opponent's attempts to extricate himself. When he tries to stand-up or pull-away, he is put back down, tumbled and brought back to 'rest' (arrest). There isn't a single punch, block, strike, or kick, in the whole kata!*

The 'namni ashi' (so called 'returning wave kicks', where a leg is momentarily lifted to be near the knee of the opposite leg before being placed back down) are not kicks, or – as has been suggested in the past – even foot sweeps; they were designed solely to give extra kinetic impetus (at key points) to changing a detainee's position and using that extra impetus to retain control of the detainee and thus prevent his escape. In my classes we usually refer to this movement as giving extra 'oomph' to the application. The raised leg is used in similar fashion to the way a baseball pitcher raises his leg before pitching the ball.

Just how or why Naihanchin has been so misunderstood is of less importance than putting it right, because the Naihanchin (part one at least) is practiced with the *incorrect* application – by several million people worldwide!

An extremely 'eclectic' version of Naihanchin (1, 2 & 3) has even found its way into the Korean art of Tae Kwon Do, a modern

Karate-based style favouring high kicks and dating from the 1950s. In Tae Kwon Do the altered Naihanchin is referred to as Po Eun Hyung, although why – other than for reasons of cultural appropriation – an obviously altered form of Naihanchin bears the name of 'Po Eun' (1337–1392), a Korean Confucian scholar and public servant during the Koryo dynasty, I can not say.

In Po Eun Hyung (Pattern/kata), the namni ashi (returning wave kicks) have been altered and are practiced as low side kicks. The trained eye will notice that this 'Hyung' was based on the Japanese Shotokan Tekki kata, rather than the Okinawan Naihanchin. In fact, Po Eun Hyung begins with the opening movement from the Shotokan kata Kanku (Kusanku) and also contains tell-tale elements of the Shotokan kata Jion and Empi.

There have been some (more recent) attempts to radicalise Naihanchin and present it as a catalogue of 'back alley' style, *extreme* 'neck-breaking', 'face-smashing', 'head-stomping', violent 'carotid artery striking', 'save your life' techniques. But such approaches betray the dispositions of the people who teach it that way, rather than reveal the genuine method catalogued in the quan/kata. The 'break the neck', 'knee the face' type approach, can never properly, adequately or credibly account for the exact and entire sequence of Naihanchin, nor can it account for *every* technique in the kata or for its very specific order. Such an approach also generally demonstrates applications that *deviate* considerably from the kata. Applications based on reasoning such as; 'life's tough', 'the kata (Naihanchin) was designed to cripple, maim, kill,' etc, reveal a lack of proper understanding of Naihanchin. Moreover, as mentioned in chapters one and two, modern 'combat Karate' systems certainly offer more direct means of getting results without the need to justify or attribute blatant brutality to the noble antique kata.

The correct applications of Naihanchin allows for the practitioner to arrest an opponent, move him to the side, bring him to his knees, tumble him and disorient him (if necessary), and cope with every (anatomical) permutation of escape attempt made by the incapacitated opponent. All with firmness and vigour, *but never with callous brutality!* The opponent is never struck, or kicked when he is down, and he is at all times accorded the opportunity to cease struggling and conform.

Motobu Choki

Of the early recorded Okinawan practitioners of Naihanchin (and there were many), Motobu Choki (1871–1944), another (some time) Itosu student, was a devotee of Naihanchin kata. It has been claimed that his classes consisted mostly of Naihanchin practice followed by 'Kumite' (Lit. 'meeting hands') – sparring of Motobu's own devising. He made some credible attempts at unravelling the Naihanchin mystery too. His approach to Karate differed quite markedly from other practitioners of the day. Motobu was interested in 'applied Karate', not just in the endless repetition of solo kata, the common approach to learning and practicing To-te or Karate at that time. Motobu questioned what he saw or was taught, particularly its efficiency or application in real fighting, something he claimed to (and did) have much experience of. In fact Motobu had many more actual fighting experiences than the people who taught him kata. One complaint made by some of his students was that 'things' (techniques in general and applications in particular) were always changing. I think that Motobu, preoccupied with practical applications, developed his Karate as he went along, making changes whenever he thought it necessary.

Nagamine Shoshin trained under Motobu for six months and stated in his *Tales of Okinawa's Great Masters*, (Boston, Tokyo: Tuttle, 2000) p.102:

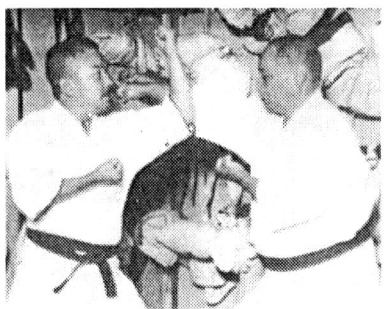

Konishi blocking Motobu's punch

> ... his [Motobu's] teachings were so provocative that
> I constantly pondered the value of his advice ...
> (Parenthesis mine).

The most notable difference in Motobu's Karate was the distance he used. Unlike much modern Karate, Motobu's applications were all carried out at close range. Photographs of Motobu's assistants attacking him, illustrate that their attacks lack the 'polish' of later 'Karate' punches, but the distances are realistic – the players aren't out of range.

In modern Karate, Japanese Budo (weapon) distances are often applied, giving much modern Karate a 'long range' look. Using the modern methods, it is often the distance taken (away from an attack) that nullifies the attack. The blocks seem to be an afterthought. In Motobu's case the block is an essential part of a strategy that included several elements common to accepted Southern Chinese Kung Fu; namely the cultivation of simultaneous attack and defence, the use of a close range, the trapping or monitoring of the opponent's free hand, and the employment of low kicks used in combination with a grasping or unbalancing action.

Motobu got close to Chinese (Quan-fa) style applications through his own efforts, and at a time when the actual application of kata seem to be misunderstood – and were relatively unimportant to many other teachers. Whilst Motobu's applications were undoubtedly effective, they were still a little crude, and the tradition of Naihanchin being a ballistic kata was too strongly entrenched in the minds of teachers and students alike (and still is!) for even Motobu – with his somewhat maverick revolutionary zeal – to challenge, so he built his Naihanchin applications accordingly – on blocking and striking techniques.

Although Motobu taught Karate on mainland Japan for a number of years (allegedly teaching there before Funakoshi did), he met with only limited success. In my opinion this was due to several factors, namely that Motobu spoke mainland Japanese rather poorly, and at times his speech would have been largely unintelligible. Also it seems he presented himself as a rather rough and uneducated individual. But perhaps the most telling difficulty for would-be Japanese students of Motobu's Karate was the lack of aesthetic form necessary to capture their attention. In short, Motobu's interpretation of Karate (unlike Funakoshi's unfolding Shotokan) was very un-Japanese.

On the plus side, Motobu, along with others, was responsible for keeping Naihanchin solo kata very much alive, in an environment in which its eminence or centrality was being reduced. Indeed, it became somewhat eclipsed by a multitude of hybrid kata stemming from Itosu and other sources.

Returning to the subject of Naihanchin proper, one of the most confusing elements in observing the solo kata is the clenched fist used throughout most of the kata. It is apt to make the observer believe that the clenched fist denotes a blocking or punching action. In this case the special type of clenched fist traditionally used in the kata and illustrated below denotes anything other than a punch.

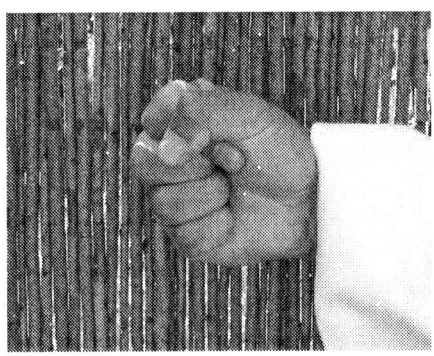

Naihanchin fist-clench

The traditional Naihanchin fist-clench omits curling the last joint/digit (closest to the fingernail) of the forefinger in the clench, thus encouraging the practitioner to concentrate on the *little, ring, and middle fingers in collaboration with the thumb.* This unique method was devised to produce a grip that is used in lieu of the double grips that would be applied to an opponent's wrists in application. *In short, Naihanchin fist-clench is a training device for developing and maintaining a strong grip. It is not a 'punch' fist.* Examples of this 'grip' can be found in *Dynamic Karate* by Nakayama Masatoshi (a student of Funakoshi Gichin), (London, Ward Lock, 1966) p.75. The Naihanchin fist-grip or 'clench' can also be observed in Funakoshi's *Karate Do Kyohan* (London, Ward Lock, 1976) p.17.

For those who may be interested, Ohshima Tsutomu, the translator of *Karate-Do Kyohan*, and model for most of the photographs, can clearly be seen using the Naihanchin fist-clench in the *'Tekki' Shodan* kata, on page 124 – photograph 18, on page 128 – photographs 38 and 39, again on page 129 – photograph 3; in the *'Tekki' Nidan* kata, on page 130 – photograph 5, on page 131 – photograph10, on page 133 – photograph 22, on page 135 – photograph 34, and in the 'Tekki' Sandan kata on page 136 – photograph 3 (right fist) and on page 138 – photograph 15. A stylized version of this special fist was drawn by the famous Japanese artist Kosugi Hoan for the front cover of Funakoshi's second book, *Rentan Goshin Tote-jutsu* (1925).

The Naihanchin fist clench is still used by some Shuri-te (Shorin Ryu) stylists to this day, yet its proper use remains unknown!

Like Sanchin, Naihanchin uses two fundamental categories of movements or techniques, based on whether a wrist is twisted and rotated clockwise or anti-clockwise, with the elbow being twisted into the centre until it can no longer move, or being twisted and locked outwards. These two categories of movements can be further sub-divided into two types of grips; the 'scabbard' grip and the 'sword' grip. Together, these movements 'divide' an opponent's strength, where one arm is twisted inwards to effect either the restraints or the tumbling techniques.

The Scabbard Grip

There are only three specific subduing or tumbling techniques that can be performed using the scabbard grip. The trilogy of techniques possible using the scabbard grip is repeated three times in the solo form (and in the two-man drill). Those familiar with the three Tekki kata of Shotokan or the three Naihanchi(n) kata of Shorin Ryu will see these three techniques repeated in each kata, where in modern times they are usually considered to be a hook punch, a middle-level forearm block and a combined middle-level and lower-level forearm block. In application, these techniques are used (in Ko-do Ryu) to tumble and disorientate an opponent in order to subdue, arrest and hold him fast. Moreover, they are the only three techniques anatomically possible from the scabbard grip.

The Sword Grip

A series of different subduing or tumbling techniques can be performed using the sword grip. In application, the Naihanchin sequence illustrates consecutive techniques punctuated by the three scabbard grip techniques, which together make a complete series of subduing techniques.

Naihanchin techniques that flow from the sword grip progressively subdue an opponent who classically is reduced to his knees and subdued with both wrists being cross-locked. Should the opponent continue to struggle and try to pull away, he will be tumbled (to disorientate him) and 'locked up' again. If the opponent tries to stand up, he is simply brought back down again, tumbled to disorientate him and locked up yet again. Naihanchin offers a series of *six* such techniques that are interchangeable responses to someone quite literally 'resisting arrest'!

Single hand extrapolations (though not genuine Naihanchin) can be used, mainly to separate out the sword and scabbard grips making them and their application less difficult to see, understand, and use. In single hand extrapolations, the opponent is made to kneel, sit, tumble, or lay down prone or even supine. The person being subdued is given only one direction in which to escape based on whether the elbow is in or out. The opponent should never be allowed escape from a hold or tumble in the direction in which he was first put into it. The importance of this will become apparent. I next detail the socio-political context of the original Naihanchin application in Ming Dynasty (China) civil arrest techniques, in order to reinforce the foundation of my argument

Ming Dynasty (China) Civil Arrest Techniques

China maintained a huge civil service during the Ming dynasty. At that time, China was administered by crown officers whose duty it was to ensure the smooth running of their allotted regions and, collectively, the country. The civil service was somewhat unwieldy, cumbersome and intensely bureaucratic, but paradoxically, it was relatively efficient. Government was entirely centralised and over-dependent on the emperor or his representatives, yet elements of the Confucian-based administrative hierarchy wielded considerable authority. Crime, as ever, was a fact of life; so was corruption and drunkenness.

On a local level, the 'Shen Shih', 'gentry', formally educated holders of at least the 'xiu cai' (flowering talent) degree, were figures of civil authority without 'formal' positions. The Shen Shih can be likened to the squires of eighteenth and nineteenth century England. Connected to them were types of local militia, private armies whose job was to enforce and keep civil order.

A social phenomenon of the period was the enormous power wielded by the eunuchs at the Imperial court. At the beginning of the Ming dynasty there were approximately ten thousand eunuchs, and by the end of the dynasty, a staggering seventy thousand plus exercised an enormous and disproportionate level of control over the entire nation. For example, the infamous eunuch Wei Zhongxian practically ruled China as a virtual dictator during the 1620s.

It was against this backdrop that, incredibly to modern Westerners, intellectually conservative Chinese law enforcement officials remained determined to operate within the social parameters demanded by Confucian ethics. Philosophically, the Ming dynasty re-enforced neo-Confucianism, but there was a large scale move away from reading and writing texts, to an emphasis on *personal conduct*. So, neo-Confucianism permeated out into all areas of social behaviour and even into the civil arrest tradition. Eventually, neo-Confucianism filtered down to Okinawan To-te, for those practitioners like Matsumura Sokon, Itosu Yasatsune and Funakoshi Gichin, who were sufficiently educated to understand its civic value, and enthusiastic enough to promote it.

Late Ming was a time when royalty and holders of high office greatly feared assassination and grew increasingly uncomfortable in the presence of weapons. The 'Shen Shih' became troubled too, and the carrying of arms became associated with banditry, corruption and the ever present threat of military coup or civil disorder. And there were plenty of people who could be angered or even mobilised.

The result of these situations was that, with the increasing population, the carrying of weapons was discouraged in civil society, and the unarmed 'civil arrest' traditions gained greater prominence and began to be refined, systematised and formalised. It is from this cultural and political milieu that Naihanchin most probably arose. It is also from this period that Japanese Ju-Jutsu begins to develop as an outgrowth of Chinese techniques, imported to and synthesised in seventeenth century Japan, where they were used amongst the civil population for the same or similar reasons as they were used amongst the civil population in (parts of) China.

After the collapse of the Ming dynasty (1644 or 1645), the Han (the indigenous Chinese people) were, as I've already stated, totally forbidden to bear arms or practice Martial Arts at all. With regard to the actual numbers of people under discussion; in 1650, the population of China still stood at about one hundred million despite being in decline and being ravaged by plague, famine, warfare, and other socio-economic reasons. By 1750 China's population had almost doubled to some two hundred million.

Putting the Grappling Legacy into Context

I wish to re-iterate that civil arrest 'grappling' techniques were not intended for competitive use then, nor can they easily be used for such now. They were not designed to be used confrontationally. Their applications are therefore not viable in modern 'cage-fighting' or prize-fighting tournaments, as I made plain in chapter one. However, like any well-designed tools, they were undoubtedly practical when used by skilled operatives, and under the appropriate circumstances.

But what were those circumstances?

I re-stress the following point because of its central importance to the proper understanding and appreciation of Chin-Na, which (like later Ju-jutsu), was most likely used to prevent the escalation of violence where one or more parties were armed (or *about* to become aggressive). Chin-Na techniques are the archetypal techniques of controlling the hands, arms, wrists, shoulders, and therefore an opponent's posture (and consequently nullifying any harm he can cause). But, they work best under circumstances of surprise, pretty much pre-emptively; for example, just before an opponent decides to reach for and/or draw a weapon. Indeed, once a weapon was drawn, an altercation would most often have serious consequences. Chin-Na, if applied suitably (at the right time and in the right way), could prevent this. Such techniques were never intended (as I explained in chapter one) to be used (for example) after a sword was drawn. The only sensible chance against a weapon was (is) to be armed oneself! Western Karate enthusiasts need to consider this point very carefully, because the context of (and for) the use of Chin-Na is vital to being able to understand and appreciate it and the (relative) value of Sai kata.

Practice with experienced training partners would have been essential in order to develop Chin-Na proficiency, but the techniques were never intended to be used mutually. It was not the case that one grappler would apply a lock and the other would apply a counter lock. Such a format is actually a characteristic of wrestling, and Naihanchin is unsuitable for inclusion in a wrestling format. The locks were designed to be as functional as possible, but, like all things, they have their limits.

Unfortunately, some modern Martial Artists can't accept this, and it seems difficult for some modern investigators to see beyond their own cultural perceptions; particularly when it comes to the possibility of effecting civilian arrest without resorting to brutality and using, specifically, the techniques masterfully set out in Naihanchin. This is because they base their perceptions and misconceptions on the (relative) size, strength, attitudes and behaviour of those around them, and make their investigations within, for example, contemporary Western cultural parameters.

What I mean, here is, that some modern investigators, obsessed with the challenges (not to mention the threat) of brute strength, have failed to grasp or understand such techniques in proper context, both cultural and physical. Further, that they have only recently been exposed to the demonstrable order, sequence and technical function of Naihanchin as a grappling sequence, has left some of them grudgingly admitting that Naihanchin is not a fight against multiple opponents after all, yet they are still determined to pick flaws in its inability to solve the problems of the 'bogey man', the monster, the 'six foot something' aggressive belligerent spectre of their personal nightmares.

Not content that the ancient, logical and well-ordered techniques of Naihanchin were designed to be used largely against unwary and inexperienced civilians, or to prevent weapons play, and then under Ming dynasty cultural and social circumstances, some modern investigators demand that the techniques instead work under the modern conditions and circumstances they insist on imposing. Having tried to apply the (thus far published) ancient techniques of Naihanchin against their colleagues and friends, many of whom are often trained Martial Artists, their frustration – due to lack of proper training and a misunderstanding of context and purpose – becomes complete. It remains a self evident truth that those who are indeed trained in Martial Arts or are just plain strong, or know, or suspect what is about to happen to them can take evasive action and thwart Naihanchin techniques, *just as they can any techniques.* This is the reason why I am not here treating of competitive or fail-safe 'total combat' strategies that can satisfy the fears or demands of those who have less than a complete understanding of Naihanchin.

The Physical Factors

Control over a person by manipulating the wrist and elbow joints of that person (as advocated in Naihanchin and similar methods) is proportionately easier to achieve if adversaries are 'slender of limb' and the operative is sturdy. This is due to the relative amounts of torque-force (twist) and gripping power the twenty-seven bones of the human hand can generate. Everyone's hand is designed the same way in terms of these bones, their connective tissue, ligaments and supporting tendons, but, the musculature can vary, as does the all important spacing between the ulnae and radius (the two bones in the lower arm) which is what ultimately determines the thickness of the wrist. If the bones in the forearm are relatively far apart and the forearm is of regular length (or slightly shorter) you get the classic thick-wrist (and usually accompanying stocky build) of the 'grappler', the sort of individual I suggest was eminently employable as a civil arrest officer in Ming dynasty China.

I would like to clarify the issue of relative strength, in terms of achievable human torque. As with all other human achievements, there is a limit to human capability. For example, it is unlikely that a normal modern human will ever be able to jump twenty feet into the air, unassisted. Similarly there is a maximum amount of (relative) torque-force a human hand can generate. So, even large, strong modern Westerners, some of whom increase muscle mass and strength through weight training, etc. are still restricted by their supporting ligaments and tendons, and therefore in the relative power their *hands* can generate (hence the heavy 'strapping' of wrists, ankles and knees seen in Olympic weight lifting competitions). Even with increased overall arm or body strength/weight, one can only generate a *finite* degree of force or strength in or with the wrist (joints). In short, the leverage and torque that the human hand can generate is more efficient if a ten-stone man applies torsion to the wrist of a seven-stone man, than if a twenty-stone man attempts to apply torsion to the wrist of another twenty-stone man. Under such circumstance other procedures might prove more productive. Of course, an example of the worst case scenario might be a seven-stone man, trying to grapple a twenty-stone man, which is the sort of unrealistic expectation some people have of Chin-Na.

Yet, Martial Artists are expected to be like Superman. They must have an answer (a technique) for every situation, and *win at all costs*. They must also be able to beat, grapple, arrest, *anyone and everyone*, even by defying the laws of physics if necessary. Above all, their 'holy duty' is to be able to defeat the bigger guys, you know, the guys everyone fears, the big strong angry 'bad guys'. This is a common misconception.

'The bigger they are, the harder they fall' is the fervent and devoted mantra (sacred chant) of the initiated hopeful – another (potential) misconception. In actual physical conflict, the bigger they are, the harder they (can) punch! Sometimes the bad guys get away. Regrettably they sometimes win! Similar situations obviously occurred in China (and Japan). Just as today, the police don't always 'get their man'.

Civil arrest techniques were (and still are) used by public servants for and on behalf of the public, and or the ruling powers they serve, to keep or restore public order. For example, Judo ('pliant way') has been practiced by the police in Japan since 1886. Their judo practice includes 'Renkoho Waza' (arresting techniques, also known as 'come along' techniques), designed to assist in controlling suspects. These techniques principally control the suspect's posture by the application of locks to the wrist and elbow-joint of the suspect. No brutality should be employed.

Restraint without brutality was the ideal in Ming dynasty China, just as it is for example, in modern Britain, where police officers are expected to conform to a code of conduct, behaviour and ethics, even when faced with the most appalling violence. The fact that they largely do so, or at least try to, is commendable, but that is precisely why society dictates the mores and values that police officers must abide by, and hires (and sometimes fires) candidates accordingly. Alongside the code of conduct, the behaviour, and the expected general deportment of serving officers, there are recommended procedures, protocols, official techniques and approaches used to effect arrests, and process suspects and detainees. These protocols are professed, 'signed-up to', and form the basis for how officers conduct themselves (or otherwise).

Then there is reality! Harsh, brutal and in dire need of results! One can certainly see that on CCTV film footage taken over any weekend in many major cities, worldwide, where the hooligan element pits itself against the representatives of authority – the police. Ming dynasty China, although arguably a much more conformist – Confucian based – society, historically had its civil troubles too.

Size and strength are important factors in many types of policing. I was a police cadet in the Hampshire Constabulary (UK), during the mid 1970s, when the 'beat bobby's' equipment was still traditional and basic. Now, the rules have changed, and the police are far more comprehensively equipped to meet modern demands. In contrast, I think Ming dynasty civil arrest officers would, just for starters, have been better positioned socially, and probably much better fed, than for instance, the average country peasant, and (like today's doormen or 'hospitality operatives') would doubtless have needed to be physically compact and solid, if not actually imposing.

Sometimes, law enforcement officers break the rules; procedures get ignored, brutality is dished out, and the wrong person sometimes gets arrested and traumatised to-boot. Ming dynasty China was no different in that respect. Naihanchin was an official template, the epitome, the 'doing it by the book'. But then there was probably 'reality'.

In respect of such grappling techniques used by 'gentlemen' (officers/warriors), I can not stress enough that the general idea was to extend civility if not 'courtesy' to the opponent (drunken person?) whilst trying to preserve something of his dignity and one's own. The over simplistic and inaccurate common portrayal of feudal warriors as either bloody 'kamikaze' cutthroats, or as remote sage-like Supermen (who indulged in a little bit of 'head-lopping' from time to time), has merely been exploited for entertainment shock value. This 'treatment' has been very much at the expense of historical accuracy and the presentation of a balanced view regarding the *nobility* of legitimate feudal groups both in China and Japan; cultures who's Martial Arts are now probably studied by more people (around the world) than at any time in history.

Master Funakoshi and the Creation of Tekki Kata

Funakoshi Gichin possibly began learning Karate as early as 1884 when it was still taught secretly on Okinawa. When Funakoshi settled in Japan in the 1920s he taught fifteen kata, a large number by the standard of the time. The Karate historian Kenji Tokitsu suggested that Funakoshi had studied only (the three) Naihanchin and Kusanku kata, and had only learned the other kata superficially, to provide him with more teaching material. Certainly, Funakoshi was not involved with the development of, or apparently even present when the Pinan kata were devised and introduced by Itosu.

Graham Noble explains that Funakoshi did not study Karate via the 'Shihan Gakko' (Okinawan prefecture school for teachers). In effect, he learned privately and had (probably) quit learning from, or training with, Itosu by 1905. Mabuni Kenwa (Shito Ryu founder and a later Itosu student) 'corrected' the Pinan kata of Otsuka Hironori (founder of Wado Ryu and a Funakoshi student), and it has been claimed that this is evidence that Funakoshi learned them imperfectly. It has further been suggested that Funakoshi hastily learned the Pinan from Mabuni. There are certain anomalies in Funakoshi's versions of the Pinan kata (which he renamed Heian) and other kata, that can certainly be explained that way.

The Shotokai Karate master, Harada Mitsusuke (graded to fifth degree black belt by Funakoshi), was puzzled once when he was told by an Okinawan ex-pat in Brazil (during the 1950s) that his

Passai kata was incorrect. Harada Sensei felt compelled to check back with his sempai in Japan. Needless to say, the Passai kata of Shotokai Karate (from the lineage of Funakoshi, via Egami Shigeru and on to Harada Sensei) is very different from that of Shorin Ryu. An academic comparison between the Shotokan/Shotokai, and the Shorin Ryu Kata, can easily be made by comparing the kata in the book *Karate – Do Kyohan* by Funakoshi Gichin, with the kata illustrated in *The Essence of Okinawan Karate* by Nagamine Shoshin.

In a demonstration Funakoshi gave at the Kodokan, the Mecca of Judo, in 1922, he performed his favourite kata, Kusanku, and his assistant Gima Shinken (1896–1989) demonstrated Naihanchin. As noted earlier, the (three) Naihanchin kata were the foundation of Itosu Anko's teaching until he created the Pinan kata to teach in schools. Funakoshi spent ten years learning only the Naihanchin kata, and that is the focus of our attention here. A widening of the Naihanchin stance produced the characteristic low/wide 'Kibadachi' stance used in modern Shotokan. Gima Shinken had this to say about Kibadachi (*F.A.I* Vol. 5, No. 4):

> As regards stances, I feel that some present-day Karate-ka over-exaggerate them. For example, I think Kibadachi (Horse stance) is often over-exaggerated.

Funakoshi changed the name of Naihanchin and several other kata, probably for political reasons. A Chinese-based art with obscure Chinese-sounding names of kata, or with pronunciations of names in Hogen Okinawan dialect, would have had less appeal to the expansionist and militaristic Japanese authorities of the day who regarded the Okinawans as 'yokels' and held the Chinese in contempt.

Applied Naihanchin – General

Naihanchin catalogues a specific sequence of continuous interaction between two people, one of whom continually grips and repeatedly arrests (i.e. restrains the movements of) the other (person who has been 'captured' – 'detained'), tumbling him where necessary if he resists. It is the movements of the 'arrestor' that are recorded in the solo kata.

The 'detainee' is 'compelled' to kneel down and made to change from standing-up to kneeling or being 'tumbled' etc. Naihanchin compels a 'detainee' to kneel down by quickly and increasingly applying pressure to one or more of his joints in such a way that he instantly feels that lowering his body is the only thing that he can do to reduce or prevent the pain.

Applied Naihanchin

The 'arrestor' initially applies both hands to one arm of the person he intends to subdue. Gripping both the lower-forearm and the fingers simultaneously, the 'arrestor' twists the trapped and bent wrist of the 'detainee' and forces that 'detainee' to one side, compelling him to walk and 'move-on'. When the 'detainee' resists the 'arrestor' (by trying to remove the arrestor's top gripping hand and thereby relieve the pain and break the control), the 'arrestor' applies his hands, each in a single-handed 'crossed' grip (one scabbard grip and one sword grip), to the captives hands, simultaneously *dividing* and unbalancing the 'detainee' who is left 'floating' off-balance and standing (momentarily) on one leg.

356

Selected Naihanchin kata techniques

The arrestor turns at the waist whilst 'folding' his 'sword grip' hand in toward the crook of the elbow of his opposite arm. The double 'lock' this produces, swings the 'detainee' around, with his balance and centre of gravity shifting from the previous weight-bearing leg to the other leg. The result is another momentary loss of balance. The arrestor then turns his waist, and facing front again, consigns the 'detainee' to the ground, subduing him with the first 'side lock up' (lock up/arrest position).

The arrestor, maintaining both grips, continues to control and repeatedly subdue the 'detainee' every time he attempts to extricate/assert himself. The arrestor remains on his feet throughout the interaction, whereas the 'detainee', initially on his feet, is thereafter brought to his knees, or is returned to, his knee(s) (and/or buttocks) each time he resists.

A detainee who struggles, will be 'tumbled' as required, and 'arrested' at one of two positions of advantage called 'lock-up' positions. Thus he will repeatedly experience having either the 'side lock-up' or the 'front lock-up' applied to him. If the 'detainee' (when in either of these 'lock-ups') makes no attempt to extricate/assert himself, then the arrestor may be content to merely maintain that position – the detainee is thus arrested.

It is worthy to note that the author does not assert that the detainee in the original use of Naihanchin actually tumbled or rolled smoothly. This device merely allows the user to see continuity between solo kata and its two man application. In strict application the detainee is first bought to his knees and given the opportunity to submit. If he continues to struggle he is promptly 'dumped' on his back (illustrated by pictures 6 through to 11, page 366).

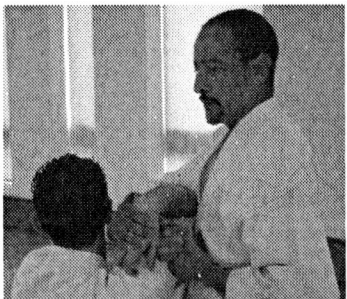

Naihanchin Side 'Lock-up':
Motobu, Solo, Applied

Naihanchin Front 'Lock-up':
Motobu, Solo, Applied

Within the kata sequence, the 'side lock-up', (the initial position used to bring the detainee to the ground) is applied three times and is 'broken out from' three times, and the 'front lock-up' is applied four times, including the final position (the end of the kata), which means that the 'front lock-up' is also broken out from three times.

What distinguishes which of the *three* responses from both the front and side 'lock-up' positions (catalogued in the kata) is used, is simple. It depends on whether the 'detainee' is at your side and has a broken posture, (as is the case the first time the 'lock-up' position is applied on either side) or, the 'detainee', after having been tumbled, comes to rest more squarely placed in front of you and is therefore in a stronger position by virtue of a having a straighter back, more leverage and greater traction. The final option (catalogued in the kata) indicates what to do if the 'detainee' tries to stand up from either the side 'lock-up' or the 'front lock-up' positions, in which case he is rapidly 'divided' and brought back down again.

It is this symmetry (three responses from each of the two 'lock-up' positions) that provides the formula and in turn illustrates the correct ordering of the kata which has, over the years, become confused and modified, largely from ignorance of the function, through to the breaking of the complete sequence/formula into three separate kata. Indeed this breaking of the complete sequence into three 'kata' merits further attention here. Moreover, this is what has caused anomalies in the openings of Tekki Sandan (Naihanchin 3) in modern Shotokan Karate, which has at least two 'official' variations centring on confusion over how it opens. If the entire kata is to be broken, either to provide modular training or because of space limitations, *it should only really be broken at the front and side 'lock up' positions!* Of course, this will produce – as it has in the past – problems with how to start the next kata/section, as Naihanchin 1, 2 & 3 are really one continuous sequence.

Orientation of the Arms in Naihanchin

The key to understanding the orientation of the arms lays in the opening movement, i.e. which open palm is on top. This 'key' is often ignored with the left palm on the back of the right hand being favoured as a mere 'formal starting position'. It is much more than this, being actually the key (within Naihanchin) to which grips are being used with which hand – which hand uses the sword grip, and which uses the scabbard grip. Left palm on the back of the right hand means a left sword grip and a right scabbard grip is being used, and of course visa-versa. Using this key, one can recognise the confusion of directions and the jumble of subsections commonly seen in published versions of Naihanchin.

In Naihanchin application, the arrestor maintains two crossed grips. As long as both people are facing one another, their linked left arms and linked right arms will cross over/under each other. Each time the detainee completes a rotation (a tumble to, and usually from, the ground), the orientation of their arms (i.e. which pair is over/under) switches. The appropriate orientation of the arms is fundamental to the functioning of each of Naihanchin's techniques.

A 'block/strike' kata can usually have its component parts (interdependent movements) and/or their mirror-images broken down, mixed and matched, and placed in different orders to create (superficially at least) different kata without adversely affecting the applications. This is because the attacks against which the kata practitioner defends himself – before counter-attacking – are independent of, and unaffected by each other. Naihanchin, however, does not function in this way. In

Naihanchin application, each technique occurs directly as a result of the technique that preceded it, which is why it is presented in the order that it is, and also why the order should not be changed. The only exception to this can occur at the crucial lock-up points, where subsequent responses depend upon the 'detainees' actions, i.e. does he try to stand up, or is he only capable of trying to pull away whilst still kneeling?

Somewhere, sometime, the application of Naihanchin was lost, and the (long) solo kata was split into sections and combined with their mirror-images to create three shorter kata (or sub-sections). Naihanchin kata as performed, for example, in Wado-ryu Karate, consists of the shodan 'sub-section' only, and is therefore incomplete. However, this sub-section does at least contain three 'lock up' to 'lock up' sections, and therefore the basic technical material, ultimately made more comprehensive in the nidan and sandan subsections.

The Reconstruction of Naihanchin's Original Sequence

My colleague Dave Franks and I actually began to unravel the application to Naihanchin by starting with Shotokan's 'Tekki Nidan'. It occurred to us that key movements in all three Tekki (Naihanchin) kata were somehow based upon an opponent's arms being somehow crossed. Just how or why, we did not know at that time, so we began to experiment.

Later, several 'anomalies' occurred to us:

1. Naihanchin Shodan when 'mirrored' (repeated opening to the left) lacked the opening movements and the first crossed half step. This inconsistency is usually explained by claiming (or assuming) that the first cross-step and the hand positions

accompanying it are purely symbolic. This is not the case. Indeed, it is because of these very movements that the entire kata unfolds.

2. We also noticed that in Shotokan's Tekki Nidan (unlike Shodan) there is no formal opening position, and the kata does not even start with the heels together as it does in (Matsubayashi) Shorin Ryu (shotokan's Tekki Sandan also lacks a formal opening).

This led to the further realisation that the Shodan sub-section leads perfectly into the Nidan sub-section, which leads perfectly into the Sandan sub-section! It soon became clear that Naihanchin was *one* continuous sequence, and a continuous grappling sequence to-boot! Its continuity had been obscured in part by the very re-ordering of the sub-sections into three kata that do not maintain the integrity of the two fundamental grips – the sword and scabbard grips.

Each of the three sub-sections has just two components; the application of the techniques required in the original sequence, and their repeat performance in mirror-image. Most importantly, it soon became apparent that the Naihanchin performer seeks to (does) establish and continually re-establish control over a *single* opponent who is being subdued by grappling.

Some current 'versions' of the Naihanchin (mostly Shodan sub-section) have been 'improved upon' without those responsible ever realising that they were dealing with a grappling kata/sequence. Such alterations were undoubtedly made to make the movements in the solo kata seem more effective in application (as blocks and strikes), but such are illogical and misleading in the context of Naihanchin's true purpose – now revealed. It was therefore very necessary to study fairly accurate and conservative versions of the sub-sections (kata, Shodan through Sandan in both Shotokan and Shorin Ryu Karate). We (the researchers) therefore found the black and white photographic records of Nagamine Shoshin and Motobu Choki to be invaluable.

Once we realised that each of the training-partner's hands operates a separate single-handed grip, and that it is not practicable to alter the grip type – sword-grip or scabbard-grip – of either one (let alone both) of these grips throughout the proper sequence, the format and application, and therefore the true order of the solo sequence became clear. The solo kata's mirror-repetition is merely a repeat of the techniques initially practiced on one particular side of the body. For completeness, the techniques have to be mastered on both sides of the body and with both hands. The operator (the arrestor) would have to be able to capture either hand of the soon-to-be 'detainee', and proceed accordingly.

Naihanchin contains six 'lock-up to lock-up' sub-sequences. Three begin at the 'side lock-up' and three begin at the 'front lock-up'. This provides the arrestor with a series of re-arresting procedures with which to completely frustrate the detainee's attempts to escape.

During research, most discoveries came from 'hands on' experience (by trying out each idea with a training-partner), and eventually, after some protracted explorations which sometimes led us into dead ends, Naihanchin's methodology became apparent. Many a scenario, which initially seemed reasonable, was subsequently found lacking, and the beginning of the kata (and therefore the purpose of the whole thing) in particular, raised many questions. For example: we speculated that the Naihanchin performer is initially gripped in a cross grip fashion on one or both wrist-joints, and he then 'reverses' these grips, and therefore the roles? When we ran with this; why? – was quite rightly the awkward question frequently raised by people outside our group. Another tricky question was that, given the efficiency of the first subjugation technique, was the purpose of Naihanchin to force a miscreant to the ground immediately? And if so, how or why does the rest of the kata unfold? If the training-partner can be forced to the ground immediately, why then isn't he?

The conclusions we reached are clear and to the point. Naihanchin is a pro-active civil arrest technique. Its original operatives were most likely not interested in publicly demonstrating their expertise or competence in the entire sequence. For the Naihanchin operative, the task in hand was to remove a miscreant from the scene, without the use of weapons or brutality – If the detainee struggled, then …

From these investigations, and the successful answering of many difficult questions, the 'arresting' function of Naihanchin became apparent, and its dignified and restrained nature duly revealed itself.

Naihanchin Kata
(Shodan through Sandan)

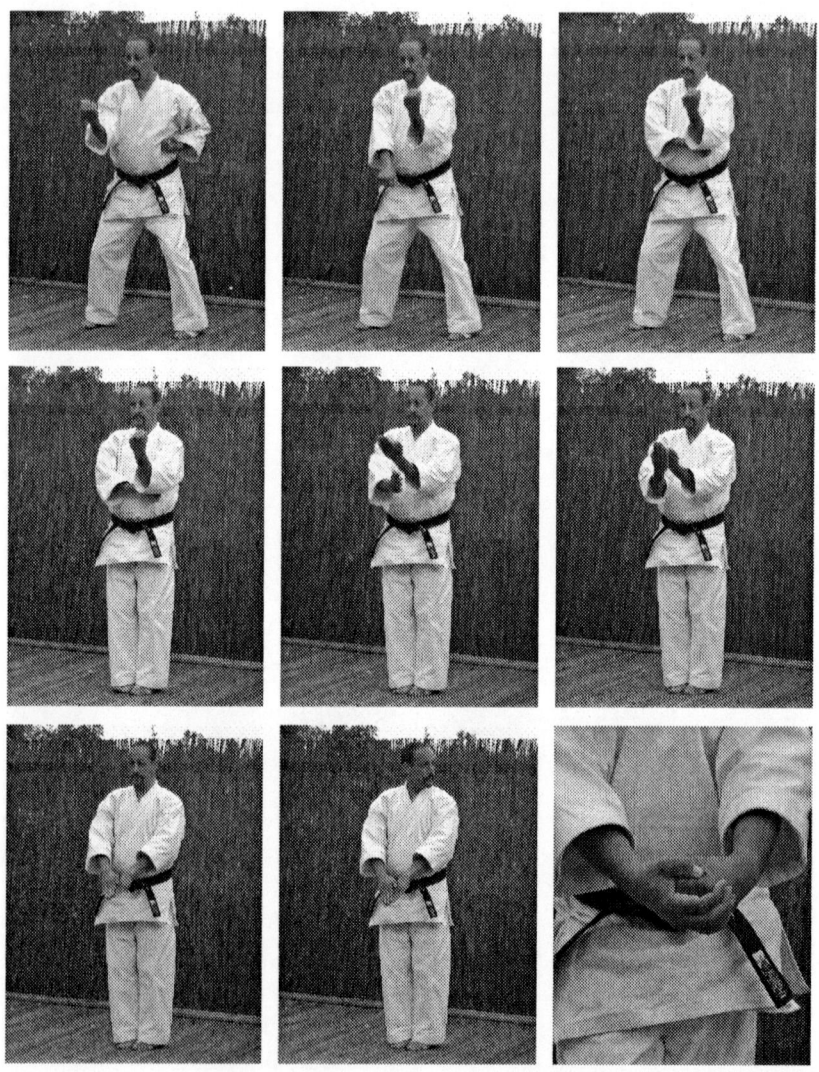

Repeat kata on opposite side

Modern Naihanchin 'Joining places' – Shodan to Nidan

Modern Naihanchin 'Joining places' – Nidan to Sandan

Modern Naihanchin Nidan's Extra Step

An extra step was added to Naihanchin Nidan (section two) presumably to make it similar in length (i.e. co-equal with the other two 'kata' in the distance the practitioner travels during the performance of the kata). We (the researchers) only became aware of this extra step after a full understanding of the Naihanchin formula was reached. The inclusion of this extra step draws the 'detainee' too far to one side for the 'arrestor' to maintain proper control. This can be seen in the film under the section titled 'The club', where two practitioners (not wearing gi's) play out all that can in fact be done if the extra step is included. Indeed, the inclusion of the extra step decreases the efficiency of the kata and represents an inferior and complicated technique, operated at a junction at which the 'detainee' should simply be tumbled using the augmented arm positions that are the whole point of Naihanchin Nidan (or section two of the Naihanchin sequence).

Chapter Nine
Kobudo

Old (Uechi Style)
Kobudo Sanchin Kata
— Section One —

then turn

front view

of sequence

return to

normal view

then turn

Old (Uechi Style)
Kobudo Sanchin Kata
— Section Two —

Old (Uechi Style)
Kobudo Sanchin Kata
— Section Three —

Old (Uechi Style)
Kobudo Sesian Kata

*now slide
forward*

The kata still faces the same direction here, the angle is now simply changed to illustrate the techniques from the side

The next sequence is shown from the front/original angle

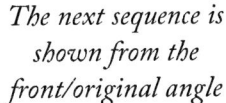

then turn 180°

*then face original
direction*

Afterword

SOMEWHERE, FAR BEYOND academic or intellectual considerations, far beyond culture, race, gender or age, there exist fundamental realities connected with Karate that are directly related to social, psychological and physiological balance for all humans. Only disturbed people revel in violence, and, in short, our bodies all generally work in the same way. The creators of antique kata understood these points in the context of producing timeless, humane, armed and unarmed classical techniques that are as civilly responsible as they are effective. Followers of the traditional methods reject brutality and refuse to adopt hostile or negative philosophies or unhealthy anti-social attitudes. Moreover, violent stereotypes depicting Karate-ka as 'dangerous' and violent, misrepresent the art and reveal only the dispositions or desires of those who portray the art as such.

Embracing inappropriate belief systems may expose one to unnecessary danger. Such paths invariably lead one into peril. True Karate is not concerned with false paths and unrealistic claims, nor are its exponents 'pitted' against the world, or against any particular enemy. Today, the real value of Karate lies in the opportunity it provides to develop physical prowess, resolve *interior* contradictions, generate and maintain a healthy body and mind, and ultimately serve society. That is undoubtedly its greatest value.

Appendix
A note on Karate Kicking Techniques

UNTIL ITS CONCLUSION, research is a job in progress. I can now conclude, however, that having learned my lesson from the *one* kick and the *one* 'knee raise' in Seisan kata, that most kicks in antique kata, are for the same purpose; to kick aside/away the opponent's trapped weapon, or to kick at the hands grasping it.

Stylised kicks (kicks without contact) are notoriously difficult to land in an unarmed situation and a determined opponent instinctively steps forward to avoid further punishment, and not backwards, as they do in the movies. It is not easy to kick a prepared opponent for real, particularly in the groin, a technique often praised as being effective.

In American PKA (Professional Karate Association) full contact bouts, a certain number of kicks (originally eight) must be thrown to avoid losing points. This does not necessarily attest to the efficiency of kicking techniques. No doubt, kicking techniques can be very strong, but problems lay mostly with delivery, particularly when the target is moving. Finally, it's ironic that in the popular 'Kyokushinkai' tournaments and similar, participants don't wear head-guards. Punching to the head is forbidden, yet full powered kicks to the head are allowed! Having said that, Kyokushinkai Karate-ka carry their hands in boxing fashion, and the style undoubtedly produces some extremely tough fighters.

Short Glossary of Terms

THIS (ROUGH) TRANSLATION of basic terms includes some crude phonetic spelling to help with pronunciation.

Chuan-fa (Chuan-far) Chinese, 'fist art', more popularly known as Kung Fu, 'hard work' (See also Quan-fa)

Dojo (Doe-joe) Japanese, place where the 'way' is practiced – the training hall.

Goju Ryu (Go-joo ree-ooh) A leading Okinawan Karate style

Jutsu (Jutsoo) Japanese, method or technique

Kakie (Car-key-ay) Okinawan, 'pushing hands'

Karate (Kara-tay) Okinawan/Japanese 'Empty hand'

Kata (Ka-ta) Okinawan/Japanese, 'form', choreographed (solo) sequence of techniques

Kihon (Key-hon) Japanese, fundamental/basic

Ko-do (Coe-doe) Japanese, 'old way'

Kumite (Koomi-te) Japanese, meeting hands (sparring)

Naha Te (Nar har-tay) Okinawan Naha (city) 'hand', defining the other branch of Okinawan Karate

Naihanchin (N-eye-han-chin) Chinese/Okinawan, 'internal divided conflict'

Quan (Chuan/Kwan) Chinese, 'fist' (form), choreographed sequence of techniques

Quan-fa (Chuan-far) Chinese, 'fist art', more popularly known as Kung Fu, 'hard work'

Rokushu (Roc-kew-shew) Okinawan/Japanese, 'six variations/varieties'

Sai (Sigh) Chinese Okinawan – a pronged civil defence weapon (tool) used in pairs

Sanchin (San-chinn) Chinese, Okinawan, Japanese, 'three conflicts' or 'battles'

Sanseirui (Sahn-say-ruhe) Okinawan/Japanese 'thirty six'

Sanseru More common phonetic spelling of the above

Seisian (Say-shan) Chinese, Okinawan/Japanese, 'thirteen (steps/hands)'

Sensei (Sen-say) Japanese, father/teacher

Shorin Ryu (Show-rin re-ooh) Okinawan Japanese generic term associating Karate with the Shorin Temple (Shao-lin in Chinese)

Shotokan (Show-toe-can) Japanese, from 'Shoto' the pen name of Funakoshi Gichin, the founder, and 'kan' meaning (roughly) hall. Currently Shotokan Karate is possibly the market leader in Japanese Karate

Shuri Te (Shoo ree tay) Okinawan, Shuri (city) 'hand', defining one of the two branches into which Okinawan Karate is usually divided

Sifu (See-foo) Chinese (Cantonese), father/teacher

To-te (Toh-tay) Okinawan/Japanese, 'China hand' (Chinese hands – Quan-fa)

Uechi Ryu (Way-chee re-ooh) An Okinawan Karate style preserving some original Chinese Quan-fa forms

Wado Ryu (Wah doe re-ooh) 'Harmony way', a (relatively) modern Japanese Karate style first registered during the 1930s

Selected Bibliography

Chaplin, Greg. "A Meeting with Master Xia Bai Hua."
Fighting Arts International 67, vol. 12, no. 1 (1990).

Draeger, Donn F. *Classical Bujutsu: The Martial Arts and Ways of Japan*, vol. 1. New York and Tokyo: Weatherhill, 1973.

Draeger, Donn F. *Classical Budo: The Martial Arts and Ways of Japan*, vol. 2. New York and Tokyo: Weatherhill, 1973.

Franks, David. Several private communications, 1993-1997.

Funakoshi, Gichin. *Karate Do Kyohan*. London: Ward Lock, 1982.

Higaonna, Morio. *The History of Karate: Okinawan Goju Ryu*. USA: Dragon Books, 1995.

Johnson, Nathan. *Zen Shaolin Karate*. Boston: Charles E. Tuttle, 1994.

Johnson, Nathan. *Barefoot Zen: the Shaolin Roots of Kung Fu and Karate*. York Beach Maine: Weiser Books, 2000.

Jou, Tsung Hwa. *The Tao of Tai Chi Chuan*. Boston: Charles E. Tuttle, 1980.

Lao Tzu. *Tao Te Ching*. London, 1985.

McCarthy, Patrick. Private letter, 1995.

Nagamine, Shoshin. *The Essence of Okinawan Karate-Do*. Boston: Charles E. Tuttle, 1976.

Nakayama, Masatoshi. *Dynamic Karate*. London: Ward Lock, 1966.

Noble, Graham. "The First Karate Books."
Fighting Arts International 90, (1995).

Noble, Graham. "The Master Funakoshi and the Development of Japanese Karate." *Fighting Arts International 34*, vol. 6, no. 4 (1995).

Noble, Graham, with Ian Mclaren and Professor N. Karasawa. "The History of Japanese Karate: Masters of the Shorin-Ryu." *Fighting Arts International 50*, vol. 9, no. 2 (1988).

Index

working, 28, 38, 42, 48,
80, 88-91, 100
double-hand technique, 304
Draeger, Don F., 87, 171
Dragon
Chuan, 146
Enter the, 129
Standing, 321, 329, 331,
332
Laying, 329, 331

E

elbow, 280, 281
control punch at, 313,
314, 317
locking of, 54, 98, 144,
304, 306, 309, 311, 344,
345, 350, 352, 358
striking of, 74
Empi, 251, 339
exhale, 298
eyes, 268

F

feet, 84, 185, 298, 358
fist, clenched
Naihanchin, 342, 343
Sanchin, 68, 258, 284
Juji Uke, 265
Fists of Harmonious
Righteousness, 129
Five Ancestors Kung Fu, 134,
153, 283
float, 145, 151, 291, 317
Fong Sai Yuk legend, 154
force borrowing, 148-150, 164,
271, 272, 279, 280, 310,
313, 314, 317
foundation kata, 73, 183, 290, 301

free fighting, 18, 37, 52, 163
Fuzhou, 135, 153, 190
Funakoshi Gichin, 41, 127, 355

G

Gate System, 144, 280
Gima Shinken, 355
Go, 202, 225
Goju-Ryu, 57, 59, 214, 226, 233,
289, 302
Gojushiho, 30, 58
grappling, 98, 337
and civil arrest, 53, 55
legacy of, 348
missing techniques of,
108
samurai, 172
grip escapes, 134, 149, 276, 319
gripper, 332
guard position, 284
guards, 281

H

Hard, *see Go*
harmonizing, 148
healing knowledge, 178
Higa, Seko, 219-221, 223-226,
228, 229
Higashionna (Higaonna),
Kanryo, 67-69, 135,
136, 190-196, 223
Higaonna, Morio, 187, 188, 195,
196, 199, 216-219, 225
high kicks, 18, 36, 52, 129, 148, 339
horse stance, *see Kibadachi*
hyper-extension, 245

I

images, 151, 152, 240
Itosu, Yasutsune Ankho, 58, 63,
    84, 126, 135, 260

J

Jion, 339
Johari, Harish, 298
joints
    manipulating of, 22, 54,
    98, 121, 142, 168, 350,
    356, 364
    hyper-extension of, 209,
    245
    in hand, 280
Jou Tsung Hwa, 146
Ju, 202, 225, 289
Ju-jutsu, 95, 142, 244, 347, 348

K

Karasawa, Professor N., 200
Kendo, 36, 42, 137
Kempo, 146, 212, 251, 263
Kibadachi, 264, 355
kicking, 52, 87, 91, 93, 397
Kiyoda Juhatsu, 189, 197, 198,
    201, 203, 208, 213, 217,
    218, 222, 224, 237
knee damage, 245
Kobudo, 8, 9, 19, 22, 24, 27, 48, 53,
    55, 58, 65, 135, 238, 375
Konishi, Yasuhiro, 341
Kusanku, 99, 205, 238, 250-259,
    339, 354, 355
Kyokushinkai, 57, 397

L

Laying Dragon, 329, 331
Leopard, 146, 329-333

Lee, Bruce, 94, 95, 129, 241
Lohan Quan, 284

M

Mabuni, Kenwa, 63, 114, 206,
    213, 263, 354
Mahayana Buddhism, 150
Matayoshi, Morihiro, 263
Matayoshi, Shimpo, 217
Matayoshi, Shinko, 217, 218
Matsumora, Kosaku, 132, 174
Matsumura, Sokon Bushi, 120,
    174, 250, 260, 347
Mawashi uke, 149, 203, 204,
    287, 288, 322, 332
McCarthy, Patrick, 61, 108, 152,
    186-188, 190, 193, 198,
    237, 337
Mclaren, Ian, 200
meditation, 22, 145, 148, 149,
    175, 215
Miyagi, Chojun, 63, 67-69, 75,
    132-135, 140, 157, 158,
    186, 226
Miyazato, Eiichi, 224, 227, 289
Monk Fist Boxing, 152, 154,
    186, 198
monks, 145-149
Motobu, Choki, 93, 122, 139,
    264, 340, 364
mudra, 151, 152

N

Nagamine, Shoshin, 20, 21, 29,
    64, 127, 137, 140, 156,
    158, 170, 186, 189, 256,
    269, 340, 355, 364
Naha-te, 16, 57, 61
Naihanchin

Ko-do Ryu
Classical Karate
Association

The kata techniques presented in this book have
been developed in association with members of
the *Ko-do Ryu Classical Karate Association.*
The 'white crane' is a bird whose actions were
allegedly studied by the Karate and Kung Fu
masters of old. Tradition has it that they imitated
the actions of the bird and copied its graceful
patterns of movement and defensive abilities.
Today, the white crane is incorporated into the
logo of Ko-do Ryu Karate, which continues
to pass on these valuable kata teachings.

www.kodoryu.com

Printed in the United Kingdom
by Lightning Source UK Ltd.
112097UKS00002B/13-39